NAJA

BY

NORA PHILIP FRY

Nora Philip Fry

Bloomington, IN Milton Keynes, UK

authorHOUSE™

AuthorHouse™
1663 Liberty Drive, Suite 200
Bloomington, IN 47403
www.authorhouse.com
Phone: 1-800-839-8640

AuthorHouse™ UK Ltd.
500 Avebury Boulevard
Central Milton Keynes, MK9 2BE
www.authorhouse.co.uk
Phone: 08001974150

This book is a work of non-fiction. Unless otherwise noted, the author and the publisher make no explicit guarantees as to the accuracy of the information contained in this book and in some cases, names of people and places have been altered to protect their privacy.

First published by AuthorHouse 3/6/2006

ISBN: 1-4259-2141-8 (sc)

Printed in the United States of America
Bloomington, Indiana

This book is printed on acid-free paper.

DEDICATIONS

To my father who always believed in me but died before seeing the book published.

To my mother who gave me much encouragement.

To my brother, George, who in the first instance inspired me to write this book.

To my husband, Arthur, who waded through pages of manuscripts, always there to support and encourage my endeavours and uplift me when the going was rough.

ACKNOWLEDGEMENTS

I wish to thank numerous people who assisted in small ways by directing me to various sources for information required to complete this book.

CONTENTS

INTRODUCTION

I sat on the floor of the living room clutching at the limp body of man's best friend. With tears welling up, blurring my vision, I gazed down at the inert form of my dog, Judy Freckles. She had been a good friend, accompanying me on many of my northern journeys. Her death was inevitable, not just because of the very obvious malignant growth on her neck but also by the laws of nature which determine that a dog is elderly at fourteen years.

The fateful night came when her time had all but run out. At midnight she became restless, raising her head periodically. It almost seemed as though she were searching the room with her eyes for the last time. My husband and I carried her into the sitting room on her bed and I lay down close to her on the floor, stroking her and talking to her through the night. She fell into a deep sleep, never to awaken again. In the morning, unable to rouse her, I observed her laboured breathing and made the decision to call the veterinarian to come and aid her to a gentle, final peace. The nearest veterinarian hospital was located some twenty miles away and due to a heavy calving delivery schedule he was unable to come. As things turned out, I was glad. I cradled her lovingly in my arms. Very soon after, she took a couple of big breaths, opened her eyes wide and looked right at me, then she was gone. I was happy that I was with her in death just as I had been with her in birth. I will never forget her eyes opening as they did as though she was bidding me a last farewell. Her moment of death will be treasured by me forever. I had lost a dear loyal friend. She saw me through many trials and tribulations in my travels and brought me much comfort. Never again would I feel her nuzzle against me nor feel her moist, long tongue touch my cheek in affection. Long walks would not be quite the same.

Death was no stranger to me. I had witnessed human death many times in my career. I watched helplessly as some patients died in the north of Canada, having attempted everything medically possible within the scope of my training and the tools I had to work with. Ultimately, in isolation, the weather factors had a bearing on mortality. When the weather was totally inclement, the planes would not fly. That decision and the fate of the patient had to be accepted.

Mixed with the sadness of my loss, my mind simultaneously became flooded with happy memories of my adventures in the Northern Hemisphere. Still holding on to my dog, I talked to her as though she were alive, telling her of the joyful occasion when I saw her born under my bed in Bella Bella, British Columbia. It was my way of a tribute to her.

I reflected on the frequent aeroplane journeys, many of them emergency flights, made in an effort to reach a southern hospital with a patient who needed treatment beyond a nurse's capabilities, some barely clinging to life. The thoughts just kept flashing through my mind like flipping the pages of a book, rapidly, conjuring up images of life and death dramas repeated over and over in various isolated posts I found myself in. The bid to evacuate a patient always brought personal risk by flying in changeable Arctic weather conditions for hundreds of miles, especially carrying out night flights which the government did not support.

My nursing career with the Federal Government of Canada, which lasted almost a quarter of a century, had been stimulating and challenging. It allowed me to participate in the care of the Native Indians and Inuit in landscapes and far off places with historical reference. The exposure to other cultures was both educational and rewarding. I am forever grateful for the opportunities that left me with such memorable episodes in my life.

I talk about the loss of my dog whom I loved. She was my child, but I speak within the book also of the deaths that occurred with frequency within the Indian and Inuit communities. Some were self-induced, some were individuals too sick for even modern medicine to save, while others would have undoubtedly had a greater chance of survival if located in the south with its advanced technological amenities.

My story is a personal journey from my humble roots in Scotland to the barren wastelands of Canada. There is so much more to the lives of the people I served than the romantic notion of tepees, igloos and dog teams. Although there were cultural differences, I found, as human beings we were not so unlike. We do share emotional feelings of love, fear, anger, anxiety and this, along with human mortality, is the same for all races. It was for me, I believe, the time of my greatest personal growth. I invite you to journey with me. Fasten your seat belt. We are off in a twin otter aircraft, making haste from Baker Lake, in the Northwest Territories, with a young Inuit boy on board, writhing on a stretcher, dangerously ill. Time is essential for his survival!

CHAPTER ONE
THE EARLY YEARS

Since I left my native Scotland and landed on Canadian soil some thirty-five years ago, I have been asked frequently as to why I decided to immigrate to this great land, particularly when the rest of my family remained in Scotland. It is a question that I have not been able to fully answer. Many Scots who have become naturalized Canadians have told me they came because of greater opportunities and to experience a higher standard of living. I would have to say that adventure probably was my only motivator. I had recently qualified from my nursing programme in 1965 and was fully employed at the Royal Infirmary in Aberdeen, Scotland, and in that era one could surmise that my position was very secure, unlike the present generation who often have to relocate to where the jobs are. Although the salary was not high, the need to find a better economical environment was not a need nor a conscious desire.

When I was still a child, my brother, who is four years my senior, would enthusiastically show me places on the map and talk about travelling to these distant lands. I wasn't particularly interested in seeing foreign places, but at this young age I had already formulated my utopian plan for the future: that I would first train to be a nurse, marry, raise a family and live a sedate life in the countryside, surrounded by a menagerie of pets. Never in my wildest dreams did I foresee the interesting, exciting and challenging life that would evolve and sometimes lead me to live a lifestyle far removed from the comforts that I had envisioned for myself.

In the classroom and from the history books I studied, I learned of explorers such as Sir John Franklin, Roald Amundsen and James Knight, and of their travels to the Arctic, never imagining that I would someday be so near to the areas of their explorations. Because of my Arctic adventures I would later come to appreciate those courageous men of history.

I duly made my entrance into the world in 1941 in the city of Dundee, Scotland, I am told, in somewhat of a hurry. The need to hurry seems, thus far, to have been an innate part of my personality. Prior to my arrival, the war was already two years under way and on the eve of my birth, Clydebank, in the southwest of Scotland, was heavily bombed. Luckily my family were well removed from there. My father had not been accepted for the army because of an existent foot problem and one which had left him with a slight limp. Nevertheless, he was required to do his duty for his country on the home front. As an air-raid warden, he had been up most of the night on duty and in the early morning when he arrived home, my mother informed him it was time to go to the hospital. My birth occurred on March, 15th, which is the "Ides of March" and according to history, Julius Caesar was assassinated on this date after receiving an ominous warning. My innocent arrival into the world came at a time when my country, being at war with Germany, was by then experiencing the hardships of such an encounter. In those early years I was too young to understand about war and as long as my basic needs were met, like any child, I was happy.

When I was about two or three years old we moved from Dundee to a small town called Huntly, in Aberdeenshire, where as a family we lived with my grandfather, my grandmother having died previous to our arrival, not allowing me a chance to know her. I have, I feel, a vague recollection of discovering a type of hand bomb at the garden gate of his home. There was talk from time to time of this episode when I was growing up, so it is debatable whether I remembered the actual incident or learned about it through conversation. Given the curiosity of children, it was fortunate that I informed my mother rather than tampering with the object, otherwise I would not be writing about it today. In due course, the army personnel came and disposed of the unwanted object.

I do however, have the memory of a soldier running with his clothing ablaze across the barracks compound, presumably gasoline on his clothing having caught fire. Northeast Scotland was not affected by the bombing as much as England, so perhaps that is why I have little memory of the war, but I do recall tales of my grandfather being in the First World War and soon afterwards captured at Mons. He was imprisoned at Sennelager, Westphalia, Germany, for the remainder of the war.

We moved on from my grandfather's house to another small rural town called Insch, also in Aberdeenshire and, out of necessity due to a housing shortage, we lived with my other grandparents until I was school age.

Finally we moved into our own home. I remember the prisoner of war camp located about two or three hundred yards from our back door. I can still visualize the rows of Nissen huts, with smoke coming out of the chimneys and the camp being surrounded by a high barbed wire fence.

Still ringing in my ears are my mother's admonitions not to talk to those men but to come home straight away. One day, on my way home from the bakery shop in town, with a loaf of bread tucked under my arm, a prisoner, with a shaven head, standing by the fence called out to me, "Little girl give me your bread." At the same time he extended his arm through the fence in anticipation of receiving some. Remembering my mother's instructions, I clutched the bread harder and ran home terrified, and no doubt eager to relate the encounter to my mother while at the same time handing over one very squashed loaf of bread. We did not know how well the prisoners were taken care of at that time or whether the man was truly hungry, but certainly rations were part of life for the general population. I have since met with an ex-prisoner of war who married a Scot and settled in that community. He assured me that as prisoners, they were well fed and taken care of. As they did not pose a threat to security, the men were used as labourers on the farms. Towards the end of their confinement the restrictions became more relaxed and they were allowed to visit local homes. Many took an interest in the church services and became choir members.

I do recall the ration books and I understood the lean times. The highlight of my young life was being handed those ration books, one for each family member, and on a Friday night purchasing the allowed four ounces of sweets per person. I can still visualize the wee candy shop run by Mrs. Donald and jars, all in a row on the shelf, filled with tempting, mouth-watering sweets. It was a hard decision to choose from such an assortment and to know this bagful had to last a whole week. Usually they were wolfed down in the first day, but later my parents would produce their preserved rations which they shared with us.

Living in rural Scotland, and money being scarce, there was not all the equipment and organized entertainment that youths of today have at their disposal and perhaps take for granted, but rather we made our own amusement. Many times the open fields were our playground. I know that not all our playtime was innocent and many times, regrettably, we wreaked havoc amongst the growing crops. Perhaps that was a less innocuous type of crime in comparison to the present age where the use of drugs, weapons and violence are an all too common event in society. Our misdemeanours, if we had been caught, would have been dealt with rather severely. We were in awe of the local policeman.

I grew up fearing aeroplanes and remember well my frightened reactions. When an aircraft flew over the fields I played in, I would run screaming, covering my ears with my hands as protection from the awesome engine sounds that frightened me so, and eventually flopped down on my hands and knees with my hands over my head. No one had taught me to do this nor do I ever recall as a youngster sharing my fears with my parents, but this fear stayed with me well into adult life, and only after flying repeatedly in the Canadian North did this feeling dissipate. During the more recent Gulf War, the pilots would fly their planes very low on their practice missions in Scotland, creating a temporary return of that fear for me.

My childhood was a happy and very ordinary one. We certainly were not well off, but my mother skilfully sewed clothes for me, often by cutting garments which belonged to adult family members and creating a pattern to fit me. I was so proud when the teacher liked my two "new" coats I wore at different times. I would tell her proudly that my mam had made them, sporting at other times the newly hand knitted twin-set with the handmade skirt to match. Nothing was wasted in those post war days. Many times I sat with my mam, a skein of yarn wrapped around my outstretched arms whilst she would roll the wool into a ball ready to be reused in the making of another piece of clothing. At the young age of four I was taught both by my mam and grandmother how to knit. I consider that to be a good attribute today. Many people are beginning to again appreciate hand knitted items of clothing.

Before I started school, the doctor had said, "Those tonsils need to come out." I had them removed at the village hospital by the local general practitioner. There was not a great deal of pomp and circumstance in those days. When I close my eyes I can still see myself, a four-year- old, walking down the hospital corridor with my small hand clasped in the larger hand of a kindly nurse, having just said goodbye to my mam. We stopped en route so that I might be perched upon the "throne" with the brown wooden seat to make sure my bladder was empty before the anaesthetic. She reassured me as we continued our walk. Finally we entered a room that was rather unwelcoming and austere, and before me stood a long table. This was the operating room. I was gently lifted onto the table and immediately strapped down. As I lay there I was aware of a funny smell and a man dressed in a white coat with his back to me, busily working. I did not know what he was doing. Suddenly and without warning, a piece of cotton wool with a foul odour was pressed against my face. I called out, "M-a-a-am." I remember only waking up with one mighty sore throat. I went for surgery at two o'clock in the afternoon and was discharged home at five o'clock. Still, that was better than having it done on the kitchen table as some medical procedures were done in days gone by. I woke up in a small ward, the only other occupant being a male patient. I remember him talking quietly to me as I screamed for my mother. I vomited over the bedding and can still recall an older nurse coming in and scolding me, telling me to use the basin sitting on the locker if I was to vomit again. Her impressive words to me that day were, "Stop your crying, or I'll skelp your backside!" I never forgot her remark and refused to acknowledge this nurse on a chance encounter later. To look back at this total event frightens me more as an adult than it probably did as a child. As you mentally visualize the scenario it makes you realize how vulnerable a little child is, having to place their trust in those around, there being no other option. I was very happy to see my mother later that day.

When I arrived home my mother and grandmother put me to bed and then tried to persuade me to eat a blackcurrant jelly that wobbled in the bowl presented to me, intended to soothe my poor throat. I was not amused by the gesture.

I attended the rural school at Insch and started two weeks after my fifth birthday, in March. There were no nursery or kindergarten schools in those days. My mother took me to school for the first two days and oh, how I cried in class, but within a week I had settled in with my new schoolmates. When I recall the slate board and slate pencils we used, compared to the students today, using computer technology, I feel rather ancient.

While standing in a circle to learn the alphabet in that first week, I made the grave mistake of asking my friend Irene what time it was. I must have been feeling weary and wanting to go home. My friend answered that she didn't know, and that little episode earned both of us the strap. Some introduction to school! I can still see Ms Anderson with her hair in a tight bun at the back of her head, bespectacled and kneeling down in front of us to administer punishment. The school years went by and I had both successes and failures on the way. The biggest resentment I felt from my school years, which remained with me for a very long time, was when one teacher continually compared me to my brother who had preceded me through the school system. In her eyes I just never measured up to his standards and the comparison was always, of course, made in front of the whole class. The following grade was not much better. I had an older male teacher who impressed upon my mind the idea that I would not amount to much in life. So much for a vote of confidence! I never forgave those teachers for their derisive attitude towards me and for the long-term hurt it left within me. I was only ten years old and those formative years were so important for ones self esteem. I struggled with feelings of inferiority for many, many years and it took working as a nurse in a remote Arctic community to bring about that confidence and self worth that I had so lacked.

I attended the Episcopal Church with my parents and also briefly attended the Sunday school. I don't remember how briefly that really was but the scenario was one where only my brother and I attended, because the majority of the village children attended the Presbyterian Church, located elsewhere. Seated in front of us, the minister started the hymn singing, my brother and I singing along in the background and being drowned out by the melodious sounds emitting both from the Reverend Duthie and his harp, which he sometimes played instead of the organ. We probably felt self conscious of the fact that there were only two of us there and soon we stopped attending. Reverend Duthie was quite the art collector and a friend of the Royal Family of Holland. I recall seeing the shiny black limousine parked outside the manse on one occasion when Prince Bernard and Queen Juliana were visiting him. How his friendship with them came about I am not quite sure.

It was during those years after the war ended that my dad seized upon the opportunity to enrol in a nursing program in Aberdeen. Jobs in the post war days were not very plentiful in the rural areas. The training was for three years and dad had to be away from home. Each week, on his day off, he would journey by train to visit us, only to return to work a day later. How happy I would be, skipping along the road to the railway station to meet my dad, stopping on the way to pay a quick visit to my grandparents who lived within view of the station. I missed him a lot when he was away and felt joyous when we finally moved to the city and he was able to come home every day.

In our modern society, men and women are interchangeable in the job market with less focus on what are male/female oriented jobs. Not so in my father's time. A male nurse was still a new concept and many times my father was not afforded by the medical doctors the professional courtesy that he deserved and certainly the reigning attitude that prevailed then would not be acceptable in this day and age. My mother had previously worked in a hospital as a nursing assistant before marriage, and also with convalescent children in Linmoor Home. It was in this environment that I grew up wanting, from age five, to be a nurse. With my little neighbourhood friends I often played nurse, wearing a piece of white sheet, representing a cap, tied around my head like the army nurses. At an early age I had a good knowledge of the bony anatomy and could very accurately take pulses.

Because my father had entered into nursing, I often had fun poked at me and sometimes very uncharitable statements were made which offended me greatly. One of the early memories I have of growing up in Scotland was that when a new student arrived in school or the neighbourhood, one of the first questions asked would be "What does your father work at?" I never experienced this in Canada. It must have been based on class distinction learned from the older generation. I would at times rebel at this question, always scared of rebuke and hurt feelings, and would refuse to say.

By the time I entered the nursing world, some nine years after my father graduated, this narrow-minded bigotry still prevailed, but this time I met my opponents head on. There was a discussion about men going into nursing and a bit of laughter. At that point no one knew my father was a nurse. I stood up in my class and bravely announced that my dad was in fact a male nurse and a good dad, and in doing so, exposed their narrow-mindedness. I never heard that subject raised in my presence again. I entered into nursing school at the tender age of seventeen and a half, and when I look back, I was but a child myself, full of innocence.

I left school at age fifteen and no amount of coaxing would persuade me to stay on. Life in a Junior High School in a city setting was just not for me. The attitude of the children in the small village school was quite different. They showed much greater reserve compared to the boldness I witnessed in the behaviour of the city students. That, along with the tyrannical treatment meted out by the gymnastics teacher, was enough for me. I had so much enjoyed going to the gymnasium and I was considered good enough in sport to win races and compete successfully. I had played netball well previously but, by the time this particular teacher was finished screaming at everyone and intercepting every move while playing netball or field hockey, there was no longer any joy left in the activity. Of course, instruction was important, but she took it to the extreme. I would deliberately leave my gym shoes at home rather than participate, knowing full well the penalty for this action was the strap. The number of whacks was increased with each forgetful episode in an attempt to restore the memory. How could I, a student, tell her my memory was perfect, which was more than could be said for her bullying methods. The day I left school, I felt a free person. I was, of course, too young to enter into nursing and so to fill in the time I worked in a chemist shop. It was a good experience, especially being allowed to help with the preparation of some prescriptions. Certain powders had to be compounded and some elixirs had to be mixed by adding ingredients. Learning to read prescriptions and the meaning of the symbols would prove to be very useful in my nurse's training.

After my hospital interview, I had to sit an aptitude test. I was accepted to train as a Registered Paediatric Nurse, which would be a three-year program. On September 19th, 1958, I arrived at the nurses' residence accompanied by my parents. All students were required, as part of the conditions of employment, to live in residence for two out of the three years. This first residence was not attached to the main hospital. It was a Victorian House, three storeys high, located in a prestigious area of town. There to greet us on that first day was an old spinster who, prior to retirement, had also been a Nursing Sister. Following the preliminary introductions, I was escorted to my room, located on the third floor. I was informed that this would be my home for the next three months while I attended the initial stage of training. The training would be conducted in a classroom setting within the hospital. Afterwards, we all would move into the hospital residence for most of the training, with the exception of our night duties, whereupon we would again return to this Victorian-styled building. I met some of my co-workers to be, who were located on the same floor. Shortly afterwards, my parents hugged me and wished me well. For the first time, I was all alone and had to fight back the tears. Even knowing that I was only a bus trip and four miles away from them did not seem to console me. I was fortunate, unlike some of my colleagues who had left the Isle of Skye, the Shetland and Orkney Islands and further south. There was much excitement that evening, acting giddy as teenagers do. Some of those new friendships that day blossomed and became lasting ones.

We walked daily to and from the hospital situated about two miles away. Again there were more preliminaries, acquainting ourselves with the classroom routine and being instructed on the many protocols of behaviour befitting a nurse.

Following the initial three months of classroom instruction we were assigned a work area. My placement was to a medical ward where I spent the next three months. As well as the ward instruction we received, each of us was an integral part of the workforce. The workday was twelve hours long and if work was not completed at the end of a shift due to circumstances beyond our control, we were required to stay even longer to facilitate the patient or for clean-up purposes. Many times we worked broken shifts on the same day, which curtailed one's own activities, having to be mindful always of the time to go back on duty.

It was in this setting that I had my first serious responsibilities in nursing duties and also my first encounter with human death. I had only been in the ward two months when a little girl died and the poignancy of that moment will always be with me. As nurses we had to carry out the last offices which meant that within an hour of death we washed the body, cleaned the teeth, brushed the hair and packed all the orifices before placing the little one in a shroud. These shrouds had a ruffle collar like those worn by choir boys. If the season was appropriate, as it was in this circumstance, we were sent out by the ward sister to the hospital garden to pick snowdrop flowers and to afterwards place these between the clasped hands of the deceased child. It was heart-wrenching to see this little angelic figure lying so still before us and to know that medical science had failed to keep her alive. Such sadness filled all of our hearts, but one had to quickly regain composure because the other children needed our care and their questions on death had to be acknowledged. The relatives arrived and behind the closed curtains you could hear their sorrowing. Thankfully, at that stage in the profession, I was not required to deal with the grieving relatives, but only with my own emotions. This death was not an isolated occurrence and the event of death was repeated in this unit many times, as well as in other wards and facilities that I've worked in over the years. This was the beginning of learning control of one's own emotions and to be somewhat resilient in the face of adversity.

Throughout training we moved back and forth from the classroom to various wards, spending two or three months in each setting. For me, a surgical ward was next on the agenda. The nursing sister in this ward was easy-going, but in spite of that I was more inclined to the caring of long- term medical cases. When a child went to have surgery, we would often have to accompany the child to the operating room. Donning a mask and gown, we were allowed to watch the procedure being performed. We remained in the background more as observers, and perhaps it helped to prepare us for the event of working in the operating theatre, scrubbing and assisting the surgeon. During a night shift, in yet another surgical ward where I worked, I heard of a boy having a leg amputated. I was glad I did not have to witness that operation.

I remember the surgical Ward Sister, who had a speech impediment, being very thorough about the sterilization of instruments and syringes which were not disposable in my time. Her words were ,"Nu-r-r-se, if the syringe needs boiling for five minutes then you must do just that and the doctor can wait!"

We admitted our share of road accident victims, which included some very serious head injuries. We did not have an intensive care unit, so the children's playroom was sometimes commandeered to care for these types of cases. There we had adequate space for all the equipment needed. It was a good location, as often the child had to be kept in a hypothermic state.

We would pack ice around the child and open the veranda doors wide, as well as running a fan. It was not the most pleasant temperature to work in. Confidentiality was always impressed upon us, particularly with accident victims, so that there were no erroneous leaks to a member of the press.

The ear, nose and throat ward did not exactly thrill me. Perhaps it was because I had to witness the removal of tonsils and see the children cry because of their sore throats. I could relate to their suffering. As soon as they were awake, they were fed ice cream to soothe and reduce the throat swelling, but invariably they vomited. I still recall the combined smell of blood, anaesthetic and ice cream.

I was in my third and final year when the Ward Sister called me aside and told me my father was waiting to see me. I was a bit perplexed, but did as she bid. My father quickly told me the reason for his visit, informing me that my mother had been in a vehicle accident. I think at that point I froze until I had established that she was alive. It was a great relief to know that she was, but unfortunately, she was now a patient at the Infirmary, having sustained a serious fracture to her femur. To make life simpler for me, I was placed on night duty by the Matron so that I could do some household chores in the morning and keep things functional at home. By this time I was now living at home. We could not afford to hire a house-keeper, therefore my dad, brother and I all pitched in. Had we been in possession of the modern equipment of today, the laundry would have been an easy chore. Unfortunately we still had the old hand-washing board, a copper boiler used to simply boil all the whites, and a hand-operated wringer. It was tiring to come home after a twelve hour shift and do a weekly wash, but it had to be done and I was happy I could do my part. While still in uniform, and before going home, I would be allowed to visit my mother at the infirmary for a short time in the morning. This was a privilege afforded me by the other professionals, even though visiting hours were rigidly adhered to. I would also go in the evening when the official visiting hours were in effect. For four months this continued. I had expected my mother home after three months, but at the commencement of her physiotherapy she collapsed with a blood clot in her lung. This meant she would spend extra time in hospital, creating more anxiety for me and a longer time on night duty, the shift which I loathed.

As part of my extra time on night shift, I was assigned to the isolation unit, taking my turn like all the other students. This area was reserved for those with infectious diseases. This unit was at the end of a long corridor, and as the name implies, it was indeed isolated. I cannot say that it was very busy while I "served my sentence," viewing my term there as just that. Adjoining the isolation ward was the orthodontist clinic which one entered through a swinging door. If it was windy outside a draft would creep in and all night long I would listen to this eerie creaking sound of the swinging door, like something from a suspense movie. It was just my luck that during my three month stint working there, a murder had been committed in the city. Our community was a relatively quiet one and a murder shocked everyone, especially with an unknown killer loose. One of my classmates was on duty in the emergency room when they brought in the victim, a small girl. When the nurse attempted to see where the blood had come from she was horrified to see that the little girl's throat had been cut. She was very shaken by the incident. Nurses, like the police, often witness traumatic events in the course of duty.

In the isolation ward was a small office. When sitting at the desk, the nearby windows, which overlooked a main road, were at my back. The window was similar in style to that of French doors and opened outward, but no matter how warm that room became during the night, I would not open them, purely out of fear of someone climbing in. The killer was caught a long time after I had left the city but not before a little boy was also murdered by the same man.

Given that the hospital was on the ground level, we had our share of visitors with tiny legs, commonly known as cockroaches. It gave credence to the stories that creepy crawlies come out of the woodwork and things go bump in the night! Ugh! How I hated them. Only a few would come into the office and I refused to stand on them and hear that crunching sound. Instead I armed myself with a small spray bottle of ether. As they approached me, I aimed a few squirts, and for the rest of the night I would not be bothered by them. They would revive towards morning, but I became very brave at that point, knowing I was going off duty. Many more of these existed in the kitchens of the other wards. The caretaker would do his nightly rounds, checking on our heating and hot water supplies. He wore what in Scotland is referred to as "tackety boots" or hobnailed boots. He would delight in switching on the kitchen light and trampling on as many of them as possible as they scurried into dark recesses.

I did a term on day duty in isolation and found that quite pleasant compared to nights. I had only one little boy to care for. He had been placed there because of his fragile condition. He suffered from cystic fibrosis. I would spend hours reading and singing to him, becoming too attached for my own good. A few weeks later, when I came on duty in the morning, I saw at once that his bed had been stripped, with the rubber protector draped over the end of the bed. I recognised the significance and my face crumpled on seeing this. My little friend had died during the night. When the cleaning lady saw me come through the door, and knowing of my deep affection for the lad, she hurried forward to comfort me.

I went home later that day and went upstairs quietly. My mother sensed there was something different in my demeanour and asked what troubled me. I told her about the little boy. She comforted me, at the same time rationalizing that I should not allow myself to become too emotionally involved with patients as I would face death many times over. It was good advice.

A spell in the outpatient department was refreshing, especially the emergency room. People got injured, we fixed them up and they went home happier than when they came in. Occasionally there were fatalities, but I was never present when those were brought in. It was in this place that the senior nurses taught me to do suturing. A small rubber teddy bear was used for practice when we had a spare moment. An arm or leg was torn off only to be reattached. He certainly was a war-torn inanimate object. It was not part of our duties to suture, but I did become quite adept in the skill, never realizing it would be a great asset in my Arctic experiences, where no instruction would be given to me, yet it would be a frequently performed task.

The three years had gone by quickly. The final examinations were over. I had passed and was now entitled to call myself a Registered Nurse for Sick Children. The training in Britain was different from that of Canada in as much that only trained nurses in paediatrics could work in children's hospitals.

During my training, I had already developed my plans for the future and was ready to put them into effect. I would go on and train in adult diseases. I had already been accepted at the Western General Hospital, in Edinburgh. I could have done the same training at the Royal Infirmary, in Aberdeen, but because my father was well known there through his work I elected to go to an establishment where I could be accepted on my own merits.

Some of my colleagues also elected to further their nursing experiences, while some stayed behind to become staff nurses, still others opting for marriage. Matrimony was not allowed when we were students and perhaps the applied wisdom meant there would be no interruptions to studies, nor loss of management's investment in our training time, by pregnancies occurring and thus leading to a drop-out problem.

I journeyed to Edinburgh to begin the next part of my training. Because I had already been a Registered Nurse, I did not have to repeat the first year, but rather started in the second year, thus omitting the basic anatomy and physiology components and elementary teachings. I thoroughly enjoyed the training and was more mature to cope somewhat with the many situations that did arise. My studies were again a combination of classroom and ward experience. I believe that this system was an excellent teaching method, combining book knowledge with a practical application, giving appropriate instruction and guidance on the job which lead to proficiency in our future duties. Ups and downs were all part of the training, but I like to recount some of the more illustrious happenings while moving from ward to ward gaining knowledge. The work hours were a little different and better, but we still did our share of the grave-yard shifts.

Two of my favourite stories occurred in the cardiac ward during my night shift. Because it was a cardiology ward, we were allotted three nurses instead of two. I was a third year student then and was placed in charge with a first and a second year student nurse on the team. We did have patient cardiac arrests from time to time, but managed to deal with the stress of these dramatic moments. We had a system that was put into effect quickly, one that brought a team to our rescue and the patients' aid. In spite of the hard efforts, many were not successfully resuscitated, the heart already too severely damaged from previous attacks. But there were other nights when the work load was lighter and not all the beds were filled. We could afford to be a little more light hearted. The call bell in the male ward rang out on one of these nights. The men had rung because an elderly male patient, suffering from senile dementia as well as his heart condition, was attempting to climb out of the window. Fortunately this ward was located on the ground floor of the two-storey building. When I approached the individual, he became quite aggressive and lunged at me with a pair of crutches, which at one point he held raised above his head. I kept advancing towards him and with assistance got the gentleman back to bed. Later he decided to take off again. This time, when we were summoned, we were just in time to see him head out at a running pace down the main corridor. He was very tall and his hospital gown did not fit very well, being rather on the short side. Apart from this scant garment, he was naked, making quite an apparition before our eyes. As we advanced on him, he seemed to speed up. Finally, and rather unceremoniously, we got him back to bed. His jaunt must have tired him as during the rest of the night he remained quiet. A day or so later the male supervisor did not have such a fortunate encounter with this man. As he leaned over the bedrails to talk to the patient he received "five of the best" in the eye. I was on my nights off and did not witness the event. Undoubtedly, nursing can be hazardous to one's health!

One male patient frequently awakened during the night. I usually made him tea and, perching myself on the side of the bed, I would join him in a "cuppa" if the workload would permit. We would whisper in the stillness of the night, the silence interrupted only by an occasional snorting sound emanating from the man across from us. I think my patient just needed some human contact and reassurance, his heart condition not being very good. The patients would develop friendships with their room mates, but sometimes when a death occurred, it cast gloom over the others. In the wee small hours, when one cannot sleep, problems seem to be so magnified. I never begrudged time spent in comforting patients.

The second year student that worked with me, together with many of her classmates located in other wards, did not like the meals left out for us and complained about this often. She would bring on duty different types of food to dine on instead. One particular night she arrived with a whole chicken and was going to cook it in the large adjoining kitchen. I did not mind as long as her duties were carried out. The night supervisor, this time a female, came to do her rounds, and from the hallway I could see her lift her nose in the air to determine from whence this delicious aroma was emanating. Following her sense of smell, she headed for the kitchen, all of us close at her heels. I thought we were about to be disciplined, but all she did was lift the lid, sniff and remark how pleasant it was.

About two weeks later, I received a note from the junior nurses, stating that they intended to prevent anyone going to the dining room. This was their form of protest with regard to the food. I did not agree and said so. I felt it better to attend the dining room and in the morning take the complaint to the proper authorities. They were determined and neither I nor my other colleagues scattered throughout the hospital, ate in the dining room that night. The gesture was recognised by the night supervisor, who also dined there. She called all the senior nurses to her office immediately. We all stood in a semi circle while this rather petite woman condemned our actions. Of course, we were really the innocent ones. She demanded an explanation and became more aggressive with our silence. I could not stand this anymore. Stepping forward, I explained about the feelings the staff had towards the culinary efforts of the cook. Her five-foot-two frame stiffened. She glared at me and then she went in for the attack. Talking back or defending oneself to that generation, was not well tolerated. I had to stand submissively and let her blow off steam at me as though I were the culprit. I was against all of this in the first instance. Then came the ban order stating, "There will be no more cooking in the kitchens!" I came to realize that the combination of my co-worker cooking food in the kitchen and my stepping forward to make a statement, seem to incriminate me. Until the day I left the hospital, I believe I was seen as the one who orchestrated the whole episode.

I was seconded to another hospital for a specific module of training not to be had in our own facility. I was alone on the evening shift, which meant I would be off duty at nine o'clock. The room off to the side of the ward was called the sluice room, where the urinals and bedpans were emptied and sterilized. The actual equipment used for emptying them was called the hopper, which was attached to the wall. As one opened the door in a downward motion, a jet of water cleaned away the offending matter. It should have turned off after I used it that evening, but there remained a constant stream of running water. I was unable to make contact with the caretaker, so when I mentioned it to my male patients they came up with many suggestions, the last one being to close off a valve. Dispelling my concerns over turning off all the water supply, they demonstrated that everything else was functional, so I went along with the idea.

I came back on duty the next day and turned the valve back on again and went off to report the matter to the caretaker. I was not able to reach him right away. This was strange, but a little later I met him coming downstairs from the ward directly above us. He looked a bit disgruntled as I was telling him about the hopper, but he interrupted me to say that they did not have water upstairs earlier and that some damn fool left the plug in the sink upstairs. He went on to say that when the water came on again they had water alright, overflowing water! I kept dead silent. My turning on the valve again had caused the problem.

In 1964, I graduated once again. The comradeship that had developed had to be put aside as we travelled our separate ways. Many of us continued with our studies at various locations. I chose to study midwifery in the Aberdeen Maternity Hospital. This was quite a rigorous course, working all day and at times attending doctors' lectures for two hours afterwards. Following lectures, we stayed behind in the classroom to practise the deliveries with the use of models provided. As I suffered very badly from migraine headaches, which started during my Edinburgh studies, I found it hard sometimes to keep going between the constant pain, the pressure of studying and the combination of long working hours. I did, however, survive and passed the oral, written and anaesthetic examinations. I had been accepted for the second part of midwifery at the Elsie Inglis Hospital in Edinburgh but, at the last moment I felt this subject was not my forte and decided to cancel. I would admit that the event of delivering a new baby into the world was both an exciting and gratifying experience, but having done the ten plus required deliveries, I was satisfied.

During one episode of instruction, given by the Ward Sister in the post-natal department, I was suddenly pounced on and asked what I would do in an isolated situation if my patient had a postpartum haemorrhage. I think at this point my midwifery interests were on the wane and I had not been listening very closely. I was unable to give the answer expected of me. My silent thought, in reaction to the question and the subsequent embarrassment was, that it was unlikely I would be in this isolated scenario being presented to me, therefore I would not face such a predicament. How was I to know that this situation would indeed face me in an isolated area in the Arctic? With no one around to help me I had to recall the instruction, which as a result of that hospital episode, was well seared into my brain.

From the post-natal ward I was designated to the milk kitchen to learn how to make baby formula and sterilize bottles and nipples. Somewhere in this time frame, five of us had the notion to go to Canada. I cannot remember how or who made the suggestion but we talked enthusiastically about the possibilities. As the time grew nearer, the others had a change of heart. My mother, on hearing of this, thought I would also decide not to go, but I was determined at this stage to follow through, even if it meant landing on Canadian soil and returning home soon afterwards.

CHAPTER TWO
EMIGRATION

The decision was made, I would emigrate to Canada. Contact had to be made with the Emigration Department and the necessary formalities had to be addressed. Meantime I was employed at the Royal Infirmary, Aberdeen, as a Staff Nurse in a private patients ward which also included taking care of any sick nurses. Soon afterwards, the Ward Sister was called upon to go to the Orkney Islands to fill a temporary position as the Matron. I was invited to take her position as the Acting Ward Sister. I felt comfortable with the work and had I stayed I am sure I would have obtained a permanent Ward Sister post .

In due course I obtained a job in the Toronto General Hospital in Ontario and, with my qualifications, I was able to acquire Canadian registration in nursing before landing in Canada through the help of the Royal College of Nurses in Britain, of which I was a member. Many nurses from overseas were required to sit nursing examinations in Canada because they lacked the paediatric or midwifery components. Until those subjects were successfully passed, they did not receive a registered nurse's wage. Because of the different fields of training I had, I commenced my duties on full salary. I considered myself fortunate in this regard.

As to the emigration protocol, I was required to journey to Glasgow to undergo a complete physical examination which included a tuberculin test and chest x-ray. Several documents had to be filled out and I had to indicate that I had a job, available accommodation and some finances to subsist on, so that I would not be a burden to the Canadian Government. I always feel a little rankled now when I see illegal immigrants being allowed to stay in a country where they are unemployed, have little or no funds to sustain themselves, and who have not had medical clearance before entering.

There was an element of anxiety during the preparation process. I had to arrange my flight, obtain travellers cheques, buy a couple of suitcases and decide from my meagre wardrobe what I should take. At that time the airlines were quite strict with the amount of weight allowed on board, so one did have to be selective. An air of apprehension lay heavy with me, not only because I was leaving my family behind, but I was embarking on a journey to a faraway land which felt like a trip into uncharted territory, and at twenty-three years of age I felt unsure of myself.

In due course, the 12th of July, 1965, arrived and I was winging my way across the Atlantic. My feelings were a mixture of shock and excitement. At the last moment everything seemed to happen so fast. I nervously toyed with the heart-shaped locket around my neck. It had been given to me by my brother as a parting gift and at that time it was the most immediate link to family members that I had. The aircraft, which was a DC10 and operated by Air Canada, was smoothly cruising at an altitude of thirty-three thousand feet. The hustle and bustle of boarding was over and the preliminary safety instructions had been delivered, making us aware of the emergency exits on the aircraft should a situation arise, the use of the oxygen masks and the location under our seats of our "Mae Wests," the inflatable life jackets. The thought of coming down in water was scary for me due to my overwhelming fear of water. I checked quickly to see that my life jacket was under the seat. There was a lull in announcements as we awaited the arrival of our meal and it allowed some time for reflection on the past weeks.

Without doubt the goodbyes were painful. The staff at work had given a small party for me and a day later my personal friends and other colleagues treated me to dinner at one of the nicer hotels in town.

The evening before travelling south, my parents and I dined at my brother's home and when it was time to leave it was hard to say good-bye to him, my sister-in-law, niece and nephew. The following day we left the north of Scotland and travelled south to Prestwick by car. I was accompanied by my parents and an aunt and uncle. We stayed overnight at a bed and breakfast but I did not sleep. All the fears, real and unreal, seemed to jump out at me in the dark stillness of night.

The following day came too quickly. After breakfasting we had some time to spare, and as we were in the vicinity of Scotland's well-loved poet, we made a car trip to Robert Burns' cottage. After an enjoyable interlude, we drove to the airport. My father had his cine-camera with him and wanted to preserve this sojourn of mine for posterity, so we all took our places and posed for the camera. I was clutching Hamish McGonk. This was a little stuffed mascot which rather looked like Humpty Dumpty, fully dressed in his highland regalia. He had been given to me by a patient who had made it for my trip.

I was wearing a light coat the day I flew to Canada and although the sun was shining it was cool. We did have a shower of hail stones, rather unusual for July. When we went inside the airport my mother discovered that she no longer was in possession of her handbag. She was upset enough that her daughter was leaving for Canada but became doubly so at the loss of not only her handbag but the contents therein. She recalled she had it last at the cottage. It was decided that together with my uncle she would make her way back to the cottage some distance away in an attempt to retrieve the bag. They said their goodbyes to me and hoped to return before the flight left. I felt terrible, both because of her loss and because my mother seemed to be snatched so quickly from me, particularly when I had not mentally composed myself yet for the parting. Fortunately the plane was delayed one hour because of mechanical trouble and this provided the possibility of them returning before my departure. However, I was nervous about my first flight, particularly as I still retained some fears of aeroplanes from my childhood. Then the second announcement was delivered, stating that a further one-hour delay was anticipated as the mechanical problem had still not been fixed. I had visions of the wings coming off mid Atlantic and with all the upheavals going on, I decided to have my first beer. Not being accustomed to alcohol it did help to tranquillize me and it added a little cheer. Then suddenly, my mother reappeared clasping her purse triumphantly. Someone at the Burns' cottage had found it and it was returned with the contents intact.

Sometime later the announcement was made for all passengers on flight number such and such to proceed to the departure lounge. This was it, the great moment of adventure, only I wasn't feeling too adventurous at this point. We all hugged and everyone choked back the tears and, it seemed, we were all determined to keep our emotions in check. We joined a small procession of travellers gradually winding their way to the departure exit, some of whom were also emigrating and some returning to Canada from a vacation. Whatever the reason a great deal of tears were shed that day. My family were temporarily distracted and looking at something behind them. I seized the moment and quickly made a dash through the exit to show my passport and by the time they looked around, I had gone through the barrier. I called out to them, blew a kiss and disappeared into the lounge, the tears streaming down my face. I couldn't bear the thought of that last drawn-out hug and knew my composure wouldn't have lasted much longer. Safely inside, a female voice spoke to me in a strong Glasgow accent and inquired if I too was emigrating. The relief of finding another "orphan," as I felt I was at that precise moment, was wonderful. We became immediate friends and were able to share our feelings of loneliness.

Soon the loudspeaker boomed out the message we had been waiting for and in orderly formation we passed through the last barrier to the outside where a blast of cool air greeted us. We made our way across the tarmac, climbed the stairway and at the door of the aircraft I took a final gulp of Scottish air and gave a wave in the direction of the visitors' deck in the hope my family would see me. I could not get over the size of the plane and how many people it could accommodate. We were all given assistance to find our designated seat and instructed regarding hand and overhead luggage. My new friend and I were soon parted but we were reassured that once the aircraft was airborne we could freely walk about and visit, which we did. When the craft was fully loaded one could hear the throbbing of the engines and then feel a gentle movement as the aeroplane nudged forward, taxied down the runway, turned, hesitated, and then we were off. The take-off was smooth and on reaching the appropriate altitude it seemed to glide with the grace of a bird in flight. In seven hours we would be in Canada.

Our first stop was at Shannon Airport, in Ireland. Never having set foot in Ireland before, I persuaded the stewardess to allow to me to step down, as the doors were already open, so that I could stand on Irish soil. Amused at the request she permitted me to do so.

The time passed quickly, what with visiting, mealtimes, coffee breaks and a movie show, not to mention, for some, a sleep. Although I was tired out from the excitement and the general hubbub of the past two days, sleep eluded me.

With heart pounding, and ears popping, we were now in descent mode. It was a little bumpy at times as we bounced through the clouds, but soon buildings were visible, as was the St Lawrence Seaway. We were about to land at Dorval Airport, in Quebec. As the wheels touched down on the runway, a round of applause was given, presumably to show appreciation to the pilot and crew for a safe deliverance. This was not our destination but it was our first port of entry into Canada and therefore we were required to be checked through customs and the immigration authorities. We were not treated very cordially, being herded through the customs buildings by an irate French-Canadian female. Fortunately, because of the initial flight delay in Scotland, we were processed rather quickly so that we could re-board our flight for Toronto. Once again safely aboard, the protocols were again reiterated for our own safety.

The doors of the aircraft opened and I felt a blast of heat. We were in Toronto and it was apparently ninety degrees Fahrenheit, with high humidity.

Like the other travellers, I collected my luggage from the carousel. Suddenly I felt very lost and weary. I had envisioned someone from the hospital being there to welcome me as a newcomer, but no one came. Lacking relatives or acquaintances in this new land, I felt very alone. It wasn't long before my Scottish friend rescued me. She had been met by a group of friends and she quickly organized them into taking me to my destination.

CHAPTER THREE
A LANDED IMMIGRANT

I arrived at what was known as the Foreign Nurses' Residence. I bade farewell to my new friends with the promise to keep in touch and once again I was alone. I entered the residence where an elderly woman greeted me from behind a desk in the front foyer. Placing my heavy suitcases on the floor I announced my name and indicated I was a new employee. Without emotion I was assigned a room located on the second floor. I enquired about the lift and she informed me there were none. I would have to manage my suitcases up the two flights of stairs on my own. For the short duration of the conversation, I was fascinated by the appearance of a plastic tube that came out of the side of her mouth and was threaded up and over the ear on that side, only to disappear into somewhere not visible. It gave her a forbidding appearance and that, combined with her indifference towards me, was just another dimension to deal with that day, which had indeed been long.

I picked up the suitcases and, with a key in my hand, I struggled to the second floor, stopping every so often to get my breath. On reaching the landing I located my room, opened the door and stood motionless for a moment. I had lived in several residences in my training years and was well aware that these rooms fulfilled a purpose, but this room had to be the most stark and unwelcoming one I had ever been assigned. I looked around, first at the bed, which was the army barracks type, painted white at least, and covered with white sheets and a white bedspread. At the bedside there was a very small white mat. Alongside was a white bedside table. In another corner was a chest of drawers with a mirror and to provide relief from the stark white this item was made of dark wood. I walked over to the open window, to observe the view, and to my horror it was fitted with heavy metal bars. I looked across the road, my view being the side of a large brick building, with no doors or windows. I found out later that it belonged to the Red Cross. If I craned my neck I could just see a main thoroughfare which later that night and thereafter, to my chagrin, was always bustling with activity and the sound of sirens. My immediate reaction to my surroundings was that I must have entered a psychiatric ward quite by mistake, one with maximum security, because it did look more like a hospital than a bedroom.

Being unaccustomed to the humidity and heat, I went in search of something to quench my thirst. I approached the elderly lady at the front desk and asked if any beverages were available. She gave me directions to the main nurses' residence where apparently there was a "pop" machine. I dodged in and out of buildings through numerous doors until I finally reached the correct site. This residence, with ivy clinging to the nice stone walls, appeared to be more like the nurses' residences in Britain, with more character and warmth to it than the one I was residing in. I was shown downstairs to where this "pop" machine was situated and instructed to drop in a quarter. All I had in my possession was paper money and travellers' cheques, and on seeing the perplexed look on my face the proffer of a coin was made by a resident. Success was mine! Clutching my cold drink, I made my way back to my quarters, musing to myself that I now knew what a "quarter" and "pop" were and how to operate the soft drinks machine.

I had barely started my unpacking when there was a tap on the door and a chubby young woman about my age entered. She introduced herself and proceeded to tell me she was next door to me and working as an assistant nurse. We chatted a while as I went about my chores. As she talked I was never sure if she was looking at me until I finally realised that the poor girl had a glass eye. I was glad of the company and found her very congenial but later, as the weeks went by, I learned of her dramatic mood swings, and sometimes when a greeting was given to her, the door of her room would be slammed shut for no obvious reason. There were only a few people living in the building: two African nurses whom I barely saw and one English girl who expounded to me about Canadians having a thin veneer of sophistication. A German girl also resided there, and whilst I was relaxing in the communal sitting room one morning, she came in. It wasn't too long after, on hearing my accent and verbally confirming that I really was a Briton, that she proceeded to lambaste me because of the war. I quickly ended the conversation by saying Germany had started it and they had lost, whereupon I left.

The next morning, in spite of my exhaustion from the previous day's travel, I had to present myself for work. I had to go through many formalities which included instruction regarding the type of uniform and shoes to be worn and the various places to purchase these. I was introduced to the ward staff and given a tour of the facility. As good fortune would have it, I met an Irish nurse in the dining hall and she offered to take me shopping for my uniforms that evening. The following day, I appeared fully regaled in a Canadian nurse's uniform and already began to feel like one of the gang. There was a fair amount of friendly teasing when I would pronounce certain words with a heavy brogue, but it was all taken in the spirit it was given. I soon fitted in, but there were various terminologies used that I had to familiarize myself with. The system was different in several ways, but the human race remains the same in their needs, and in the way they experience fears at a time of illness, so that adaptation was not so complex.

I worked on a large surgical ward where there was a predominance of cancer patients. In Scotland, I had worked a fair amount with cancer clients and in those days, we were not allowed to use the word cancer, so I was quite taken aback when patients in Canada would openly discuss their illness. I was not quite prepared as how to respond to them. I discussed this matter with the nursing staff and they convinced me of the necessity of this knowledge and taught me that patients have a right to know so as to put their affairs in order. I did not think of this as being a cultural issue, but more a different approach.

I made, in all innocence, a few faux pas. One of these occurred in the evening before a certain gentleman went to the operating room. He was to have an enema, so I assembled all the necessary equipment required for the procedure. One of the nurses caught me heading down the corridor complete with tray in hand and asked what I was doing. I explained and was told laughingly, male orderlies give enemas to male patients. When sutures had to come out I learned that the doctor, not the nurse, removed these, and when any intravenous fluid required to be changed, the intravenous nurse did this. This was somewhat boring as I was used to carrying out duties with more responsibilities.

By this time, I had met a Scottish nurse who was looking for a roommate to share her accommodation. We got along well and I found it thrilling to live in my very first apartment instead of institutional living. There was a snag: we were always on opposite shifts. It's not that I depended on her for total friendship as I had already established my own circle, but as I worked quite often until twelve midnight, I did not relish walking to the subway to wait there for a train home and then afterwards walk along the poorly-lit street by myself. This made me feel a little nervous. I started to think about getting out of the city when one night at work an older nurse mentioned that someone had been murdered in an area close to where I had to walk. Even though this had happened a long time ago, it put thoughts

24

into my mind. I enjoyed the work immensely but suffered from bouts of homesickness. There was an elderly patient in the ward who also came from Aberdeen. On hearing her accent I would become weepy, spending a portion of each day in the bathroom at work, wiping my tears, until I looked in the mirror one day and told myself I could go home at any time. This seemed to set me straight.

There really was a great deal to do, but city life was not too appealing to me, and it was around this time I met a nurse, of English origin, who was leaving Toronto to work in the north. It was a government position with Health and Welfare, Medical Services Branch, and it meant working on an Indian Reserve with the Cree Natives. It sounded interesting and I desired a quieter place to work. She gave me all the necessary addresses to write to and in a very short time I had a reply to my letter. I was accepted immediately, not even being required to produce references at that time. My training background seemed to suffice. I had only been in Toronto for eight months and now I was about to embark on a new adventure. I have often wondered what my life would have been had I not immigrated and joined the Federal Government.

The steady motion of the train and the sound of the wheels on the track had an almost hypnotic effect on me. I remember closing my eyes and just allowing my thoughts to drift at will. I had plenty of time to reflect as the train meandered across the vast expanse of prairie land. I had boarded the train at 9.45 pm and was directed to my roomette in carriage number seven, and room number twenty-seven. This way of travel was all very novel for me and I had to familiarize myself with my surroundings. In the roomette I had my own toilet and wash-hand basin. In the evening my seat was converted into a bed which the porter on board prepared. When the porter appeared, I was not at all sure of the tipping protocol, as just a few hours before I had had an awkward moment.

My roommate had got me safely by taxi to the railway station in Toronto and as we drew up to the curb, a portly gentleman, of African descent, stepped forward as the vehicle door opened. He reached down to assist me with my luggage. I protested, but he was quite insistent. I, wanting to be mannerly, stepped back and allowed him to do so. I thanked him profusely for his help. After the suitcases were placed on the floor by the ticket counter, I was still aware of his presence and, not being too worldly, I had not realised the significance of this. I thanked him again and, in a booming voice, he said, "Ain't you goin' to tip me?" Very embarrassed, I fumbled in my purse. I had no idea of what would be considered an adequate tip and, at the same time, I felt I had been conned into this situation at his insistence, so I gave him the smallest denomination in coinage that I had. He wasn't at all impressed!

I thought about the farewell dinners and the bustling about prior to departure. I had arrived in Toronto with a couple of suitcases, but as I had collected extra belongings, I had to purchase a trunk to accommodate everything. I had become quite skilled in packing, utilizing every square inch as taught to me by my mother. I had made arrangements for the trunk to be picked up and sent on board the train I was travelling on.

After my evening meal on board, I returned to my room. Unable to concentrate on reading I decided to go to bed, whereupon I had no problem falling asleep. During the night there were a few stops and shunting noises that disturbed me. I sat up and looked outside and could see in the clear sky a beautiful full moon and a galaxy of stars which seemed to dance. The snow lay heavy on the ground and the treetops looked as though they had fine wisps of cotton wool hanging from them.

The following evening one of the porters, who somehow knew I was a nurse, asked if I would check on an elderly woman in the next coach. She was feeling ill and they were not sure if at the next stop the following morning the lady should be taken off the train to a nearby hospital. I agreed and was escorted to the invalid's room. She was a delightful lady in her eighties, travelling alone to Alberta after visiting her son in Ontario. After introducing myself as a Registered Nurse, I asked her a few appropriate questions in an attempt to establish her medical problem. It seemed that the journey alone was proving too much for her and she appeared more anxious than ill. She was perspiring with her nervousness. After sponging her forehead, I ordered up some tea. I was convinced there was no emergency occurring and I advised the porter accordingly. My patient and I spent an hour or two chatting over our cup of tea. Soon she was relaxed and laughing. I made sure she was comfortable and settled before bidding her goodnight.

After breakfast I visited her again to find she was feeling quite well. At this point, I had to say good-bye and gather my belongings. Soon we would be arriving at Winnipeg, Manitoba, where I was, upon arrival, to proceed by taxi to the downtown core. A hotel room had been booked for me, but first I had to arrange with the forward baggage department to have my trunk sent on to Wabowden Station by rail and subsequently by air freight to Norway House.

The next day, I made my way to the Medical Services Branch office for documentation and instruction with regards to the ongoing journey. That completed, and after meeting many of the staff, I had some free time to look around Winnipeg. In the evening I reorganized my suitcases in readiness for the next leg of my journey.

The following day a social worker met me at the hotel as had been arranged earlier. She had a baby and two five-year-olds with her. I was to escort these children back to their home at Norway House. This was not an unusual event. The children had been brought to Winnipeg for medical treatment and on discharge it was the practice, if possible, to have someone going into the community to escort them back to their parents. With her help we travelled to the airport by taxi and prepared for our departure. Within the hour the much awaited announcement was made over the loudspeaker. It was, at last, boarding time and those with children were allowed to pre-board. With my young charges I crossed the tarmac to the waiting aircraft with its engines roaring, and ascended the steps. The aircraft was a DC 3, which was much smaller than the one I had left Britain aboard some eight months before. I felt quite excited. Comfortably seated and having secured the children and myself with the seatbelts, I busied myself in removing the layers of clothing from the baby. It wasn't long before everyone was on board, the doors were closed, and we started to taxi down the runway. The stewardess began the customary instructions as to what we would have to do should there be an emergency landing. I was only paying half attention to the announcement as I was busily preparing to feed the baby. Prior to take-off we were given the usual candy to suck while the aeroplane got airborne. The swallowing motion helped to prevent eardrums popping. Of course the baby was too young for this, so I had been advised to let the baby suck on the bottle. The child's feed time had been delayed because of the boarding procedure, but soon the irritable child was soothed. The bottle barely empty, my little charge was soon in the land of nod. This was my first encounter with the North American Indians. I looked down at this beautiful angelic face with the long eyelashes and tuft of black hair and glanced over at the other two fastened securely in their seats. I sensed I was going to be happy in my new posting.

The time "flew" past quickly, no pun intended, but I cannot say the journey was entirely uneventful. As we proceeded through dark heavy clouds an electrical storm caused considerable turbulence. Needless to say the children became a little frightened, clinging to me. Although somewhat anxious myself, I had to put on an air of calmness, making a game out of the situation each time the plane hit air pockets, causing the plane to lurch. Not yet being a seasoned air traveller, it was a great relief when the storm abated and we were making our descent into Norway House.

CHAPTER FOUR
NORWAY HOUSE

The landing was a smooth one. In an orderly manner the passengers made their way down the steps to where a crowd was waiting. Over the years that I spent in the north, I found that the arrival of an aeroplane was indeed an event, and usually drew a crowd of people for a variety of reasons. The plane brought the mail to isolated communities, along with fresh meat and vegetables and sometimes a loved one returning home. Such was the case when I arrived. Amongst the sea of faces were the parents of the young charges I had just escorted from Winnipeg. I was greeted by an Englishman who introduced himself as the Director of Nursing from the hospital and, following the initial courteous greetings, I handed over the children to their appropriate families who were quick to embrace after their separation.

There was a lot of snow about. I did not realise at the time that the plane had landed on a frozen lake. Perhaps it was just as well, as it took me some time to accept that the ice was thick enough to safely hold an aircraft, or people on machines of transport such as skidoos and bombardiers. I learned that bombardiers were considered the local taxi service. These vehicles were painted a dark blue colour and their shape bore resemblance to a gigantic beetle on caterpillar tracts. There were windows on each side of the vehicle, rather resembling portholes on a ship. On the roof there was a hatch door, so positioned should the occupants require an emergency exit. I asked numerous questions on the short trip to my quarters, one of them being about this mode of travel. Its usage would become commonplace for me. I would eventually get used to the bumpy and noisy rides. The hatch was opened in readiness, they explained, if they were unsure of the ice conditions on the water at certain times of the year and particularly where a joining of two rivers occurred, creating a weakness in the ice at the juncture.

My new home was in the nurses' residence, a modern building and pleasantly decorated. My bedroom was quite spacious with the window facing towards the hospital, located some one hundred yards away. The residence was part of the compound, that is to say, a number of other buildings, which included homes for the married staff, were also situated near to the hospital. I later came to enjoy this arrangement of living in close proximity to the various staff members as it made me feel like part of a large, happy family. The familiar scene presented again: unpacking and making acquaintances with the other residents, followed the next day by a tour of the hospital. It was during this tour that a remark was made by the administrator and one that I never forgot but did not necessarily heed. He announced, "When you work with the government don't rock the boat." I thought at the time it was a strange remark, but in the latter years of my career I would understand the repercussions that follow such an action.

The hospital was a wooden structure, painted gaily in yellow and red and had a bed capacity to accommodate thirty-five patients, comprising adults, children and babies, but during my stay there I witnessed fifty-four in-patients on one occasion at least. There was a delivery room, emergency outpatient facilities, an x-ray department and a small, well-equipped operating room. The wards were small, each holding four to six beds. As well, there were two children's wards, a newborn nursery and an isolation room. Any major illness or injuries had to be flown south to Winnipeg in a chartered aircraft. I spent the next few days shadowing the Head Nurse in order to learn the routine. I found out very quickly that there should have been a complement of thirteen registered nurses to cover all of the shifts and days off. Instead, there were only four of us. Needless to say a new staff member addition was greeted with enthusiasm. There were local native girls working as nursing aides, perhaps totalling five or six, whose duties were quite different from ours. There had been a dentist on staff, but he had resigned before I arrived. The medical staff should have consisted of three doctors, but one had also just recently left, leaving a vacant position which never was filled during my stay. The Zone Director, himself a retired surgeon, was mainly involved in an administrative capacity concerning medical matters.

The fact that we cared for different age groups within the facility provided us with a varied and interesting work opportunity. The adult in-patients had many of the usual complaints which included high blood pressure, cardiac symptoms, occasional mental health problems and diabetes. The children, on the other hand, presented with the infectious diseases that they are subject to at the various ages of growing up, particularly where immunization protection had not taken place. Impetigo was common, often seen following chickenpox or a scabies infection. Pneumonia and croup were quite prevalent at certain times of the year and these children were often desperately ill, requiring a great deal of nursing care. Many were placed in oxygen tents, and with intravenous fluids, steam and antibiotics they usually pulled through. Meningitis, too, would appear from time to time. Then of course there were always the injured patients from accidents who appeared at the emergency department for treatment. The more seriously injured or ill cases were admitted in order to monitor their condition.

One of the first matters I needed to attend to was to have a parka made. We already had snow and frozen lakes, and I only had a sheepskin jacket from Scotland and a pair of dress boots. I was directed to send my measurements, along with my choice of colour and type of fur that I required around the hood of the parka, to The Pas, located further north. In the meantime I ordered a pair of mukluks to be made by a local Cree woman. All that was required from me was an outline of my foot. There were different combinations used in the making of these boots. Some were totally made from moose hide and others made with red and navy burlap material for the leg part and only moose hide for the foot which were how mine were fashioned. Sometimes, for a baby, they were made from deerskin, which was very soft. The decor around the top of the boots was beautifully embroidered while others had a floral arrangement done in colourful beadwork. To complete these, a trim of rabbit fur was often placed above and below the decorated part. Either moose hide made into thongs, or wool yarn woven into ties with pompoms attached at the ends, were used to secure the boots, adding yet more colour.

The Natives hunted the moose for meat and used the skin to make articles of clothing, but mainly for making the mukluks. After the hide had been cleaned, it was stretched on a wooden frame and placed over a smouldering fire. In this way the hide was tanned, taking up to two weeks or more. Meantime, the meat was cut into strips and hung up to dry. The meat looked and felt rather leathery, but it remained edible for a long time. In the early days the dried meat often would be pulverized. To this, animal fat and berries were added to make a mixture called Pemmican. This could be stored in a skin bag and be used as a nutritious meal while travelling.

In a short space of time my beautiful, warm parka arrived. I was greatly relieved, because temperatures often reached minus forty degrees Fahrenheit. The inner part of the coat was made of warm, white duffel which is similar to a woollen blanket, lined with green satin, and the outer part, referred to as the shell, was made of dark green grenfell, a material which kept out the wind. I was told that the grenfell material on the coat exterior had been used by a Dr Grenfell who had been an English missionary as well as a medical doctor in Labrador, Canada. The hood was very warm and windproof when worn up over the head. The white fox fur trim felt soft against the face as well as providing further warmth. Loving animals and appreciating their beauty, I would never elect to use the fur of an animal again. They did not deserve the cruel treatment meted out to them by humans. Many of these animals were trapped, and no doubt suffered greatly without having a rapid or humane end to their lives.

The northern location of Norway House meant that the only way to access the settlement was by boat or float planes in the summer, or a plane landing on the frozen ice on skis in the winter. The community is located approximately three hundred miles from Winnipeg. It was isolated geographically because of the non-existence of a roadway. I had been told that the total circumference of the community was about ten miles. The first Norway House post was established near to what is known as Warren's Landing and had been destroyed by fire. The Norway House that I came to know was situated on the south-east corner of Little Playgreen Lake and built in 1827. The first settlers to the area had been Norwegian axe-men, hired to cut a road to a place called York Factory. Norway House was once a thriving community of forty-five hundred people of Cree and Metis backgrounds, and was a significant post for the Hudson's Bay Company in its trading network. The York boats, so named for the Hudson's Bay Company at York Factory, were suitable for travel on the lakes, carrying twice the cargo of furs and supplies. They would carry the furs through Norway House to York Factory from where they would be freighted to England. The boats were propelled by oars or a square sail. Boat-builders were recruited from the Orkney Islands, off the coast of Scotland. It has never ceased to amaze me, as I learned through my travels, how important the Scottish adventurers were to the growth and future development of Canada.

Because of travel costs, one did not hop on a plane each weekend and take a trip, but rather remained in the community, in most cases, until vacation time rolled around. My needs were simple as I already had accommodation and meals provided. The clothing I required was very basic, consisting of long woollen underwear, known as "long johns," heavy sweaters, scarves and mittens, and of course the parka and mukluks for outerwear. The Hudson's Bay Company, being the only store, provided a potpourri of merchandise, from fresh and frozen foods, clothing and camping equipment, rifles and ammunition, trapping paraphernalia, as well many other important items essential to living in isolation. The Hudson's Bay Company building was quite old and near to the store was the jailhouse, above whose doorway was the date 1856. The jail was in use until 1892 and finally used as a storage place for gunpowder.

I hadn't been at Norway House very long when a native I worked with made the remark during our conversation, "You white people." I remember being taken aback, as I had never thought of a skin colour difference and consciously looked at her colour and mine. I believe that was my first introduction to racial differences. I did not, at that time, realise there existed the deep-seated, antagonistic feelings of the Indian people towards the white man. Over the many years I worked with the native people, I gained an understanding of their resentments. I cannot blame them for their mistrust of us because of the broken treaties and having our belief systems foisted upon them, thus destroying their cultural ways and stripping away their dignity and right to control their own destiny. I wanted to learn as much as possible about these people and felt very proud to serve them. I tried to learn some words in the Cree language, but I was unsuccessful as the pronunciation was hard to master. I had further plans to travel to other Indian Reservations and knew that I would encounter different languages, so I did not really apply myself to the true art of learning. They, on the other hand, were smarter than I, as most of them had mastered the English language, although at times we required an interpreter for the older generations.

There was a local court case scenario shortly after my arrival whereby a young male Indian was on trial for causing bodily harm to another male, a gun being used as the weapon. I attended the trial out of curiosity on my off-duty time. The young lad in question asked the judge to have an interpreter present. It was a long and dragged-out procedure, involving a three-way conversation. At one point the accused did not like some part of the evidence presented, and in good English raised his objections. "Right", said the judge, "if you can answer like that and understand, we will dispense with the interpreter!" The trial continued at a more rapid pace.

I learned that there were treaty and non-treaty Indians at Norway House. The treaty natives lived on the reservation some five miles away at Rossville. They were given a treaty number as a means of identification. The Federal Government was, as a result of the signed treaties, responsible for the healthcare, housing and transportation of these people. In July each year there were "Treaty Days", whereby a small annuity was given to family members. I believe this was in the region of five dollars per person. In times gone by, ammunition necessary for hunting and equipment for fishing were given, along with food supplies such as flour and lard. Although I never attended the event, I was told that the Royal Canadian Mounted Police dressed in their red tunics for the occasion, and a carnival was held that day in celebration. The village at Rossville consisted of a church, a school and a number of homes.

The children were educated on the island in one of two schools. One was Roman Catholic, run by the nuns and the other was non-denominational. The natives at that time lived in small houses where overcrowding was not unusual. There were two churches: one Roman Catholic and the other Anglican. I attended the small, simple, beautiful Anglican one. I would be amused at the casualness of the late-comers arriving at the church service. At times, when the prayers were under way, a sudden loud noise could be heard from the rear as the heavy portal opened and the tardy individuals, adults and children alike, entered. A clanging sound followed when the door was allowed to swing freely to a close, followed by a loud click as the door latched, shattering the place of peaceful reverence. With a scurry and a shuffle, intercepted by coughing and "ahems" they took their places alongside the other worshipers. Meantime, the already present congregation were twisting their necks to see who had arrived. The singing voices were melodious, but somehow each note seemed to be elasticised to the full, causing a little musical chaos for the organist who was several notes ahead of everyone. Religious services were also held at the hospital for the sick, the ministers and priests being able to speak the Cree language. In the mid-eighteenth century, Reverend James Evans, a Methodist minister, lived amongst the Crees at Norway House. Having difficulty in teaching them to read from the English alphabet, he devised the syllabic characters, thus creating a written Indian language.

Time passed quickly. I loved walking, and once I was convinced about the safety of the ice there was no stopping me. Because of the frozen lakes, there was scope to walk in different directions in the winter time. A favourite walk was through the beautiful forest trails. It was not unusual for me to be accompanied by several dogs on these walks, and I must say I enjoyed not only their company but also watching their high jinks in the snow. There was one occasion when travelling in the woods I came upon a group of local Indians, males and females, drinking alcohol, but with the presence of the animals, I felt safe - not that there was any animosity, which was as well, my not being adept as yet in dealing with intoxicated individuals.

There were very strict rules with regard to dogs. Many puppies were born only to become strays. These grew to be adult dogs, often forming themselves into packs, and at times, an order was issued to shoot them on sight. Everybody was warned ahead of time, so it was the individual's responsibility to contain their pets, otherwise they would be classified as a stray and eliminated. I always found this so distasteful, but apparently there had been occasions where children had been knocked down and savaged by these hungry animals. It was a fact of northern living and had to be accepted.

Another enjoyable trek was crossing the frozen lake to visit the home of an old Norwegian fellow who was married to an Indian woman. The walk could be very invigorating on a cold day, especially with no trees for protection. I had been taken there initially by an English nurse, who loved to walk as I did, and she introduced me to the couple. We really had to find different ways in which to amuse ourselves and we did this by visiting, having parties, even attending an occasional movie which was shown in a small, work building used by the hospital carpenter. Once in a while I would go down river to a home and watch an Indian woman do her intricate beadwork.

I had not realised we were so surrounded by water and small islands. Everything was frozen at the time of my arrival, in March, and gave the impression of a solid land mass. The days got longer and warmer as spring and then summer rolled around. It was not long before I became acquainted with the "mosquito." It seemed they liked new blood, and I was constantly plagued with their biting which produced welts over all exposed areas of my body. Sometimes the bites caused my eyes to be puffy, not to mention the constant need to scratch, making me very irritable. Some people were immune to the mosquito attacks, and, in later years, I too must have built up an immunity as I would only have a hint of annoyance. I was given some old wives' tales as to how to avoid them, but I was not convinced that the odour of garlic was any more tolerable than the bites, so I opted to take my chances along with the help of an antihistamine cream. Worse was to come when I was chased by the horse flies which seemed particularly fond of wet skin!

It was in the summer time that I requested to work permanent afternoon shifts which meant starting at four o'clock in the afternoon until midnight. This time schedule was a satisfactory arrangement for me as I never liked early mornings. It also allowed me to go out in the hospital boat in the mornings and cross to Bull Island where my friend Marlene and I would make a fire to roast wieners. This was all very adventurous for me. I had never been in small boats nor experienced barbecues or weiner roasts before. It was while in a bathing suit and in the boat with my skin wet that these horrible horse flies would attack. Invariably, they struck it lucky with me, managing to gouge out pieces of skin. I was always afraid of water, but I did not let that stop me travelling in this manner, nor spoil my trips. I wore my life jacket, which was a must. Failure to comply might have restricted us in the use of the boat. Some of my hospital colleagues had to be in the boat with me as I depended on them to drive the outboard motor. On discovering my fears, one day they sat, arms folded, and refused to take the boat out, saying it was time I learned to drive. Reluctantly, I positioned myself at the rear of the boat and awaited their instructions. They were very patient with me and I was able to successfully take the boat out into the lake and dock it again. The lake was used by the amphibian aircraft for landing, and, of course, as I started out for the first time, a float plane came in to land, and although it was well past me, the wash effect was felt, disturbing the water enough for this beginner to be very aware of the swell. With great calmness, my colleagues instructed me on how to cut the waves.

There were times, when on boat trips, we would have to return home rather quickly because of an electrical storm. They were fairly frequent, and I remember walking to the residence in the dark on several occasions and seeing the sky light up with the sheet lightning. Everything around would be illuminated while it lasted. No thunder could be heard to give a warning, just these eerie flashes in the quiet of the night.

During the summer, I ventured on a longer trip by boat. It was one I would not readily forget. A few days before, I had read the hospital notice board. Mentioned was a fishing trip to Spider Island. The invitation to sign up was extended to any staff member who was off duty and interested. It was not unusual to have these opportunities, and, of course, I wanted to see and do as much as possible, so I signed my name. As it turned out, I was the only female off-duty out of our scant staff. On the appointed day, the male Director of Nursing, an Indian guide and two other married men from the compound and myself set off. We had to be back by early evening as all of us from the residence and married quarters were going on a barbecue to one of the islands. When we left, it was a pleasant morning, the water was calm, and with the sun shining, the temperature was conducive for travelling. From Norway House we first crossed a part of Little Playgreen Lake before reaching Lake Winnipeg. I cannot recall the exact distance but twenty miles was mentioned to me. The entire trip was in the vicinity of forty miles. An Indian guide was at the helm of the boat and he knew the safe channels to take us through. I sat up at the front of the boat, exuberant with the anticipated adventure and gulping in the pure, fresh air. Quite a spray of water was thrown up as we sped along, but I didn't mind. I was having a good time.

On arrival at the island our clothing was quite wet. One of the men made a fire on the beach as the rest of us gathered driftwood. Being summertime there was no real concerns over the wet clothing and after standing by the fire for a while we were soon relatively dry. The men fished as I wandered about on the beach picking up the gnarled pieces of driftwood, trying to make something in my mind's eye from the many tortuous shapes. I always found strolling on empty beaches, searching for some treasure that might have drifted from afar, a form of total mental relaxation. We had taken a picnic lunch of sandwiches with us and eating out in this manner was enjoyable. I only wished another female had been with me for company, but it didn't work out that way with the staffing situation.

Black clouds were looming ominously above us and the men decided to head back. They would have to be content with their "fishy tales" of the one that got away! All aboard again and homeward bound. The first part of the trip was smooth, but soon the temperature changed and the wind volume increased, making travel a little bumpy! The weather was not improving as we pulled into Warren's Landing to replenish the fuel. By this time we were all wet and shivering from the cold spray. Although it was summertime, I remember observing how white the tips of my fingers were with the cold, and it was necessary to keep them under my armpits for warmth. Off we went again. By now we were approaching Lake Winnipeg, which is the sixth largest fresh water lake in Canada. It is known, at times, to have very high waves although it is not considered a very deep lake. The Director of Nursing, who was very afraid of the water due to a bad experience earlier in life, had his eyes covered with a towel. I believe, because he was so terribly afraid, it made me strong. The situation was serious. Without a doubt this was like being in the middle of the ocean. One moment the boat was tossed upwards on a wave, only to be thrust down again. It made steering very difficult, and it could have resulted in the boat capsizing. I was unable to swim, but with the storm in full swing and the coldness of the water, perhaps, that was an inconsequential matter. Each time the boat was plunged down, some water came in. We tried desperately to bail out the water using a tin mug. In spite of my unhealthy attitude towards water and harbouring the belief we were going to drown, I became very calm, which to this day amazes me. Thanks to the ability of our Cree guide and perhaps a guardian angel watching over us, we survived. Meantime, waiting anxiously at the dock, were the other staff members who had delayed the trip and barbecue, hoping we would arrive safely. As we pulled in, there were great yells of relief all round as a bunch of drenched, cold individuals clambered over the side of the boat onto terra firma. A detailed description was given of the exploit. Each of us talked through one another in our excitement and determination not to leave out any details. After a hot shower and a quick change of clothing, off we went by boat to our barbecue, undeterred. The water was calm, but as we were not travelling far, I had nothing to fear.

I had a wonderful sense of freedom in my off-duty hours, but there were trials and tribulations at work. The lack of staff brought its own problems. On the evening shift that I had elected to work, I was the only Registered Nurse on duty with three Indian aides. It was always a busy shift. There was the usual routine work which included giving out medications as prescribed, wound dressings to change, blood pressure checks and a variety of treatments to complete. Checking and replenishing the oxygen tanks and administering to the many babies on steam inhalations, or in oxygen tents due to their breathing difficulties, was time consuming. Many required to be fed by bottle and as they gasped for breath, the chore was prolonged. Apart from this, there were emergency patients that came to the hospital. Their medical conditions could range from minor incidences to much more dramatic episodes, at times requiring evacuation to a larger hospital in the south.

Located in the outlying areas were Nursing Stations, which were manned by either one, two or three nurses depending on the size of population and the availability of nursing personnel. In these areas there were no doctors. Instead, the nurse cared for the health of the entire community, diagnosing illnesses and providing treatment, as well as conducting a public health programme. Some babies were delivered at the Nursing Station, but usually any firstborns and from the fifth pregnancy onwards, including those expectant mothers with suspected abnormalities, were sent to us for delivery care at the hospital. This applied also to other medical conditions that were beyond the scope of the nurse or in cases that required constant care. The Nursing Station staff made radio contact every morning with the hospital doctor and in between times if a health problem could not be resolved.

On the evening shift the radio was on at all times, and, from time to time, we received calls from our colleagues for assistance. We would then call the on-duty doctor to give them advice. Patients were often transported by plane from the Nursing Stations at the end of the day and on my evening shift it was not unusual to receive a number of patients all at once whilst in the middle of in-patient care. Of these new arrivals, sometimes a native woman would be in full labour. It was my responsibility to admit the patient, assess the stage of labour and inform the doctor who normally did not come until just prior to delivery. We would have to gauge the timing so that the doctor would not have to wait around. The fact that I and others similarly trained could have managed an uncomplicated delivery was neither here nor there. In this setting the doctor had to deliver the baby. As I was in charge, I would assign a native aide to sit with the woman in her labour and assist me by timing the contractions, but I had the hardest time keeping the aide in there. As soon as the woman would make a sound, they would run out of the room to get me, believing the baby's arrival to be imminent. At times I found the aides hiding in the kitchen or another ward with the door closed. This was most frustrating when I had so many other responsibilities, and had to go looking for them. When a patient was very ill or well established in labour, either a nurse from the Nursing Station would act as an escort in the transportation of the client, or if this was not a viable option, a hospital nurse sometimes flew in to accompany the patient.

In off-duty hours there were chances at times to fly into a Nursing Station, at the invitation of the pilot, when there was not an emergency, but where the pilot may have had cargo or mail to deliver. Such was the case when my friend Marlene and I had the opportunity to travel to Cross Lake. The aircraft was very small, a 180 Cessna. It had room for the pilot at the controls and one passenger in the back. We two joy riders managed to squeeze into the back seat. Luckily in those days, slimness was on our side, but in spite of that it was still quite cramped. I think too, that the young pilot was happy to have company. The trip going in was uneventful. We visited for a while and had coffee with the nurses, but the pilot decided he would rather have beer. Somehow, he accidentally burnt his hand, but it was not a severe burn, requiring no more than a light bandage. When it was time to take off, the senior nurse did not want us flying with this pilot who had been drinking. She tried to persuade us to fly out the following day on one of the larger, scheduled flights. We felt we could not wait, as we were to be on duty the next evening. The pilot was eventually coaxed into staying, his schedule allowing him to do so with no pressing cargo deliveries. We left very early the next morning and had no sooner got airborne when the pilot said, "We are going back", the reason being there was freezing rain on the wind shield. The senior nurse was still uneasy about our safety, but we rationalized that the alcohol would now be out of his system and we would be alright. Some time later, we took off and flew back to Norway House with the same pilot. This adventure must have caused quite a stir, because the following day we were on the "carpet" for this escapade. Our safety, they said, was very much their concern, and there were to be no more joy rides! Certainly, to look back now I can see the foolishness of our trip, but

I did not see it in the same light when younger. It was good that the senior management curbed such activities. Perhaps the next time we may not have been so lucky, as crashes did indeed occur. Forty years later I have recently met with my friend and we enjoyed recalling the episode.

One evening a sixteen-year-old girl was admitted to the hospital having been delivered of a healthy child by a local Native "Midwife." They brought her in because she was experiencing an inability to void urine. On arrival, it was obvious that she was a very ill young lady. When the Zone Director was advised of her condition, he instructed me to pass a catheter into her bladder and place her on an antibiotic regime. As I proceeded to examine her, my findings indicated that she had a very hard, ridged abdomen, and along with her falling blood pressure, pulse and temperature changes, convinced me that she had a ruptured uterus. I was unable to pass the catheter into her bladder due to swelling, bruising and lacerations from the delivery. How this poor young woman must have suffered at this local "Midwife's" hands. It was totally unnecessary with the hospital nearby. She was very restless, and in a short time showed deterioration in her condition. Both the local doctors were away from the area, and in their place were two medical students from Winnipeg. I called them, and following an examination of the girl, they tended to agree with my observations. The next line of communication was back again to the Zone Director, the Medical Administrator, living nearby. We requested permission to evacuate the patient immediately to Winnipeg, but the request was denied until morning, as it was now dark outside.

I always thought this was a cruel decision, but he felt the risk of night flying was too great. I did encounter this policy again and again, and later I came to understand the wisdom of some of these decisions. There certainly had been pilots', nurses' and patients' lives lost in similar events. If the patient's health was deemed to be so precarious and that they might not survive even the night or the trip then it was considered senseless to expose healthy individuals to the dangers of night flying and facing the weather elements. If the patients were not so critical then it was considered they could await the daylight hours.

Excellent care and monitoring was given throughout the night to this young woman. With sedation, intravenous infusions and antibiotics, she was safely transported south in the morning. The follow-up reports indicated that after a number of blood transfusions, she was taken to the operating room to have a hysterectomy for a ruptured uterus. I believe she returned to Norway House a very long time afterwards. I was told that the family felt a sense of disgrace, because the young, unmarried girl had become pregnant, so she was not sent to the hospital at the time of delivery, nor had she attended prenatal care.

The bombardier's usage was not only as a taxi service, but it also substituted as an ambulance. There was evidence, at times, I was told, that certain individuals in one location down the river were calling for the ambulance and faking illness. On the way back to the hospital, the "ill" person would then miraculously recover beside the local drinking spot. If this occurred in the spring it meant placing the ambulance driver at risk of going through the thin ice for a needless call. Not only that, but there may have been a genuine need for the vehicle elsewhere. Because of this practice, the power to send the ambulance was taken out of the hands of the nurse on duty, and all requests had to pass before the Zone Director for his approval. An incident arose, where someone came running to ask for the ambulance as a man was bleeding from his stomach and lying in the woods. The family were told by the Director to do what they would have done in the old days, and bring him to the hospital by dog team or skidoo. I was not involved in this episode, but recall this was indeed a real emergency case. Perhaps the firm approach was to teach those that were guilty not to call wolf, but as always, the innocent usually pay the price.

One evening, I hadn't long been on duty when the emergency bell rang. I was greeted by a very heavy-set woman who towered above me. She just sat down and glared at me as though defiant. She was accompanied by another older lady. When I asked as to the nature of the problem, the older one replied that her relative was hearing voices. After further enquiry I found out that the voices were telling her she must kill herself. I promptly admitted the woman to the ward and called the doctor. She was, it turned out, suffering from paranoid schizophrenia, and was known to the staff. After sedation I thought all would be well, but before the sedation had taken hold, the patient, dressed in a hospital nightgown and robe, strode past me, her eyes a little wild. I called her name and asked where she was going. " I am going to the lake!" she snarled. I called down the hall to her and asked, "Now why do you want to go there?" Walking faster she replied, "The voices want me to drown myself!" She was far too powerful for me to restrain, so I sent my aide with speed to get male help from the compound. I tried hard to intercept her, but my weighing in at one hundred pounds against someone over two hundred pounds would have been an exercise in futility. Fortunately help did arrive in time and once again, with a great struggle, she was back in the hospital and heavily sedated.

We had some very critically-ill young babies and toddlers arrive for admission, suffering from viral pneumonia. Many were coming from the outlying areas by plane in the evening. Oxygen and steam tents had to be set up to assist breathing. On one occasion I had more young patients than I had beds. The administration seem rather indifferent to my plight, and told me to put them on mattresses on the floor. I was not amused, because I took my nursing duties a little more seriously than that. Eventually I was provided with some extra beds from the store room. In the meantime a few patients who were fairly well recovered from their illness were able to be discharged in the evening, and were instructed to return as out-patients. An extra bed or two were necessary for future admissions, should the need arise during the night. Even the discharge of these patients took effort as most of them did not live nearby, and had to go to certain designated homes located further down the river. They had to dress warmly and transportation, in the form of a boat, had to be arranged. The necessary papers, showing identification, had to be made out and accompany each person, adult or child. It all took time. Records as to which home each individual was being sent had to be kept.

I became increasingly frustrated at the lack of staff, and not being able to carry out a high standard of care. The male Director of Nursing had moved away. We had a new, female Director, one with whom I had a good rapport. I requested more staff. Of course it was promptly denied, basically as there really were no spares. I believe at that point we had gained one new Registered Nurse.

I was delighted to find that the newest nurse to come on staff hailed from Glasgow, Scotland. I enjoyed working with Sheila very much. She was an excellent nurse, competent in carrying out her duties and a bundle of fun. She had not long been married to a pilot, and one could see her eyes sparkle when she knew his plane was coming in. If he arrived when she was off-duty she would pop into the hospital en route to the dockside to meet him, hardly able to contain her excitement. Tragedy was to hit, though. Perhaps it was good she was enjoying life, not knowing what the future held.

I actually left the hospital before she did, and would not meet her again for about six years, not until I went to work in British Columbia. Perchance, I was walking through a supermarket when we bumped into one another in Campbell River. I was cordially invited to her home for dinner that night and the two of us talked non-stop in an attempt to catch up on the missing years. She told me of her husband's severe accident. The head injury he sustained was from a moving aeroplane propeller, and no one knew whether he would survive, but fortunately he did. At the time I met her she was working as a Supervisor at the Campbell River Hospital, and had a young son. I moved away from the area, and I was not to meet her again for a few years. Sadly, the last time I did meet with her she was ill from cancer. She had a strong determination to survive. If determination was the only required ingredient to overcome this scourge of an illness, then she would have been here now, but with the ravages of the disease, my dear friend lost her battle. I still miss this special person, and was very glad that we had our chance meeting to become reacquainted.

When some of the babies were admitted to hospital, depending on the projected length of stay, the parents often had to return home to their neighbouring communities by plane. Later, when these babes were ready to return home, they were accompanied either by an adult from that specific community, also being discharged home, or accompanied by an nurse escort. It was interesting on these occasions to observe the parade leading from the hospital to the nearby dock. Staff nurses and ward aides could be seen carrying the babies in a ticanogan (cradle board) on their backs in a long, orderly line to the waiting aircraft. I had carried children in this manner, and found it a good method, leaving the hands free for other purposes. The babies were lifted up into the waiting aeroplane and placed in the care of the appropriate escort.

The ticanogan consisted of a wooden frame, often painted, and attached to the wooden frame was a moss bag made usually of tartan material. Probably the tartan was introduced by the white Scottish traders. The baby was first wrapped snugly in blankets, and then slipped into this bag which was then fastened with moose hide thongs, laced through the various islets. Inside and placed under the head, was a piece of white sheeting which had been embroidered by the mother. As well as being decorative, it had a useful purpose. With the variable weather elements, the sheet could be brought down to cover the child's face for protection. A cord connected to the wooden frame was placed over the shoulders in order to carry the papoose (the Cree word for baby) who faced outwards and was able to have a view.

My understanding is that before the advent of diapers, the native women used a sphagnum moss found growing on the ground. Because it had sponge-like qualities it was used inside the moss bag to absorb the urine very effectively. When wet, it could be replaced. Perhaps this was not a bad idea given the difficulties encountered now with our modern disposable diapers that seem not to be so disposable.

There was little improvement in the staffing situation and this, along with an incident one evening, helped me to make the decision to move on to another location. A staff party was being held in the nurses' residence, and I would have been off-duty within the hour and able to join in the fun. I was finishing the charting for the evening, the patients all settled for the night shift, when someone came running into the hospital in a very excited manner. I couldn't understand the garbled message at first, but then it became clear. It was pitch black outside. Unlike the cities there were no street lights to give relief to the darkness. Two small, outboard motor boats, travelling in opposite directions, had collided on the lake near to the hospital, and people were in the water. One of those individuals was a small baby in arms. It was so dark that no one could see what they were doing, and they did not have lights on the boats. I phoned the nurses' residence to summon help, but none was forthcoming. No one responded to the call perhaps because the telephone ringing was not discernible by the party makers. I very quickly sent my aide to the residence to alert everyone. She returned, but there was no sign of action. I am not sure what the scenario was, or whether she had adequately presented a clear picture. I promptly left the hospital and raced across the compound, threw the door open into the lounge room, and in a rather indignant manner rallied them to assist at the dock.

One or two clients were brought to the hospital to warm up, but otherwise they were medically alright. The only area of concern was the young baby, who belonged to a white woman. It was tightly bundled and asleep at the time. I was told that on impact of the boats, the babe shot out of the mother's arms into the water, went down, popped up, and then just floated. The little one was asleep at the time, so that there would not have been flailing movements. We placed the baby, a boy, in a bassinette and gave him some oxygen, as his colour was a little dusky. Fortunately, all ended well, and after a good check over, no real harm to the infant's health had occurred. I went home about three in the morning, and with all the mounting frustrations, sat down and wrote a request for a transfer. The last straw for me was the amount of fussing over one child when there were so many other very ill children. It was not that he was unimportant, but many others were in worse shape. My little patients and I were not afforded the same empathy in the dilemma of bed and staff shortages. Within a short time, I would say goodbye to Norway House.

CHAPTER FIVE
YUKON TERRITORY

Once the decision had been made to transfer, it was just a matter of waiting for an available position in the Yukon Territory. That timeframe allowed the usual gathering of boxes, suitcases and trunks for the inevitable, onerous task of packing. It was during this time that I had a call from an English nurse working in Ontario. She had been a colleague of mine at the Toronto General Hospital. She was looking for employment with Health and Welfare's Medical Services Branch and wanted me to provide information regarding departmental contacts. In a later communication we arranged to meet in Winnipeg and have a holiday together.

The transfer I had requested came through and I found out that I would be filling a vacant position at the Mayo General Hospital in the Yukon Territory. I was extremely pleased to say the least. Although I knew little about this new territory, that fact made the move all the more intriguing for me.

My friend Jenny and I met in Winnipeg, as arranged. She had managed to secure a position in Aklavik in the Northwest Territories. Before going our separate ways we vacationed for two weeks in the town of Banff, in the Rocky Mountains of Alberta. The year was 1967. I could well understand why Banff National Park was and is increasingly a world-wide tourist attraction. The majestic mountains towered over the lush vegetation and the meandering rivers below. The glacier-fed lakes, deep green, mirrored the surrounding forests and one could often see the loon, with its beautiful black and white plumage and hear its haunting call. There was an abundance of mule deer, white tailed deer, elk, coyotes and squirrels to be seen. Although grizzly and black bears existed I did not see any until I returned thirty years later as a resident to the area.

Jenny and I went our separate ways and soon lost touch. So often friends have good intentions of keeping in contact, but ultimately time passes, each of us being absorbed in our own lives, addresses change and communication is inadvertently lost. There have been several situations where in recent times I have been reunited with friends and colleagues after a gap of many years. The efforts in re-establishing friendships has proved to be a worthwhile endeavour; those relationships, formed in the earlier years, seemingly endure.

I flew from Edmonton, Alberta, to Whitehorse, the capital of the Yukon Territory, and en route, touched down at Fort St John, which was inside the British Columbia border. Little did I know as I sat on board, watching the activities on the tarmac below, that my suitcases were being taken off the aircraft. Not until I arrived at the Whitehorse terminal, and after a lengthy wait by the baggage carousel, did I discover that my suitcases were not on the plane. I consulted with the appropriate authorities only to find that my personal effects had been unloaded at Fort St. John. The airline company accepted the error of misplacement as their responsibility, and invited me to purchase, at their expense, the necessary night attire and toiletries. After everything was sorted out, I hailed a taxi to take me to the hospital residence.

I attended two days of orientation, and in my allotted spare time I familiarized myself with some local history and points of interest, one of these being a sternwheeler in the dry dock area. Sometime between the mid 1800s and the early 1900s steam-driven paddlewheel boats had been built to traverse the Yukon rivers. Out of all the paddle-steamers used, only three were preserved for posterity, one of these being the Klondike 2. I was able to view this hulk of a boat as it lay beached on the banks of the Yukon river, but I was not able to go on board. Viewing did not take place until 1981. It would have been rather a pleasant experience to wander through her, trying to visualize these boats plying to and fro with their cargoes and all the activities that emerged during the Gold Rush of 1897-1898.

Whitehorse became the capital of the Yukon Territory in 1953. When I arrived there in 1967, it was still a relatively quiet town. I have always been curious about place names and learned that there were various explanations given as to the origin of the name "Yukon." In the1840s the Hudson's Bay Company established a trading post there. John Bell, a fur trader and the first European to stand on the upper banks of the Yukon River, claimed the Indians called it Yucon. The name is derived from the Loucheux word Yuchoo which means the greatest river. The first people of the Yukon, it is said, came across a land bridge from Asia, known as the Bering Strait, some 12,000 years ago.

I heard tales of gold panning, something I would experience later at Mayo. There were a number of quaint stores in Whitehorse, and the prevalence of gold was very much on display in the form of jewellery, teaspoons and knives bearing a real gold nugget on the distal end. Other items such as serving spoons made of wood, with ivory handles, had northern scenes beautifully etched on them.

On departure day, I had to travel to Mayo by car, accompanied by a male Nursing Officer. It was a gravel road, and by the time we had travelled the two hundred and fifty-three miles, I felt I was eating the dust, not to mention how hot, sweaty and dishevelled I felt on arrival at my destination. We had made a few stops on the way at places such as Carmacks, Pelly Crossing and Stewart Crossing. While near to Carmacks, I was shown the Five Fingers Rapids just below. Wanting to learn of the local history, I found an old-timer who explained it was so named because it resembled five fingers pointing in five directions to where the gold had been found. In days gone by, it was considered dangerous to manoeuvre the large paddle boats through the channels. As I passed through Carmacks, I did not realise until later the significance of this name and its relationship to the gold rush days. Indeed, most place names were derived from the many historical figures that had pioneered the land as traders, explorers, surveyors and prospectors.

With all the chit-chat back and forth, it seemed that in no time we had arrived at the Mayo Hospital. Almost at the blink of an eye, we had passed through the town, which was located on the Stewart River and at the mouth of the river Mayo. It consisted of a hotel, a couple of small stores, some decayed buildings and homes around the area. The town was named after Alfred Mayo, who had been a trader with the Indians as well as a prospector. It had originally been called Mayo Landing. The sternwheelers which had stopped there to pick up ore no longer did so after a road was built between Whitehorse and Mayo.

The hospital was a small, one-storey building, and had approximately a twenty-bed capacity. The matron, a middle-aged woman originally from Australia, was, to my surprise, known to me. I had met her at Cross Lake Nursing Station while I worked at Norway House, in Manitoba. It was she who did not feel happy about our flying in the 180 Cessna on a joy ride. The other staff comprised three nurses, a local doctor and a visiting doctor from nearby Elsa, a secretary, a maintenance man, a cook and a helper in the kitchen. The nurses and the Matron lived downstairs in the hospital building while the other staff lived in their own private homes.

I was by now used to changing routines and I settled in very quickly. I arrived in the month of October, but there was still evidence of the beautiful fall colours on the trees all around and on the hill behind the residence. A few weeks went past, and there still was no sign of my trunks, which contained all my worldly possessions, including my heavy winter wear. I had made the necessary enquiries. The railway agents were trying hard to trace the whereabouts of my baggage. As the weather grew colder, I felt a little panicky as to whether my effects might be gone forever. There was no real monetary value, but I would have been greatly inconvenienced if I had to start outfitting myself in winter wear again. Finally, I got a call to say that my trunks had been located. Someone had goofed. They had been sent to Dawson Creek, in British Columbia. I was both relieved and annoyed as the voice at the other end of the telephone insisted that I would have to prepay the shipment. At first I refused, indignant at the officials who had made the blunder and chose, on a technicality, to further delay these much needed items. The government, as part of the hiring conditions, paid for this anyway, so there was no fear that the agents would be left with the bill unpaid.

The cold winter days were fast setting in. This was the land of the midnight sun, and although the long days were enjoyed in the summer, the winter produced subzero temperatures. From December to February we lived in darkness. Not until February would we see the sun come up, and then it was only for a brief interlude. It was as well that we were, for the best part, a harmonious group living and working together, with the Matron looking after us like a mother hen. Some time later, when I had found a boyfriend, I recall her admonitions to him that I was a working girl and to have me back at a reasonable hour. She would add, "And treat her with respect." She acted as a surrogate mother, and what with my being young and naive by today's standards, perhaps this was good.

After work there was time for fun. We played many a joke on the Matron, especially when she would leave her apartment unlocked. When you are youthful you think removing the light bulb in the bathroom and covering the toilet seat with cling wrap is hilarious. If that was not enough for her to come home to, we also made her apartment look as though a wild party had just taken place in her absence with shoes and bottles strewn about and chairs upturned. Fortunately, she took all this in her stride, being very young at heart.

On Saint Patrick's Day, although none of us was Irish, we each made ourselves a green skirt fashioned out of the operating room green linen that would normally be used for draping the patients having surgery, only no surgery was done at this hospital, only baby deliveries. We went to great lengths to cut out shamrocks with which to decorate, improvising with available materials. There were no local stores to supply these frivolous items. We found a blend of Scottish and Irish music, turned it to a high volume, and danced a jig or two in the downstairs hallways, inveigling the Matron into joining us.

Mealtimes were enjoyable. All the nurses, Matron and the Cook dined together as much as possible, and before the commencement of meals, grace was said, each of us taking a turn. It created a home-like atmosphere.

Once again, because I was British, a German nurse on staff brought the fact of my nationality and its relationship to the war into focus. I terminated her introduction of the subject by reminding her that the war was over and that Germany lost, the same words I uttered in Ontario when under fire. I did not wish to have bad vibes over a situation that neither of us caused, nor had control of the outcome. An amusing incident occurred one day soon after I arrived. The same German nurse confronted yet another new nurse, because of her surname. She insisted my colleague had to be Jewish. "With an name like that, you must be!", she emphatically announced. My colleague laughed it off by saying she was definitely an Episcopalian and that our colleague must be misinformed. I thought at first when I heard the challenge that World War Three was about to be declared, but no further mention was made of the incident. I suspected that my German colleague had a bad time during the war. She spoke of being forced into the Hitler Youth, and later fleeing from Berlin. She consistently left a little food at every meal, wrapping the morsel in a serviette, which she would take to her room. Undoubtedly she suffered some emotional scars.

It was a happy time in the Yukon. We were kept busy at work but never hard-pressed with lack of staff or too many patients. The clients admitted to hospital were the natives from the area as well as the mine workers from Elsa and Keno City, some twenty-eight miles away. I have always found male patients easy to nurse, and when feeling well, often they played their share of practical jokes on us. One patient delighted in the fact that his friends would supply him, at visiting times, with alcohol which we could not find, probably for the simple reason that it was internally hidden. He was never drunk, but just very giddy and would make us laugh, although we tried to remain straight-faced and appear disapproving. After all, his behaviour contravened the hospital policies. The nice part was that most of the non-native patients were not seriously ill, but were there due to work-related injuries.

There was one elderly native male who was quite sick and required to be in long-term care. Although there was a language barrier, we could still communicate with him. He did know a few words of English, but not enough for a full conversation. He was a nice old soul, and I can still see him sitting on top of his blankets on the bed, cross legged and packing wads of chewing tobacco into his mouth. With his tongue, he pressed the offensive substance into each cheek where it was held fast to savour the flavour. From time to time, the juices collected were spit into an old tobacco can at his bedside. I found it distasteful, particularly when I required a vocal response of "yes" or "no" to a question. To witness this dark, tarry, liquid oozing out from the corners of his mouth was not pleasant, and when the answer was "yes" or "pretty good", it was more of a splutter as he tried hard to retain the bulk of liquid in his mouth. At least it wasn't my concern to get the dark stains out of the pyjamas where he had drooled. Local information given to me indicated he was the Medicine Man. Who was I to restrict this man's tobacco pleasures when he perhaps possessed certain powers.

One evening, just before my shift ended at midnight, a bat flew into the hospital through an open window. I didn't feel particularly comfortable with this situation as I always associated bats with rabies. I felt sure this creature would probably get me. I tried shooing it out with a fly swatter, but to no avail. It just perched itself upside down from a beam near the nursing desk, as though to goad me. Some time later, at midnight, the night nurse arrived to relieve me from duty, and I welcomed her appearance. Even though the winged creature was paying no heed to me sitting below, I still felt the discomfort of its presence. After giving the customary report on the patients to my colleague, together, we would eradicate this unwelcome little monster. She did not wish to share her space with it any more than I did. We tried a variety of methods, but to no avail. Finally, we opened all the exit doors. Meantime, all the patients were deep in slumber, some snoring and obviously in the land of oblivion. Were it not for the nature of the clients having back injuries, we might well have given the rallying call to arms. We held a sheet between us, and with swooping motions we hoped to dislodge the intruder and assist him to an exit. We were successful in removing him from his present bearings. To our chagrin, he went into the elderly Indian's room. The old man was in a deep sleep, so again with the sheet between us, we crept into his room on our tip-toes, having removed our shoes. With the sheet method we finally managed to expel the bat to his natural environment. As I write this, the memory still makes me laugh, especially, when I try to envision what the reaction would have been had the Indian patient awakened as we flitted about in his room. Before him he would have seen an apparition of two angels. The white sheet spread out could have, in the darkness, been perceived as angel wings. The bat, no doubt, would have been seen as a bad omen by the Medicine Man. Thankfully, no one had even been aware of our midnight performance.

Walking through bush trails in off-duty hours was an enjoyable recreational activity. Well wrapped in warm clothing, the fresh icy air was bracing, and although the temperatures were much lower than anything I had experienced in Scotland, I found it warmer because of the drier climate. My male companion, who had been an ex-patient, introduced me to the use of snow-shoes for the first time. In the beginning, I was more often lying face down in the snow than upright, but eventually I got the knack of walking in them. Where one would normally be unable to walk due to the depth of snow, these shoes gave the ability to travel. When the skies turned blue and the temperatures reached zero degrees Fahrenheit, it felt like a spring day. Heavy parkas could be removed and replaced with only a warm sweater.

I had a zest for life. Everything seemed to be going my way. I truly enjoyed my work and play hours and wanted to see as much as possible, experiencing to the full a different way of life. When my male friend offered to teach me how to shoot a gun, I was interested in participating. I knew that I would never own one or consider shooting an animal, nor be party to that deed. He, on the other hand, owned firearms legally, and along with other men occasionally hunted for moose to supplement their larder. We travelled to the small community of Keno and at the local dumpsite, safely outside the village residents' parameters, we set up some old cans in a row. I was given some safety instruction on the use of a firearm first, and some general instructions, before being handed the pistol. I felt rather nervous just touching the weapon. My only encounter with guns had been at the local fairs shooting at a moving object to win a prize, and that had been a pretty hopeless endeavour. I lifted the pistol and fired a couple of shots. This was followed by the firing of a .22 rifle used for small game hunting. Then came the .303 rifle which apparently is used for shooting larger game such as moose. Having supported the rifle butt against my shoulder, I fired. I could feel the recoil from the gun as it went off, and the impact made me aware of its power. Needless to say, I was a poor marksman. It was as well that the freezer compartment at the residence was well-filled. Reliance on my endeavours would not have sustained life.

It was during one of these outings with my friend that I had a crash course in driving a car. Until then I had no knowledge. We had gone on a trip into the bush country to visit his friend at his log cabin and arrange for the use of his skidoo, but there was no one home. The journey back was in the dark except for the moon giving illumination on a cold frosty night. My companion at some point developed severe chest pain and started perspiring. He had been involved, in the daytime, with heavy lifting. This I knew from an earlier conversation we had. He said he couldn't drive, and that I would have to manage. Being a nurse, one learns to keep calm in an emergency, but I must admit that being in the middle of nowhere, without driver skills, knowing the person was presenting with possible cardiac symptoms, made it a little hard to remain cool. We switched places and I became the driver. Once in the driver's seat, I realized it wasn't so difficult a feat. At least there was no traffic in my way nor road rules to obey, just a rough logging road. We did get back to town in one piece, and my friend was well checked out by his doctor. Further testing did reveal some cardiac problem that could be rectified with surgery.

Winter was long, but we entertained ourselves in a variety of ways. Some liked to curl and although the Scots were thought to be the originators of this sport, I showed no inclination towards the game. Guests came to dinner, we held parties and on occasion we were known to raid "Cookie's" pantry and make pizza from scratch. My English nursing friend had become engaged to a local banker from Elsa. We, as her co-workers and friends, set about organizing the customary bridal shower prior to her leaving. They would eventually move to British Columbia, and I remember how emotional Claudia was about marrying a Canadian. In a way she felt she was severing herself from her homeland forever. I could relate very well to her fears, being an immigrant too. I was sad to see them go as I had become so attached to them, Henry being like a little brother. I was affectionately known as "The Monster"; the reason for that completely eludes me now, but some fun episode precipitated the term.

Following Claudia's departure our group was joined by a policeman's wife. Although she was a very nice girl, it wasn't the same with one room downstairs empty, and with the "Mountie's" wife living elsewhere in town.

The cold winter brought its share of respiratory infections in both young and old. Such was the case of a tiny Indian baby whom I will call Benjamin. He had been born prematurely, and he had made very little progress in his weight gain. Eventually, with little to fight with, he became very ill with a respiratory infection, requiring hospitalisation. His little chest was heaving in an attempt to get air into his lungs, and his lips were a dusky blue colour. The doctor did not believe he would make it, as he was not responding to the medications. My colleague and I requested to place him into the newborn incubator where he would have a constant, controlled temperature with humidity and oxygen piped in. We were given the okay, but again the doctor said he wouldn't live anyway. We were determined to give him all the tender loving care to restore his health, almost willing him to live. We were caught up in the emotionalism of the moment and proceeded to baptize our infant charge. With some sterile water we made the sign of the cross on his forehead and said the name he was known by. There wasn't a local minister readily available in the community, and baptism had not be done. In a week or two, young Benjamin was showing great signs of recovery, perhaps due to the grace of God combined with our love. He was a patient for a long time and we just adored him, and it made us sad to see him leave. At the same time we were joyous for him to be reunited with his family.

There were never any real violent episodes in Mayo at that time. There were about three Royal Canadian Mounted Police Officers with whom we socialised, located across the street from us at the barracks. They often dropped by the hospital on the evening or night shift, and if things were quiet, would stay for coffee. It helped the time to pass when on duty alone. It was on one of these visits that a young, fun-loving "Mountie" showed this inquisitive person how to apply handcuffs. Naturally, he had to demonstrate on me, and to my horror, he attached me to a large food trolley and proceeded to leave. I wasn't too impressed with his joke, brief as it was. Fortunately he got the reaction he wanted and removed the offending irons. Taking my nursing seriously, I was afraid that at that precise moment of being handcuffed, a patient would ring for attention. At one of our parties, I met a new police constable and a young teacher to whom he had recently become engaged. Interestingly, I was to cross paths again with them in the future.

In spite of the winter coldness, I thoroughly enjoyed walking through the bush trails. The icy air on my face felt invigorating. There was a peacefulness within the solitude. The only sounds I heard were my feet making a crunching noise, walking on the hard frozen trail along with my deep breathing from the exertion. I never felt alone or afraid. There was an abundance of trees and vegetation, and animals such as bears, wolves, cougars, lynx, moose and deer were in that vicinity. Because I had never been exposed to wildlife, I didn't really comprehend the possibility of encountering an aggressive animal. I had not realised then that bears can come out of hibernation on a warm winter day.

In the spring, when they officially come out of winter hibernation with their cubs, a bear might attack when startled, feeling the need to defend their young. I do recall some old-timers saying that if a black bear gave chase, lie down and play dead. In the case of meeting a grizzly bear, climb a tree, as they are not as adept at climbing as black bears, because their claws are straighter. A recent tragic event proved that theory of the grizzly bear to be flawed. I tried to imagine the scene of playing dead and felt one would need to be very brave to do just that. I am sure if I had such an encounter, the bear would know very well that I was alive with the amount of trembling I would do. In later years, I grew to have a greater understanding and respect of the wildlife by acquired knowledge, but, with the loss of naivety, I became thereafter more fearful on the bush trails. It was and is always important to check with the Wildlife Officers about bear activity in an area.

On one such walk, not far from town, the only animal encounter I had was with two Alsatian dogs. About half a mile away, these beasts came careening down the trail towards me, barking ferociously. They belonged to a man who lived on the outskirts of the village. I am well used to dogs, so I wasn't too concerned. As they drew nearer, however, I was sure they had very unfriendly intentions, so I considered my options. One was climbing a tree, but in order to do that I would have had to go down a steep embankment to reach one. I didn't relish being stuck knee deep in snow at the moment of confrontation, lest I be further disadvantaged. I could start running back towards town, but they would have outrun me, or I could have used a stick or stones to chase them away. This might have been viewed by them as an act of aggression and provoke an attack. As these ideas rapidly passed through my mind, none of them seemed to be a viable solution. Instead, I charged down the path towards the dogs waving my arms wildly in the air and uttering some loud noises. The hoped for reaction was very evident, as the dogs stopped in their tracks, turned, and now they became the pursued. My strategy had worked, but not wishing to tempt fate, I decided to retrace my steps and abort my excursion for the day.

In February, I was allowed to escort a patient to the Whitehorse Hospital. The timing was perfect as the Sourdough Rendezvous was in progress. This was like a winter games gathering, and the day started with a pancake breakfast, as far as I can recall. There were husky dog races, dog weight-pulling contests, as well as human participation in weight-lifting and snow-shoeing events. I got caught up in the excitement of the dog races most of all. These beautiful Siberian huskies and malamutes were already wearing their colourful harnesses. The owners and handlers were preparing the double-hitch, which meant the dogs ran side by side in twos. There could be a variation in the number of dogs pulling the sled, and it was not unusual to see eight on a team. The dogs were trembling with excitement, tongues lolling out as they panted in anticipation, at times jumping up in the air, their actions interspersed with yelps of joy. They were impatient, and much harness banging occurred. They pulled against their straps in attempts to start the sled and be off. The mushers, clad in Indian mukluks, parkas, long heavy moose hide gloves and sporting furry Davy Crockett hats, were poised, at the ready on the sled, whip in hand. The pistol was fired, the signal that the race had begun. The mushers' voices, audible in spite of the spectators' noisy, enthusiastic support, shouted, "Hike!", which the dogs knew to be the command for go or to pull harder. I mentally picked the team I wanted to win and, although a very quiet person in those days, I found myself loudly cheering the team on.

A Sourdough is the name given to a person who has lived a long time in the north. The word comes from the old prospectors' custom of carrying sourdough from camp to camp. After one batch of bread was made, some of the sourdough which contained yeast would be kept back to start the next batch.

Back in Mayo it was still very cold with temperatures reaching minus sixty degrees Fahrenheit, but at least we didn't have a wind-chill factor to deal with. The sun came up at about ten in the morning and was gone again by two o'clock in the afternoon. I felt, to some degree, immobilized due to the climate and stayed near to home. In the event that one travelled to Elsa or Keno, warm sensible clothing was imperative. As well as a good parka and footwear, the use of heavy wind pants was usual. Informing a reliable source of the time of one's departure and expected time of arrival proved to be a worthwhile principle to follow should the car break down. It could have been a long wait in these conditions, and with few people on the roads, it could spell disaster. This happened to a young woman travelling with a companion. They had not advised anyone where they were going. She had been wearing long high boots, good only for city life. Their vehicle broke down due to the cold and they were exposed to the elements for some time before someone happened to come their way. We saw her as a patient at the hospital, but she was fortunate to have only a minor frostbite. I did nurse a man who had severely frozen his feet, and eventually, I was told after I had left there, he had to have them amputated in spite of the attempts to save them. A very painful process indeed for him, both physically and psychologically. The soles of the feet, once a healthy pink flesh, were just a blackened, crusted layer. He required morphine to ease his severe pain.

At last, break-up came making everywhere extremely muddy. During the winter months, when the water was frozen, a barrel was set in the middle of the river and attached to it was a wire cable connected to an alarm system. When the ice cracked the alarm would go off and the precise time of break-up would be known for that area. Bets were usually made prior to this as to the exact time when the ice would go out. This provided a bit of entertainment during the dark days. At the sound of the alarm, shops were closed and the local people headed to the river to witness the event, excitedly wanting to know if they had won their bet.

It seemed at times as though spring and subsequently summer would never arrive for me. Patience was not a virtue of mine. When it did come, it was off with the parkas and into something less bulky. Rubber boots were a must. My reason to push the season forward was so that I could visit Dawson City.

It is written by many that Dawson City was the heart of the Klondike and where the gold-rush of 1897-1898 started. George Washington Carmack, an American by birth, settled down with a Tagish Indian chief's daughter, and along with her two native brothers, Skookum Jim and Tagish Charlie, they searched for and found gold in Bonanza and Eldorado creeks, staking their claims in 1896. Needless to say, news spread and gold miners poured into the area, but the Royal Canadian Mounted Police wouldn't allow any miners in unless they had a year's supply of food and other necessities. Sometimes they had to make many trips to fulfil that condition. They made their way over the Chilkoot Pass, a main route to the goldfields, which was a test of endurance. It was said that many of these men in actual fact were white-collared workers and had never mined before. I can visualize the prospectors, young and old, arriving grubby and worn after their journey. Some came on horseback with their mule-packs following, heavily laden with supplies. Some travelled on dog teams, and others arrived on foot. Chaos existed in the setting up of the camps, cooking on open fires and the only topic being gold. At one time between 1898-1899 Dawson had a population of 16,000-18,000.

When I was there, many of the buildings were dilapidated or closed up, but still I had the sense of the history of some eighty years before. The Palace Grand Theatre had once seen packed houses where miners would be entertained by Klondike Kate whose real name was Kathleen Eloise Rockwell. She was born of Scots/Irish parents in the United States, in 1876 and was very popular with the miners. They could well afford to pay to see her show with their new-found gold. There was the option of a night at Diamond Tooth Gertie's Saloon bar. She was so named because she had inserted a diamond between her two front teeth. One can almost hear the raucous laughter and the tinkle of the ivory keys on the honky-tonk piano mingling with the revelry.

Robert Service, a poet of world renown, spent about five years in Dawson City. He was born in Preston, England, in 1874, and in 1896 immigrated to North America. He was employed at the Bank of Commerce in Whitehorse before transferring to Dawson City. I paid a visit to his log cabin where many of his poems had been written. After the war he returned to France and died in 1958, in Monte Carlo. I purchased two of his poetry books, "Songs of a Sourdough" and "Ballads of a Cheechako." At times I read these and it still creates feelings of nostalgia.

With revitalized thoughts and emotional longings I once more feel an urge to return to this land of the midnight sun. It occurred to me as I was writing about the Yukon, that as a child, my father would sit me on his knee and read aloud to me the poems "Dangerous Dan McGrew" and "The Cremation Of Sam McGee." Who knows really how much I absorbed as a child and what influence this may have had on me when I requested a position in the Yukon. Somewhere, stored in the recesses of my mind, there may have been imaginary pictures of the gold miners finding the mother lode, with me envisioning the excitement it must have generated.

I was back on the job again at Mayo, enjoying the summer and Mother Nature's brilliant colours surrounding me. There was a profusion of the fireweed plant which is the floral emblem of the Yukon. Its habitation is in moist mountainous areas, but it is also seen in burned areas. As well as giving vibrant colour, it has been used in folk medicine. I journeyed by car, making local trips, feeling quite content to view the beautiful lakes and landscapes, enjoying picnics in the tranquillity which seemed to engulf me, interrupted only by the sounds of birds and occasional conversation. We seemed to be less busy at the hospital, and with more available time, I was able to be very attentive to those admitted.

One of those patients was a local man who was well known to us, but Scottish in origin. He had progressed with his cancer condition to the terminal stage. Each day we had watched him go downhill, and all we could do was give him emotional support and make him as physically comfortable as possible by administering the prescribed morphine injections ordered by his doctor. He had been, in healthier days, a tall, well built, muscular man who now was reduced to a shadow of his former self. It was not long before death came to him. In my nursing career, I have had to witness the face of death over and over. Some say you get used to it, although I am not sure that is so, but one does develop coping skills.

For those who have not sat by the bedside holding the hand of the dying to give comfort, nor have shared private moments, thoughts and fears of a patient, only later to perform the last offices, might not understand that a small incidence occurring after death can make you laugh. In no way can the laughter be considered irreverent. Such was the case of the client we will call Joel. At the time of his demise, the local doctor was away on a six-month course. There was no locum delegated, but another doctor from the mine at Elsa could be called upon as needed. The Matron was off on her summer vacation. My colleague, the German nurse, was on duty during the day until four o'clock in the afternoon. I would follow her on the next shift. When Joel ceased to draw breath at around two o'clock that day, our nursing friend could not locate the physician. He was required to pronounce death and issue the necessary death certificate. In desperation she called upon our other colleague to assist her in officially determining that death had occurred, and to bear witness. The German nurse was in a conundrum and not altogether calm about the situation which she had reluctantly been presented with. When I arrived, she was excitedly telling me that she was sure he was dead, but on the other hand, she thought she saw the man's chest move. In the background the second nurse had a big grin on her face but stated that he was indeed gone. I was handed the stethoscope and after listening, confirmed that the patient was definitely deceased. In the silence of the room, there was an eerie feeling as we looked down at the still form which once laughed and joked with us. It was easy for the mind to play tricks when we really wished him to be alive.

Nurses are not trained in this sphere, nor in the habit of pronouncing death. Because of this fact, we had to contact a doctor in Whitehorse and explain our scenario. He then gave us the official permission to pronounce death and to have the body removed from the hospital. Due to the extenuating circumstances, we were given sanction to do whatever was necessary. There was no next of kin in this case to notify. The temperature was eighty degrees Fahrenheit outside and it was not feasible to keep the body too long in the hospital facility, especially with other patients to consider, and the fact that our own residence was located directly below. We allowed a couple of hours to pass before arranging to remove the body to the mortuary. During this interval, personal effects and equipment were gathered. The patient was still sitting bolt upright, elevated by pillows, and as well, the head of the bed was raised. We now wished to lay the corpse flat before rigor mortis set in. I bent down to use the bed crank to lower the head of the bed , at the same time talking with my colleague discussing our next duty. I was aghast as a pair of feet suddenly started sliding towards me. Horror struck, I realized that I was cranking in the wrong direction, further elevating the head, causing the corpse to slide and move towards me.

In my travels I have met many interesting characters, from people who have been prisoners of war to the old man who was a patient and had come from Norway many years before. This fellow told me that as a young man, he had been on board a ship travelling to the Americas, probably in the early 1900s. At one point he had jumped ship for his own reasons and would have been without the necessary documents needed to be a legal immigrant. All the intricacies of his case were not revealed to me, but he had compiled a manuscript of his story. However, he related to me that eventually he was caught and placed in a chain gang. Somehow, he had escaped and was on the run. In a weakened state, he was found and taken to a home in the bush-land. There, the wife of his rescuer nursed him back to life. At the time of his recovery, he went on to say, the couple took him outside and showed him a wooden box. They had not expected the Norwegian to survive, and in the meantime, the husband had made a coffin for him. I often wonder whether this manuscript was ever published, and I wish I had paid closer attention to the story.

Nursing, as well as being a worthy profession, is also physically and emotionally taxing on the system. The rewards are many, mostly coming from the feeling of satisfaction in helping human suffering, sharing in an intimate way the lives of those that place their trust in us. During illness, patients are in their most unguarded and fragile state. Whether rich or poor, we all deserve to be accorded the same decency and the same amount of care. As I prepare this book, I do wonder and fear for the future. It would seem that the more advanced our technical world has become, the more indifferent and colder humanity appears to have become in personal interactions. The swing, however subtle, appears to favour the rich rather than the poor.

Did someone mention gold panning? My ears picked up. I wanted to try this. In my imagination, I was going to find gold nuggets as large as a hen's egg. I was going to be rich! If I was feeling this excited in the 1960s, I can well imagine the atmosphere that was generated when gold was first struck. "Eureka!" I travelled through the McQuesten Valley situated below the town of Elsa, surrounded by forests and mountains, to the area where placer mining was operational to some degree. Placer is described as deposits of sand and gravel in a stream bed where gold particles were contained. The dredging and washing was known as placer mining. It was not obtained from the underground in the same way as coal mining.

Here and there were seen the remains of those large dredger machines belonging to quite another era. The different parts had to be hauled to the various locations by horses, and assembled on site. As mining disappeared, these machines were abandoned to rust and decay, leaving behind a living museum for people like myself to see.

At the site, I was handed a gold pan made of a heavy gauge steel. At the nearby creek a demonstration was given before I ventured to try. The pan was dipped into the water and in a scooping motion retrieved gravel and silt. With a circular motion the water was sloshed around within the pan, the top layer of gravel being washed out. The process was repeated a few times until some particles remained, which, in my case, I hoped would be gold. But alas!, there was no evidence that a second great Klondike gold rush was imminent. I made several unsuccessful tries in the cold water. Although somewhat disappointed I need not have worried. Paying a visit to the miner's home, I saw, set out before me, row upon row of neat little jars containing gold nuggets of all shapes and sizes. Perhaps, as Robert Service so eloquently put it, "Yet it isn't the gold that I'm wanting, so much as just finding the gold." At least I did not return empty handed. From the jars of gold I was able to select and purchase two gold nuggets which later I had made into earrings. Disappointment in turn gave way to an experience that, dare I say," was worth its weight in gold!."

By now I had resided in Canada for two and a half years and I felt a need to return to my native land and see my family again. Because I had experienced flying I now wanted an ocean trip venture on the homeward journey, stopping at various ports to visit new lands. I needed to do careful planning, considering the sea voyage would take approximately five weeks by my chosen route. Everything I owned was packed carefully into trunks and suitcases. This time I was determined that my luggage would not again be misplaced in some foreign land. The signs were done in very dark, bold print, adequately displayed.

As always, I hated the goodbyes, and at the given moment of departure I questioned the wisdom of the move. After all, I was very happy there.

From Whitehorse I travelled by plane to Vancouver, British Columbia, feeling very sad. Still, good things lay ahead. After a relatively quiet life with little traffic around, I was not enamoured with the city hustle and bustle. I felt relieved that my stay there would be short. Friends that I had known in Mayo met me at the airport. The following day, they escorted me to the dock and came on board the ship, the SS Orcades, and stayed until I got settled into my quarters. My dear friend, Claudia, had brought me a beautiful bouquet of flowers. We cried as we parted, for we did not know if we would meet again.

For me, this trip was a final return to Britain, or so I intended. I can still remember the poignancy of that moment. The ship's horn blasted a couple of times as we moved slowly away from the dockside. I, along with hundreds of other people, stood at the railings waving to the crowd below. I could just see Claudia and her husband blowing kisses and waving. I knew well that Claudia would have been wishing that she was also en route to the English port of Southampton. We had been handed streamers before departure, and every one started recklessly throwing them to the crowd below. Caught up in the fervour, it didn't seem to matter for whom those streamers were intended. It was as though everyone on the dockside waving at us were related to all of us on board. As the ship moved further away from the quay, the strains of music from the band on the shore could be heard until finally, the sound faded away as we headed further out to sea. When there were no visible traces of the dock and the people, I made my way below to meet my cabin mates who, like me, were homeward bound.

Perhaps it is sufficient to say that the cruise was a wonderful experience. I spent most of the time on deck for the simple reason that below I became very seasick. Stopovers included San Francisco, where we were allowed a short visit, just long enough to ride the trolley bus and seek a view from Fisherman's Wharf of Alcatraz, the notorious prison. Los Angeles was next on the agenda, with a quick visit to Knotts Berry Farm. We dropped anchor near the dock at Acapulco and at that point we were rowed ashore in large boats. Our strict instructions were to be back on board by midnight. There was no fear of our transport turning into a pumpkin, but it is feasible that with the ship's schedule they may not have waited for anyone who happened to be tardy. We visited the La Perla Night Club to see the famous cliff divers. They climbed to a height of thirty metres and, after praying to the Virgin Of Guadalupe, dived into the dangerous rocky waters below.

There were many activities on board, including swimming, deck quoits, movies, shopping or having one's hair coiffed. Some preferred to laze on the deck soaking in the warm Pacific sun, while others walked, some enjoyed a drink and some twirled around the dance floor. The evenings which followed our visits to the different ports, were fun, as a costume dance was held, with guests usually wearing the apparel native to the place just left. A large basket of props was left for us to rummage through in order to select a suitable outfit.

We made passage through the Panama Canal with heavy tropical vegetation visible on either side, and one could feel the clammy effects of the humidity. Different bird sounds could be heard from the rainforests. It was a most interesting experience to learn first-hand about the workings of the lock system. I had been taught about this in school, but it wasn't the same as observing the action. One moment we would be level with the dock and then gradually descend below ground level.

We stopped in the Panama ports of Cristobal and Balboa. Before landing, we were issued a warning for our safety. The ship's personnel advised that we should not carry handbags or wear jewellery and travel only in groups, particularly if taking a taxi. The reason was explained to us that tourists often were targets for muggings, and it had been known for individuals to be beaten and left for dead in alleyways. With the friends I had made on board, I went ashore, adhering to the advice given.

We eventually arrived in Trinidad. The area we passed through seemed to have a great deal of poverty. We were taken to a Mosque as a place of interest, being careful to remove our footwear before entering the temple, as was the custom. I also had the opportunity to hear and watch the steel drums being played on the sandy shore. The sound and rhythm was wonderful, and the local people danced and swayed to the beat of the music, distinctive in its own way. When our ship pulled out from the shore we could still hear the band playing in the distance.

Madeira was our next stop. We went shopping, purchasing linens that were beautifully hand cut and embroidered. Many of the shops visited offered us a glass of Madeira wine while we were browsing.

Curacao, a Dutch port, was a very brief stopover before continuing on to Southhampton, England. I was pleased to see solid ground again. Sporting a deep suntan from the hot weather we had encountered, it was a shock to the system to embrace the icy cold British weather in October. The dampness seemed so much colder than any subzero weather I had experienced in the Yukon.

I remained at home in Scotland for six months, during which time I had applied for and was offered a position as a Ward Sister in Inverness, Scotland. I turned it down at the last moment and decided to return to Canada. The decision was a very hard one.

CHAPTER SIX
YELLOWKNIFE

It was not a rumour of gold that brought me to Yellowknife in April of 1968, but rather the inability to emotionally sever myself from The Great Canadian North. I've heard it said many times of the north that there is a love/hate relationship: some love the solitude of the remote areas while others have no stomach for it. When Robert Service wrote the poem, "The Lure of Little Voices", the words spoke eloquently of my feelings and it was as though indeed those lonely places were calling me back. My feelings could best be depicted in my Zodiac sign of Pisces, the fish symbol, travelling in different directions. It spoke amply of the struggle within me, which was wanting to be in two places at the same time, my innate need to maintain my own culture, and as well experience a new one which was so different historically and appealed to the adventurous side of my nature.

Yellowknife, otherwise called Tatsanottine, was named after a small, Athabascan-speaking Indian tribe who lived northeast of the Great Bear Lake and Great Slave Lake, now called the Northwest Territories. Great Slave Lake was named after the Slavey Tribe by Samuel Hearne, a Hudson's Bay employee and a fur trader who explored the area and was the first white man to visit the shores of Great Slave Lake. The Indians there used yellow copper for crafting tools and knives from whence they derived the name of Yellowknife. Sometime between the 1800s and 1900s the Dogrib tribe massacred the Yellowknife Indians in retaliation for earlier raids against them.

Gold was first discovered in 1896 by miners en route to the Klondike. There was a gold rush beginning in 1934, and by 1936 Yellowknife was a boom town. Two mines were built, Giant and Con Mines, which were still productive in 1967. There are two occasions in the last thirty-five years I can recall which brought the town very much into the focus of the news media. One was the case of a pilot who crashed his plane with the loss of human life, which will be touched upon later, and the other was the more recent event of sabotage in the mine.

In 1992, a bitter labour dispute was under way at the Giant mine. The company had been bought by an American woman and under new management, changes were afoot. A number of concessions would be required of the union representing the workers, which included a cut in pay. Management were prepared for a walkout and ready to bring in alternate workers. A tentative agreement had been worked out, but with further discontent a majority vote called for strike action. The threat to bring in other workers became a reality. The airlifting of men to the worksite enraged the strikers. Adding to this was the fact that some of the Giant employees became "scab workers." Emotions ran high outside the gates and eventually violence erupted. Nine replacement men proceeded through the mine shaft in the shuttle car, when the wheel made contact with a detonator and the resulting explosion killed all the passengers. Initially there were two suspects, but after thirteen long months of police investigations there emerged a third suspect. The latter was eventually tried, convicted, and imprisoned.

When I arrived in Yellowknife it was still a relatively quiet community. On January 17th 1967 it was selected as the capital of the Northwest Territories and in January 1st 1970 it became a city, and in future times was to see an expanded growth. There was an old section of Yellowknife which was the original mining town, located by the lake. In the centre of the old town is a solid mass of Precambrian Shield known as The Rock. Remnants of old buildings were evident from the gold rush days. One could walk through the Indian village, referred to as Rainbow Valley, a name which aptly depicted the brightly-coloured houses painted in green, yellow, blue and pink.

Latham Island was the base for float planes. I used to sit and watch from an advantage point the hubbub as planes took off and landed. The island was named after Gordon Latham, a school teacher who became a bush pilot, later training Allied pilots during the war to develop good skills in navigation. A monument was erected in honour of the bush pilots who helped to open up the far north, and from its rocky prominence one could look down on Great Slave Lake, Giant Mine, the Latham Island and the Willow Flats below. Also located there was an old log building known as the Wildcat Cafe. It was operational in the 1930s and again in the 1950s, but at the time of my residency it was not in use.

New town was laid out in the 1940s. I was employed at the Stanton Hospital, in the new part, and presumably the facility was named after Doctor Stanton, who had been, in his time, the local health officer and played an active role in the early days of Yellowknife.

My working life at Stanton Hospital, whose occupants ranged from newborn babies to the elderly, was enjoyable. It was, at times, very busy with general patient care, deliveries and caring for the newborns, not to mention the out-patient department, which could be chaotic. There was one room set aside for any patients with a mental health problem requiring observation. It was just large enough to contain a bed, a locker and a chair. The windows were made of unbreakable glass and two separate doors were in place which could be locked if deemed necessary.

One male patient had been admitted to this room during the day. When I was on the evening shift, he had an outburst that I am not likely to forget. He had wanted to smoke a cigarette. The regulations attached to the occupants of this particular room were such that a staff member had to be present during their smoking session. Unfortunately the busy events of the evening prevented us from stopping at the moment the patient made his request. This all being explained in a rational manner obviously did not sit well with the client. An outburst of anger and destruction ensued. I was attending to the infants when I heard quite a din. On investigating, I found the side rails of the bed had been detached by the occupant who then proceeded to charge at the windows, but without damaging them, due to the safety type of glass used, but he was able to leave indentations on the wooden door which he attacked with great ferocity. A chair with metal legs was promptly mangled and bedding was strewn all over. The patient would not be calmed. In the end the Royal Canadian Mounted Police were called upon to assist. It took three officers to restrain him until I was able to inject him with a tranquillizer. His behaviour, which he was unable to control, was attributable to his illness. For the rest of the evening he slept soundly without a further episode. Following some staff meetings, it was decided that from there on in, a bed would not be supplied to that room, merely a mattress on the floor with bedding. Sometimes alcoholics who had delirium tremens were also placed in this room.

Another male patient had been admitted the day previously with some form of a mental health disorder. He was allowed to stay in an ordinary room as his behaviour did not pose a threat. He would pace to and fro in the corridor and in front of the nurse's desk. He was not violent in any way, but one was made very aware of his agitation. He had pale blue eyes, and when eye contact was made he had a cold penetrating stare. At some point during the week the doctors had decided to send these two patients for psychiatric assessment in Edmonton, Alberta, and I was given the opportunity of acting as the nurse escort. The patient who had the outburst previously was to travel lying on a stretcher, well sedated, while the second patient would travel sitting up. A police escort was also assigned, no doubt in case of any unforeseen events. The fact that we were using public transportation, I assumed, meant that the law had to ensure public safety.

. The journey went very smoothly and on landing, a police vehicle was waiting. I was advised by the policeman who met us, to accompany the ambulant patient to the waiting van. Meantime the police escort assisted in the transfer of the stretcher case to the waiting ambulance and paramedic care. I sat in the van waiting with my patient for what seemed to be an eternity. I felt uneasy due to the fact that my patient sat huddled close to me. He told me how much he liked me and asked if he could date me when he came home. "What does one do in this type of situation?" I was a little taken aback, but for safety reasons I thought it prudent to be agreeable. I was very relieved when the police escort joined us. I never heard from either of these clients again and, as I had hoped, the incident in the vehicle must have been forgotten. I did learn, however, that both patients returned to the community within a week, being considered perfectly normal.

A sad incident occurred during one shift when a baby was delivered stillborn. The mother was in her late forties and already had a grown family. The labour had been long and the delivery difficult due to the large size of the baby. Following the birth, I was handed the lifeless body of a perfect little girl who could not be resuscitated, and instructed to take her to the mortuary. It was tragic that this little human being made the journey to the outside world but was denied even that first breath. We felt very badly for the woman in her loss and also for the baby who, perhaps, in a bigger centre could have been saved. The mother, at first on learning about her pregnancy, was devastated at the thought of another child in her later years, but had come to both accept and look forward to the event.

There were a variety of outdoor activities I took part in. With friends I spent a great deal of time hiking, occasionally boating and canoeing. A group of us went on a picnic, travelling by jeep over some rugged terrain for a few miles. At the appointed destination and whilst the men folk unloaded the canoe, we put on our life jackets. We had only travelled a short distance by canoe when we encountered some rapids around which we had to portage. The men knew about their existence and instructed us regarding the procedure. The portage trail used to avoid the rapids was rocky and narrow. It was a very hot day and the effort of carrying the canoe caused us to perspire heavily. That in turn seemed to bring a cloud of mosquitoes, adding further to our discomfort.

Having finished our water sport for the day we headed back to the truck and the subsequent picnic area. All the girls pitched in, setting out on the table the much anticipated meal and refreshments. It had been an enjoyable day. Our appetites sated, we were reluctant to go home, but black clouds were looming overhead and a few drops of moisture could be felt. We barely succeeded in packing everything away when we heard a clap of thunder and down came a heavy rainfall. Safely inside the truck, we decided to wait until the rain abated. As we sat and chatted, out lumbered a large black bear heading straight for our picnic spot. How long he had been lurking nearby was not known, but undoubtedly he would have been attracted to the pleasant aromas of our food. He moved on, finding no tasty morsels. It did give us an opportunity to have a great close-up of this beautiful animal. Fortunately we were in the vehicle so that no untoward encounters jeopardized us, or indeed the life of the bear.

We also made a trip over to the Chief's Island. I was not able to meet the Chief in person that day, but when we docked the boat we visited with a family who made us very welcome, offering us tea. The man of the house climbed into his attic and brought down skins and furs to show us, which he acquired through hunting and trapping. At one point they discussed how much their ways of life had been changed by the appearance of the white man. They did not confront us in a hostile manner, but only wished to talk about the old ways. What they told us was historically true.

Skating was an outdoor sport that I was unable to master in spite of the many attempts made by friends to teach me. Perhaps, the fact that I wore borrowed skates that did not fit very well contributed to my awkwardness. It was hard to convince me that the ice was safe. I could clearly see the lily pads under the frozen water. I decided this was not for me, preferring to indulge my time in snow-shoeing and ski-dooing, with less chance of breaking any bones.

Because accommodation was not readily available in Yellowknife, I had to live in the nurses' residence, this one being built with a slight difference. Usually we were assigned a room inside the main building. In this case, the set-up was more like an apartment where one would enter through a main door into a vestibule. Off from the vestibule were two self-contained bedrooms. The outer door and vestibule were shared, with both parties having identical keys, but there were no locks on the bedroom doors. The girl sharing my communal space was a radiographer from New Zealand. As in many residences, parties were held on occasion, the entertainment taking place in the main lounge. I had attended a party that night and when most of the guests left, I decided to retire. The New Zealander called to me, as I was leaving, reminding me not to lock the outer door as she did not have her key. I had barely got to sleep when something disturbed me. I opened my eyes just as some male crawled into my bed. I let out a blood curdling sound, and the intruder bolted out of the room with me in fast pursuit. "Catch that man!" I shouted, "He just climbed into my bed!" The few guests and staff started to laugh. The offender had disappeared into thin air. I believe he was probably under the weather with drink and didn't know what he was doing. Needless to say, the door was locked from thereon in.

Not long before I left Yellowknife, the first phase of many buildings to be erected began across from the hospital. They were to be apartments, and were built on top of a rock. This was the beginning of the growth of Yellowknife as the Capital of the Northwest Territories.

The gold mines in town were active in their production. I tried to wangle a trip down both of the mines, but was not allowed because of a superstition that women would bring bad luck to the mine. I believe that this idea has since changed, and that women are now allowed entry.

The Asian influenza hit Yellowknife and the hospital was filled to capacity. As well as new patients being admitted, the in-patients, already there for a different reason, were also becoming ill from the virus. Next, the staff caught the germ, creating nursing shortages. Although I seldom got sick, I did succumb to the wretched infection and took sick leave. Most of us went back to work as soon as possible, to ease the staffing strain, although we were not fully recovered.

I had made an application to work in a Nursing Station, and towards the end of the year I had been given an appointment at Baker Lake in the Northwest Territories. Just before I left, I witnessed a show of racism by a male doctor, himself of ethnic origin and an immigrant to Canada. When I called the doctor in question to attend to a patient in the emergency room during the evening, his response was, "Is he white or native?" My reply to him was, "I'll let you determine that when you arrive, but I have a patient that requires to be stitched!" Whatever the differences were individually about race or creed the hospital was not a place to exercise those opinions, each sick or injured person having equal rights. The ethnic origins of the doctor shall remain nameless, but I believe he would have loudly shouted discrimination had the shoe been on the other foot.

I was invited by a pilot friend to take an aeroplane trip from Yellowknife to Fort Rae. He had some cargo to deliver, making the visit very brief. While he went about his business I wandered through the small village, unaware of the historical reference of the place name. Much later I learned it had been named after Dr John Rae. He was born in the Orkney Islands and on touring the Islands recently, I saw the house where he was born. He trained as a surgeon in Edinburgh, Scotland. From others' research I have learned that he joined one of the Hudson's Bay Company ships, working as a surgeon. He became an explorer and is credited with actually finding the Northwest Passage where Sir John Franklin failed. The available history on Dr Rae is very interesting but not being a historian, I will leave the reader to do his/her own research. Dr Rae is buried in the graveyard of St Magnus Cathedral, in Orkney.

CHAPTER SEVEN
BAKER LAKE

There was a pounding on my bedroom door which awakened me abruptly, and the excited voice of my colleague shouting, "Get up and hurry. I have an emergency and need help!" I literally sprang from my bed, reaching quickly for my bathrobe. I raced through the house into the adjoining clinic to see what the commotion was about. I was quickly filled in on the scenario. The small eighteen-month-old Inuit child in the cot had been brought in by the mother because of respiratory distress. The child's condition was steadily worsening. I was instructed to stay with her while the Nurse-in-Charge fetched, from the medicine cupboard, the necessary drug needed to assist in the child's breathing. Before the drug was administered, the babe went into respiratory and cardiac arrest. Attempts to resuscitate were activated, but to no avail. The child was dead. This was my heart-wrenching introduction to Nursing Station life in the far north. I had only just arrived in Baker Lake, and, in less than a week, experienced not only a death but also a totally different and highly responsible way of nursing, with no doctor to turn to, or an immediate hospital to evacuate patients to.

Whilst working in Yellowknife, a Welsh-born nursing colleague, on hearing of my plans to go north asked, "Are you not afraid of the responsibility you will face?" In my naivety, I responded that I was not entertaining any thoughts of insecurity or a change of heart. These words echoed in my mind as I remember looking at the small inert body, and indeed I did have second thoughts about this new position.

Sadly, we informed the young parents, and both my colleague and I felt the pangs of utter failure at not being able to save this little one. There were no sophisticated practices in place such as a mortuary or funeral parlour. We notified the Department of Indian Affairs and Northern Development, otherwise known to us as DIAND, of the death and ordered a coffin to be delivered to the clinic. The coffin was not the type one is familiar with in the towns and cities, but consisted of a rough wooden box built to the appropriate size and, for this, we had to wait until morning. The layout of the Nursing Station was such that our living quarters were attached to the work area. With the heat within the facility there was a concern, voiced by my colleague, that odours from the deceased would permeate to the living quarters. Based on this, she made the decision that following the washing and dressing of the child in a nightdress and diaper, she would then place the child in a plastic bag, leaving it outside the rear clinic door in order to keep the little corpse refrigerated. Although it may seem callous to the reader - and it also appalled me- one must keep in perspective that for what is taken for granted as protocol in death in our more sophisticated way of living, there had to be adaptation to our special circumstances. It was inevitable that such a method of freezing did not present the most desirable results, and when the time came to place the child in the coffin, complications arose with positioning. Even though my colleague had taken care to arrange the corpse in a proper position in a confined bag space, the body to some degree lay crooked, and consequently froze that way. Had a coffin been readily available at that time it would have been beneficial.

After this episode occurred, it was not possible to go back to sleep. It was very unsettling, and when normality was established we spent a few hours reviewing all details. The Zone Director, who was a medical doctor located in Churchill, had previously been contacted and an account of the tragedy given. Detailed documentation had to be made. Finally, exhausted and having recognised that nothing more could have been done under the circumstances, we dragged our weary bodies to bed. Had the child's condition presented at a major city hospital with advanced technological equipment, the outcome may well have been different. It was important to remember that this was the landscape into which the Inuit were born, and where the vast majority would remain until they died, in spite of the harsh elements. Nurses are not trained to take the ultimate responsibility for human life, but do very well considering their own traditional role.

That first few weeks certainly were eventful, and really, I didn't have time to consider my career options. When I arrived, my presence was very welcomed, at least, as an extra pair of hands. There had been a number of cases of meningitis, resulting in two deaths. A team of doctors arrived just ahead of me in the community and were busy taking blood samples, as well as ear, nose and throat swabs to determine the specific organisms and the possible source of the disease. The whole community was placed on antibiotics. Practically as soon as I deplaned, I was assigned to counting pills. The babies and children were weighed and for them, liquid antibiotics were prescribed and dispensed in accordance with their weight and age. As many families were large in number, the parents would leave the clinic with armloads of medicine. I was advised I would also have to take the preventative treatment.

I was very resistant to the idea and was prepared to take my chances, until my superior pointed out that if this knowledge got out into the community, there probably would be a lynch mob waiting for me! Dutifully, I took the prescribed pills and dealt with the ensuing nausea. It was some time later, when doing my home visits, I was confronted by families, asking what to do about the boxes of unused medicines. I was dumbfounded at the amount of antibiotics that finally ended up back at the clinic, and even more troubled to find out how many individuals failed to administer the medicine to their offspring. It had taken hours of laborious work on our part to prepare. In the meantime we had been under the illusion that our community was rendered safe due to the stringent measures in place. We were at least able to salvage the infants' antibiotics as the contents were still sealed and the expiry dates were still effective for safe use.

My boss at local level announced to me that as I had midwifery training, I would be in charge of all deliveries and that she, having obtained a diploma in public health, would attend to other preventive health issues such as immunizations. I didn't know any better and went along with her suggestion, even though I had always disliked midwifery. It wasn't long before I had to put my training into effect.

Almost three weeks had gone by, and now I was to deliver my first Inuit baby. It was my turn to be on call, the rotation being two days on and two off. The doorbell rang, and though I always slept deeply, I was able to jump quickly to the call of duty. The policy at that time, laid down by Health and Welfare, Medical Services Branch, was that all first pregnancies, as well as those women having had more than five, were to be sent out to hospital in good time for their delivery. Any indicators of previous abnormalities or current problems were similarly treated. There were flaws, whereby on occasion we would be unaware of the existence of some pregnancies until the woman would appear on the doorstep in full swing labour. We just had to cope the best way we could under these conditions.

In response to the bell ringing, I quickly threw on a bathrobe and stifling a few yawns, made my way to the clinic door. I was confronted with a young, very pregnant lady. It was obvious, seeing her hand placed over her belly, that she was in labour. I admitted her and assisted her into bed. At the same time I asked her a few pertinent questions and determined she was not far off from having this baby. Getting her comfortable, I speedily changed into some presentable attire for being on duty. I was on my own now, but knew I could call for assistance if required. The baby came fast, and it was quite a thrill to have delivered the mother safely, single-handed, in an isolated community. I held in my hands a chubby, healthy newborn baby girl with a shock of jet black hair and a good set of lungs, which she used to announce her arrival into the world. This little girl must now be over thirty years old. I had remembered well the teachings from the good old days, and thankfully it was an uncomplicated birth. It was not a first baby for this lady, but nevertheless, she was very happy at the safe arrival of her daughter.

The Nursing Station was physically set up like a miniature hospital and as with any care centre, there is a routine and protocol to adhere to. Following the birth, the mother had to be bathed, soiled linen changed and general post-delivery care given to make her comfortable. The baby had to be attended to soon afterwards and was carefully checked over for any abnormalities. The body temperature was recorded, the baby bathed and suctioned from time to time to remove mucous from the mouth. The mother's vital signs were observed at intervals and she was observed for any haemorrhaging, while paying close attention to the babe's colour and breathing. When all had been attended to, I had to make up a supply of glucose water which was given shortly after birth to the newborn for the following twenty-four hours, even although the mother would be breast feeding.

That, I remember thinking, was a good night's work for one person, when my thoughts were rudely disturbed by the door bell ringing once more. Lo and behold, another very pregnant woman stood before me. It was obvious from the history she gave me and the closeness of the contractions that the birth was imminent. The patient did make it to the bed, but not with much time to spare. My adrenaline was flowing by now, but I was in my element. My colleague was fast asleep while I was bringing new life into the world. Wow! Soon a little boy was born. What joy! He, too, was very healthy. The same routine care was afforded the mother and child. When reading about this type of event, it cannot be fully appreciated how extensive the workload was, when everything had to be done single-handed. Compare the same occurrence in a hospital setting, where numerous well-rested staff are available over a twenty-four hour period, each one performing their own specific duties.

Of course, after all the excitement was over, there was clean-up time, soaking items of bedding which the maid would be responsible for washing later in the day. Any equipment used such as scissors for cutting the umbilical cord, or suturing items, had to be soaked and scrubbed, and subsequently sterilized in readiness for the next case. Not having the modern convenience of an autoclave, we had to use a pressure cooker for this purpose. Although most of the nurses were young and fit, there was no denying, the work was rigorous and demanding, with sleep deprivation creating much weariness.

When the first rays of light filtered in through the window, and heralded in a new day, it was a comfort to know that sleep would not be far away, unless of course only one nurse was left on her own to man the facility. That was not an entirely uncommon situation, as I was to find out.

A final check of the mothers and newborns was made before greeting the curious staff coming on duty. As I looked down at the little boy, the newest arrival, I did not know then what future fate awaited him, and how emotional that event would be for me.

"Good morning!", the voice from behind me said, "So you had a delivery last night and managed okay. I didn't hear anything!" With a satisfied smile, I replied, "No, I had two deliveries."

Such was my initiation into Baker Lake. When I applied for the nursing position, I did not have an inkling about the dynamics of the role I was about to enter. The information and mental image I had was one of dog teams, people in fur garb, explorers and the Hudson's Bay Company, and a notion that temperatures would be very cold. The wonderful advantage of my wide-ranging nurse's training allowed me the flexibility to travel in different directions in this vast North American continent, and also to other lands, had I so desired. At that time, nurses were very much in demand, particularly in the Northern Hemisphere. The government liked British-trained nurses with midwifery qualifications, given that deliveries would be an expected part of our role. There is a change afoot now, where Inuit and Native Indians have entered into the nursing field, with some returning to care for their own people. I can look back now and be grateful that my northern experience was a great adventure and may never again be captured in quite the same way in this fast-changing world. Perhaps there are advantages to our modern world, but I feel a sense of sadness for the people in the Arctic. Their cultural ways will never be the same, and the rapid swing into our materialistic world has its pitfalls.

Baker Lake was named after two brothers from the eighteenth century: Sir William Baker, a Governor of the Hudson's Bay Company, and his brother Richard. It lies approximately three hundred miles north of Churchill, Manitoba. The community overlooks the lake and it was not unusual for me to awaken early in the morning, in the Nursing Station, to the sound of the huskies passing near to my bedroom window, panting and yelping in anticipation of the journey ahead. I could clearly make out the sound of the qamutik (Inuit sled) runners gliding over the snow as the dogs pulled their master, an Inuk, on the way to hunt caribou. On hearing this delightful sound, I never tired of jumping from my bed to make my observances, sadly sensing that the future world modernisation might make this sight extinct. Recalling the many aspects of my life in the north still thrill me. What is life all about, if not in part the exposure to a variety of encounters and experiences that help provide meaning? Had it not been for the exploits of the early great explorers, we might not have known of the existence of many races, or learned about other cultures which surely enrich ours.

The Hamlet, at that time, had an Inuit population of approximately six hundred, with the white population adding a further two hundred persons to the total. The preferred term of Inuit simply means, "The people." The word Eskimo, which was given to the Inuit by the Indians, was considered to mean "eaters of raw meat." This is currently disputed. The people of Baker Lake are the Caribou Inuit and they are the only inland Inuit community in the Northwest Territories. It was a pleasant lifestyle there for me, and it had all the fundamental requirements that I needed. It certainly did not have the frills of southern living. If individuals desired a gay, social life, the north might have proven to be a disappointment, and there were some people who could not cope in this setting.

The Hudson"s Bay Company store was located down the road, less than a mile from the Nursing Station, and provided us with the necessary foods for our varied culinary tastes. Fresh vegetables and fruit were scarce, and had to be brought in by air cargo twice a week, as was the meat supply, unless the weather conditions did not permit flying. These would have acted as supplements to the Inuit, as many of them hunted the caribou and ice-fished for trout, arctic char and grayling.

I am sure that the introduction of white man's sugary foods had some detrimental impact on their health. When the visiting dentist came to town, there was a good attendance at the clinic. In between, we gave fluoride brushings to the school children as a part of the health programme, and taught the detrimental effects of consuming sweets in large quantities.

The Hudson's Bay was also responsible for sorting our mail delivery. When the drone of the aeroplane engine was heard from overhead, I felt an air of excitement and expectancy. As soon as the clinic was over I would scurry down to the Bay and wait in a long line in the hope of receiving a letter, bringing news from overseas of family and friends.

My salary was paid by direct deposit to the bank in Winnipeg. My monetary needs were very minimal, lodgings and food generously being supplied by Health and Welfare with only a small deduction from one's pay cheque made each month in exchange. Our food supply was not only for the staff, but for any visiting personnel such as nursing officers, doctors, dentists, x-ray technicians and patients who may have been admitted.

In a room off to one side in the facility and located between the living quarters and the clinic was a large, walk-in pantry. I had never seen anything like this before. The pantry was divided by wooden partitions and on the shelves were dry food supplies such as boxes of cake mixes, lard, flour, canned carnation milk, canned bacon, raisins, baking powder and all sort of other things. It would take too long to identify the many other items of food, but it looked like a mini Hudson's Bay Store. In this era, many foods and medicines were still being shipped on a yearly basis and addressed as sea lift. Only some meats and fresh foods were required to be purchased locally. At least if planes could not fly due to inclement weather I felt secure with the adequate pantry supplies. Before I left the community, the supplies which were delivered by ship yearly were being downgraded and more items were being purchased locally. The goods were always obtained by a government purchase order. Each month, after a careful assessment of our needs was done, we would travel by skidoo, with a qamutik (sled) attached to a hitch at the back, to pick up the necessary items. Our Inuk caretaker had built a wooden box on top of the qamutik to transport the items purchased. This simplified it for us, and saved us time having to lash down the supplies to prevent them spilling over. That, of course, was not guaranteed to ward off any calamity like the one that happened on the way home across the frozen lake on one occasion. With a heavy load, we hit a bump in the ice and, as we were travelling fairly fast, it caused the skidoo, qamutik and passengers to spill. It was comical, no doubt, to witness two nurses lying on the frozen lake while the frozen turkeys skidded across the ice as a result of the impact. I shouted, "Anyone for curling?" In mock gesture we lined up a couple of turkeys and sent them speeding across the ice. Perhaps the saying, "Laughter is the best medicine", carries a lot of truth and helped keep the bad stress at bay.

It happened on one occasion that our food supply requirements were very low, possibly, due to fewer visitors or in-patients. At the same time the Hudson's Bay Company were displaying rather attractive quilts. We really were in need of improved bed coverings and, with a little bit of persuasion, we negotiated a deal with the manager. For the price of meats, etc., we came away with two lovely quilts. The quilts were itemized for billing as meat, the monetary value being equal.

There were two missions in the community, one, a Roman Catholic and the other Anglican. A little later the B'hai religion appeared within the settlement. The Anglican minister was an Englishman, and I, also being of that denomination, decided to be confirmed there. The minister insisted that I had to attend some kind of instruction, and he had the foolhardy idea that I was going to study. The thought of that did not appeal to me. Having to work frequently in my spare time and with the many restrictions the job imposed, my freedom of time was important to me. I opted to defer the confirmation until a later period in life. I met the Catholic priest in those first few weeks and was very fond of this gentle, older man. In fact, on the way to the Hudson's Bay I had to pass the mission. There frequently was a very large mound of drifted snow near to the priest's quarters, over which I had to drive the skidoo. Not yet too accustomed to the operation of the machinery, I tended to slow down at the bottom of the hillock, thus sinking the skidoo into deep snow. Consequently, Father came to the rescue and helped dig out the skidoo. In a laughing voice and a heavy Flemish accent he would admonish me thus exclaiming, "No-ra, don't slow down at the hill. Just keep going fast!" I soon got the knack.

There was a Royal Canadian Mounted Police detachment with two members in the community, one being the corporal and the other a constable. Both were married. The constable was located in a house directly across from the clinic. Shortly after my arrival I was pleasantly surprised when I responded to the house doorbell. There in front of me was the police constable, and instant recognition crossed both our faces simultaneously. I had known him from the Yukon Territory when he and his wife became engaged, and now they were my neighbours. At a later date, his wife, who had been a teacher by profession, became my part-time secretary.

Baker Lake was a quiet, law-abiding settlement, and a dry one which banned alcohol being brought in. However, rules do get broken in the best of circumstances, and there were occasions when it was evident that someone had brought supplies in from Churchill, creating a little community merriment. In addition to the other officers there was an Inuk special constable on their staff. Being of that culture and fluent in his own language had its benefits in helping to keep order, as well as for interpretation purposes.

The Federal Government assumed responsibility for the Inuit in many avenues, including education. The students attended the local school from grades one to six. For further education they went to Churchill. There was a small classroom building separate from the main school used for the nursery-age children. Their attendance there helped them in the cultural transition. Adjacent was another similar building, where the kindergarten students were taught English along with other programmes. The school student enrolment was around two hundred and thirty pupils, and there were about eight teachers diligently applying their skills for the betterment of the children's education. Two Inuit assistants, a cook and a caretaker completed the staff in this small, modern school.

The Department of Indian Affairs and Northern Development (DIAND) had a resident Area Administrator with a number of Inuit employees under his direction. He had many duties, including community development, settlement planning and was a service supplier of fuel required for the various vehicles (garbage collection and sewage removal). In the removal of sewage, a truck, affectionately known as the "Honey Wagon" pumped the waste from the septic tanks in the community. In this particular Nursing Station we did have a flush toilet for our personal use and one for the patients. Our facility effluent emptied into a large septic tank which was located under the building in an area we called the crawl space. Obviously it had a fair bit of usage, and periodic emptying had to be carried out. As a medical facility, we frequently worked in co-operation with DIAND and many other departments. In the event of a death, this department provided us with the rough box to act as a coffin. At times when we required transport from the clinic to an aircraft for a medical evacuation, either DIAND or the Department of Transport (DOT) provided this service.

Located in the opposite direction from the Inuit homes were other necessary services. Here DOT played a very important role. The airport was operated by a branch of DOT and they were responsible for maintaining the landing strip on land in the summer and the ice strip on the lake in the winter, as well as coordinating the air traffic activities, incoming and outgoing cargo, and the refuelling of aircraft. We did have electricity and oil was used for our heating. They were responsible for replenishing the fuel tanks and maintaining the hydro-electric plant by which water from the lake was chlorinated and pumped to our homes. There were quite a number of staff required for operating heavy-duty equipment, maintenance and mechanical repair. Their department had many more in-depth responsibilities. I merely wish to provide an outline, so that the reader can better understand the different functional roles of the agencies which provided us with the means to make our existence in isolation possible.

Another branch of DOT was the radio communications. This service was invaluable to the pilots and to the ships that came with the sea lift goods. They provided important navigational information with round the clock coverage of weather conditions and changes. As a nurse, I found the radio operators to be of immense value to me. All our communications to the doctors at the hospital in Churchill, at that time, were entirely transmitted by this mode. I was not very adept initially at using the radio and placed a great reliance on the operators. It could be stressful listening to and concentrating on words that could be garbled and obliterated with the atmospheric static when in an emergency situation. They were expert in relaying the doctor's messages under these circumstances.

Also at Baker Lake was the installation of a Geophysical Observatory, a branch of the Department of Energy, Mines and Resources. It is part of a Canadian network capable of recording earthquakes occurring in different parts of the globe.

The Inuit have always been skilled with their hands, this being a necessity for their survival in the barren lands. These hand skills, in the past, were used to fashion hunting weapons, in the form of spears, harpoons and fishing tackle. For means of transportation they made qamutiks to be pulled by the sled dogs. A Qulliq was a lamp, carved from soapstone. In its basin was placed seal oil, which was used for lighting, heating and cooking purposes. By using caribou skins, seal skins and various animal furs, the women were able to make warm clothing. Like other members of society, they too enjoyed and played games for their amusement, the game pieces used were often carved from bone. It isn't surprising, then, that the Inuit adapted easily to converting their skills, making crafts as a livelihood, following the Department of Indian and Northern Affairs, introduction of an Arts and Craft programme at Baker Lake in the sixties, in order to provide employment for the people. A co-operative was formed, which acted as a protection to prevent the Inuit from being exploited when selling their art work. During my stay in Baker Lake, I observed the Inuit carve animals and figures from caribou bone, antlers and soapstone which they first quarried themselves. I have in my possession some superb carvings which I treasure. One of my favourites is of an Inuk doing a drum dance. The covering of the drum is delicately made from fish skin. The carver of this piece, I am told, also made a carving of a musk-ox for Her Majesty, Queen Elizabeth of Great Britain. Today many of these carvings are seen in city shops and on display at Art Galleries. Stone plates were also carved from whence prints were made.

The women too were skilled in making carvings. They also made items of clothing from skins of the caribou, kamiits, which are the Inuit fur boot, wall hangings and drawings. These drawings sometimes were made into prints, and also reached a market in the south. Their industry was a great success. A duffle garment centre was opened in 1969 which employed quite a number of women. Some were machinists, sewing the parkas and outer shells, while others created hand-embroidered designs, adding fur trim on the coat hems and hoods to complete the garments. They made waistcoats for adults and children and duffel socks to wear inside the kamiits. Gradually, some of the old ways were reintroduced to help maintain the culture. The girls were taught sewing and the boys were taught the art of making igloos and hunting.

As a business enterprise, six cabins previously owned by the government were bought by Rainy Lake Airways and used as accommodation for visiting fishermen, as tourism was on the increase. Before I left, there were plans afoot to build a lodge.

Last, but not least, to be mentioned, was the existence of the Nursing Station. It was very much a focal point of the community, where life and death experiences were played out. As well as routine medical care, a prevention health programme was also in effect. The station was operated by the Department of National Health and Welfare, Medical Services Branch, and was built in 1957. There was a complement of four staff members, two being registered nurses, a housekeeper/interpreter and a janitor. The staff were directly responsible to the Nurse-in-Charge, who in turn was responsible to her Nursing Supervisor and the Zone Director. In those days, the director's position was held by a medical doctor who was located in Churchill, Manitoba. The chain of command crept up the ladder to the Regional Director and all the way to the Minister of Health. Following the lines of communication was deemed necessary for the smooth running of the organization, but there were times when communications went adrift.

The role of the nurse carried great responsibility. There was not a doctor on hand in the facility, and nurses were called upon to do extensive examinations, diagnose on the basis of their findings and prescribe appropriate medications to suit the malady. As well as deliveries, suturing was done, blood samples and x-rays taken, light plaster casts applied, intravenous infusions set up and generally the careful monitoring of the very ill until such times as a plane was available for the patient to be evacuated to hospital care. There were times when dental extractions were a necessary evil.

Today there are outpost nurse training programmes to help equip the nurse for the rigorous job, but I, along with my compatriots, had to do the best we could from our primary training experiences. Nursing duties apart, there also was the administration aspect and general running of the clinic, with supplies to be ordered, food stocks kept adequate, supervising the other staff and making sure that the building itself was well maintained by the janitor. Laundry, such as bedding for the staff, visiting personnel and patients, was done on site by the housekeeper with an old-fashioned washing machine and hand wringer. Coupled with her interpreter duties in the clinic, she was kept very busy, and unfairly so. She could not always apply her time to the housework duties. The caretaker was required, as part of his chores, to collect patients by skidoo to attend a special clinic held by a visiting doctor, or for those who were too sick to attend on their own. In the advent of a stretcher case, a bombardier could be requested through DIAND as we did not have our own transportation, other than the skidoo used for home visits.

The physical layout of the clinic included two small wards, each holding two beds, giving a total of four places to accommodate adults. There was one small child's cot, two bassinettes and an incubator for a premature newborn. Adjoining, was the main clinic room, fairly well equipped with rows of medications in the cupboards, oxygen cylinders, examination table and equipment and an x-ray machine. Adjacent was the small waiting room, always filled to capacity starting at eight-thirty in the morning. There was a small office where filing cabinets stored the many medical files. At the time of my arrival there was no secretary on staff. This meant that we typed all our own reports, medical and otherwise, and in my case this was a one-finger operation, not having accomplished typing skills. However, in due course and after much hinting, we were finally granted a half-time secretary.

The crawl space underneath the building occupied the entire length of the structure where the bulk of medical supplies were stored. Three months later, and after my colleague had left, a fire inspector deemed this to be an unsafe practice and a fire trap, thus requiring all the supplies to be removed. Of course, no extra help was brought in for this rearrangement, and I was left single- handed when the decision was made. At the same time sea lift had arrived and there were boxes upon boxes of medical items to be emptied and stored. Storage could not occur until new space had been created. Most times, there were not enough hours in the work day to do the many duties required of us so naturally sometimes we worked all evening. I could ill afford the time to be spent on this reorganization of supplies. With sandwich in hand, over my lunch time, I made the endeavour, making many trips up and down a ladder as well as squeezing down through the trap door to retrieve the numerous items. The new location for the goods was to be my grocery pantry. Not only had the downstairs to be emptied, but revamping of the entire cupboard upstairs was also necessary. The task was extra difficult because the crawl space was just that, and one had to move about on hands and knees.

After one month, I was beginning to be a little more comfortable with my new role when the Nurse-in-Charge informed me I would be going to Rankin Inlet Nursing Station for a month to do relief work. Happy at the thought of yet another new challenge, I did not realise until the day I arrived, that the two Australian nurses stationed there were both leaving within a couple of days and I would be entirely on my on. I cringed at the idea, being so totally fresh to the life in the Arctic and not knowing whether I was ready to cope by myself. As they were busy with packing, no one was inclined to spend much time in orienting me to the centre.

The two days flashed past and I was on my own. Well, it was a smaller community, and I imagined I would have a relaxing holiday. Feeling comfortable after a bath, I sprawled out on the couch, book in one hand and a nice cup of cocoa in the other. "Rats!" I thought as I stumbled to answer the repeated doorbell rings. "Baby come now!" blurted the person in front of me. I quickly ushered her into the clinic. It was rather obvious she was in full swing labour. I phoned for the interpreter, and in a jiffy she arrived. Through her, I learned that the woman had been in labour for some time, and it was her third baby. She had not received any prenatal care, nor was there any record of her pregnancy. All in all, this was not a good obstetrical profile for me to be confronted with in this setting. I changed into my uniform, mentally saying goodbye to my evening of imagined leisure. I set up an intravenous drip immediately in case of any serious problems I might encounter. On examination, I was dismayed at my findings. This baby was lying in what is called a transverse lie in the uterus with an arm presenting at the outlet.

The position was not the only problem. I could not find a foetal heartbeat. How I wished at this moment that I was in a comfortable hospital setting with a doctor on hand and other allied support. Although in good labour, the woman had a bulging bag of water delaying the delivery. I promptly ruptured the bag containing the amniotic fluid which instantly and forcefully shot out. She now progressed rapidly, pushing hard with result. First the arm appeared, followed by the head and the rest of the body. Sadly the babe was stillborn, appearing very emaciated with obvious congenital abnormalities. The small face did not look as it should. Had the foetus not be so small I might have had very real problems with the delivery. Even if a plane had been readily on hand, with the mother's advanced state of labour, it was preferable she delivered at the clinic with more amenities available, and in a more controlled environment than on the plane. Had she been attending the clinic, those difficulties would have been identified and the patient sent to Churchill ahead of time. The afterbirth refused to appear and some bleeding was occurring. The mother was becoming restless. I became concerned for my patient and decided to play it safe, being so far from a hospital facility. I radioed for a plane to transport her as a medical evacuation. Back came the message that the weather was out and no plane would be forthcoming until later. It was anyone's guess what was meant by later. You cannot imagine the crestfallen feeling one has when the link with the outside is cut off and you alone are responsible for a human life. I stayed with the patient all night, frequently checking the vital signs and recalling rapidly the instructions given that day in midwifery class about this very situation. I felt I had covered all aspects, and now it was a matter of waiting it out. There was a constant slow bleeding all night but not too dramatic.

Through the crackling sounds of the radio I received a message, announcing a plane was on the way. It surely felt like D-Day. It was six o'clock in the morning. Preparation had to be made for such a journey of approximately three hundred miles in an aircraft. This would be a stretcher case and I needed to make her comfortable for the trip. The patient had to be transported warmly wrapped, and the intravenous protected from the bitter Arctic cold. A sterile pack for delivery of the afterbirth was taken in case the altitude precipitated contractions, thus expelling it. The mother needed also to be comforted in the loss of her infant. Family members came to pick up the body of the baby for burial. After a certain period of gestation, a foetus is considered viable, that is to say, under normal circumstances it could maintain an independent life. Therefore, as a little human being it could be buried.

The nurse had to be adequately clothed as well. The emergency equipment supplied by the government always accompanied us in case of the aircraft coming down. The equipment consisted of a tent, an arctic sleeping bag and a stove. The plane was also equipped in the event of an emergency landing. When possible, I always made sandwiches, and took a supply of chocolate and raisins. Time did not always allow for such luxuries if a nurse was working alone at the time.

It was a relief to be on board the aircraft heading to Churchill. My colleague from Baker Lake was, by sheer coincidence, also on the same chartered flight, escorting a lady in labour with similar complications, only she was bleeding before giving birth. When we landed at the airstrip we were met by the ambulance crew and quickly transported to the hospital. Our duty was now completed, but there would be other emergencies.

Wearily, two nurses dragged themselves off to a well-deserved sleep at the local hotel. We had not slept for twenty-four hours or more. After so many hours of sleep deprivation it would seem that instant slumber would be attainable, but not so. Rather, one became quite giddy, laughing at the silliest things before eventually passing into the twilight zone.

Having recovered from a good night's rest, once again, I was winging my way back to Rankin Inlet. It being a smaller community, I thought I would not be overly busy with patients, and it would give me time to do an inventory of supplies needed. I was very wrong. Soon, I had an outbreak of an infectious disease within the community that required immediate attention. There were so many cases, contacts of cases and contact of contact patients, that eventually the Zone Director flew in to give me assistance. After a busy week, I was again on my own, the situation having quieted down.

The visiting dentist arrived a couple of days later and once more the clinic was packed. The day before his arrival, I had seen a teenager at the morning clinic who displayed signs of influenza. Advice was given to her mother who had accompanied her. At six o'clock in the evening, the doorbell rang, and the same mother and daughter stood before me. I sent for my interpreter. Better communication was accomplished in this manner, giving a more in-depth history to questions asked in order to better diagnose. The young lady's condition had worsened and I decided to admit her for observation. The process of admission was similar to that of any hospital only we did not have the benefit of clerical help. Just after I admitted her she fell into a semi-coma.

Because of the prevalence of meningitis in the north one was always suspicious, and following an extensive examination with some specific reference points being checked, I diagnosed her as indeed having meningitis. An intravenous was set up and the appropriate antibiotic was administered. In her semi-coma state she still responded to the pain stimulus. In response to her head and neck pain, she writhed about and screamed, at times half-sitting up. During one of these moments, in order to comfort her, I attempted to cradle her in the crook of my arm. I was not at all prepared for her next action. Her head was pressed against my bosom, and she suddenly, without warning, in her anguished state, sank her teeth into my breast. I would have loved to have seen a replay of both the action and the reaction. I remember releasing her from my arms, clasping a hand over the breast and exclaiming, "She bit me!" I disappeared in a flash to the adjacent bathroom to carry out the necessary inspection, and there I found, to my amazement, a lovely set of upper and lower teeth marks with the beginnings of a bruise. Fortunately the skin remained intact but this posed a dilemma for me, because this was a highly contagious disease and I was a contact in more ways than one. It was usual for us to take precautions and treat all household contacts preventatively. Previously, I had been subjected to taking antibiotics at Baker Lake for the existence of the same disease in the community, and did not wish to have another course. Under normal circumstances, I would not be concerned, but with the bite I received, I contemplated the need to take medication.

My patient was made comfortable while I awaited the arrival of a plane which I had requested from Churchill, for her evacuation. The policy was that when in doubt, take no chances with human life and particularly with meningitis. Neglect could have deadly consequences, not only to the patient, but to the overall community. When dealing with this disease, the causative organisms could be varied and only a spinal tap and the laboratory could determine that. As well as the training and skills acquired by the nurse, there was a treatment manual at each facility which was our "Medical Bible." Having carried out all the care that was feasibly possible in isolation, one tended to refer to this manual to make sure that all government procedures were in effect. When the sound of an overhead aircraft was heard, there was a huge sense of relief, knowing that help had arrived. In this case a nurse had been provided to escort the patient to hospital.

Having completed the discharge of my patient, the following day I had to set about tracing and treating the girl's contacts. This could be very extensive and time-consuming work. Some of the other duties were halted to make available time for the laborious task. As part of my responsibility, I had to notify the Zone Director of the medical evacuee, her diagnosis and condition when she left my care. It was then that I discussed my encounter with the young lady's teeth. The counsel given to me was that it might be prudent to take antibiotics immediately. That day the visiting dentist arrived, and in discussion with him, I mentioned the bite. He volunteered to give me an intra-muscular injection of the appropriate antibiotic into my hip so that it would be quickly absorbed. He gave a very good shot, considering that afterwards he told me, he only ever injected gums not "bums." At least I was able to laugh about it.

In my off-duty hours which were, of course, few and far between, I was able to walk around the hamlet and find out about the community. Rankin Inlet is located on the west coast of the Hudson Bay and derived its name from an early explorer named John Rankin. It had become a settlement in 1955 and prior to 1962, it had a nickel mine operation. The Inuit subsisted by fishing and crafting, and during my time there, a factory also produced canned maktaaq, the whale blubber, in a variety of different sauces.

Although my stay was short-lived and full of action, I found it enjoyable. There was always someone dropping in for a coffee or a meal. My interpreter, who had some personal problems in her home life to resolve, moved in with me for a week.

I was quite happy to be back at Baker Lake, and wanted to learn as much as possible from my superior, which included the general management of the clinic in all its uniqueness. There were a multitude of forms that had to be submitted to headquarters monthly, the ordering of supplies and a good working knowledge was also required of the many programmes to be delivered to the population.

The clinics for the sick were held each morning, five days a week. It was then that we determined the nature of the illness, prescribed the necessary drugs or treatment plan, and made our entries accordingly on the charts. In the afternoons, different clinics were conducted on different days. These included prenatal care, but there were some pregnancies that slipped through the loop and were not seen until in advanced labour. Such was the case of the client at Rankin Inlet. The caretaker and interpreter were very good at informing the nurses if they heard, via the grapevine, of pregnancies in the village so that we could coax the mothers-to-be to the clinic. Incorporated into this clinic was a mother-craft class, which was supposed to better equip the women in the care and management of their offspring. When I look back, those mothers with multiple children could well have educated me from their experiences, as some had delivered out on the land without assistance. However, this was part of the job, and there were some modern day, white man's techniques that proved useful. Baby clinics were carried out for the purpose of immunizations and developmental assessments - by testing the children we could establish if they were attaining correct levels of development for their age. Maternal and child care were high on the agenda of priorities, but with little staff, and the fact that illness itself was always prevalent, along with emergencies, this meant that the prevention aspect had sometimes to be abandoned. There were only so many hours in a day, and indeed, we were extended many, many times beyond the bounds of normality and suffered the consequences at times by compromising our own health and safety. Sadly, looking back I ask myself, "Who really cared about the nurses?" It took me a great many years to realise that attention to one's own health comes first, otherwise there can be a serious cost to pay.

A certain amount of chest x-rays had to be done routinely. Tuberculosis existed, and a number of Inuit who tested positive to the disease were evacuated to the Charles Camsell Hospital, in Edmonton, for the appropriate care. A number of these were children, still very young to be parted from their parents. Some remained there for one or two years while receiving treatment. After a lengthy stay in the hospital, these children would return home speaking English, understanding that language more than their own. This was hard on both the parents and child. When they were discharged home, close monitoring had to be done, which included sputum collections and intermittent chest x-rays, the due date for these being determined by the hospital doctors. Tuberculin tests were carried out in the clinic for adults, and in the school for the children. A highly positive tuberculin reading required the taking of anti-tuberculin drugs. Thankfully, treatments have advanced, requiring minimal hospitalisation and a lesser amount of pills to be ingested. Once a day, the school-aged children on this pill programme attended the morning clinic to have their dosage of medicine given personally by the nurse. Each Friday they were weighed, general health checked and a weekend supply of pills was issued to them. The regime was, and had to be, stringently adhered to for the sake of all residents. Of course we visited the school at intervals, not only for immunizing and tuberculin testing, but also for health education purposes.

One afternoon had to be set aside for home visits and, amid all this, time had to be made for office work, which included typing letters to doctors and other agencies, recording in charts and making new ones as needed. There were appointment books kept for the various visiting doctors and dentists that had to be kept updated. Reports had to be surrendered on time each month to our superiors. These reflected our workload, types of illnesses seen, management concerns and a general summary of the community. In order for the casual staff to be paid, their hours of work had to be submitted. Because there were not enough hours available in the day, so many duties were carried out in our own time. For this we were granted one extra day of holiday time a month in exchange for the hundreds of hours of overtime worked. I doubt if any other professionals gave so much, so willingly and without monetary gain or recognition by their employer. The nurses in these stations were the backbone of the service, and I feel too little recognition has ever been given to them, past and present. There were deeds of heroism by the "Nightingales" who in some circumstances gave their lives in the line of duty.

One evening, when an old lady was brought to the clinic, appearing to be very ill, I admitted her, and following a good examination determined that she possibly had congestive heart failure. She had not been eating, was dehydrated and very short of breath, and her lips were deep blue in colour. Contact was made with the zone, requesting an aircraft to evacuate her. In the meantime, the woman went into respiratory arrest. My colleague and I carried out resuscitation promptly and were able to revive her. An intravenous was set up and the necessary medications administered. We then sat with her, monitoring her condition. Our medical advisor was of course contacted.

The pilots arrived only to announce that we would not be flying immediately due to strong winds and some dubious weather reports. We had been too busy to concern ourselves with the climate. Our main concern was that we had a patient whose condition was rapidly deteriorating, and we needed to evacuate her soon. I pleaded with the pilot and co-pilot, but both of them stood firm, telling us we would have to ride it out until dawn. In actual fact the nurses were forbidden by the department to fly at night. A nurse had died on a night flight, and this decision was in place to safeguard us. The philosophy was the same as I had encountered at Norway House. If the patient was so ill, and could not last for a few hours, then it was unfair to jeopardize the lives of two pilots and a nurse against the odds. However, when faced with these predicaments, one does take chances in order to save a life. Looking back, I am grateful for the wise decision the pilots made, as their logic prevailed over my emotions.

When daylight came and the winds subsided, we were given the all clear to go. My colleague was due out for a trip as the nurse escort. The sense of relief when the plane departed was very short lived, as it soon landed again. The dear lady had died, and this time there was no recovery. We faced the sad duty of informing the family. At first we had given hope. The great bird in the sky was taking their mother off to make her well in the white man's world. They had faith in us, as well as their Christian beliefs, and we felt we had let them down.

Home visits were a treat for me at the end of the week. It meant getting out on the skidoo, and although the cold was extreme, with proper gear one did not feel the icy chill. Sometimes I would go alone, but many times the interpreter came with me, sitting on the back of the machine clutching the nurse's black bag which contained thermometers, dressings and a conglomerate of other medical necessities. The travelling distance was short, but sometimes over very rugged terrain, according to the way the snow had drifted. Some of the houses had snow piled up to the roof. In order to gain access to the doorway, one first drove over a hillock of snow then descended to the other side. Unexpectedly, the husky dogs, tethered nearby the door, confronted us, so one had to be careful when making a blind descent. These animals were not the usual family pet and therefore not always friendly. It was meant to be that way, as they were a working dog used to pulling the Qamutik for the hunter on his mission to kill the caribou.

The clients we visited varied in their needs. Some were new mums, some were follow-up clinic patients and some were the old and infirm who were unable to pay us a visit at the clinic, but not so sick that they needed to be admitted. A tall Inuk male, quite elderly and with white hair, was pointed out to me on one of these visits as he walked by. This was the Shaman or Medicine-man. It was said he came from a different place originally, as he was taller than most. Looking back I wished I had attempted to find out more about him and the old ways, which was indeed my loss. The Shaman, was believed to have healing powers and the name means, "He Who Knows." He had social standing due to the belief that he could communicate with the spirits, and this gave him authority in the community. It was also believed that he could bring about good and bad. To what extent he was consulted during the later years, I do not know, but judging by the heavy attendances at our daily clinics, there had been a shift to our ways as far as medical healing was concerned.

It was exhilarating to travel around in this manner, and we were always graciously received. The Inuit laughed easily, and through the interpreter many a joke was shared. One very elderly lady, in her late nineties and the oldest inhabitant in the settlement, had a number of tattoos. They were on her cheeks, forehead, chin and arms. When I enquired as to why this was done, she laughed and said it was for beautification. I never saw any males tattooed, it was primarily women. When I asked what her recipe for longevity was, she replied through the interpreter, that taking life easy was the secret, and she was very amused at the "Qallunaats" question. "Qallunaat" was the Inuit name given to the white man. I have been told it means "one with distinct eyebrows" because the white man seems to have more growth on the eyebrows than the Inuit. As to her answer of an easy life, I doubt if her generation had known anything but utter hardship.

My colleague announced unexpectedly that she had given her resignation, effective at the end of the month. I felt sad at the prospect of losing my partner who had helped me so much in adjusting to this new environment, but she was ready to move on. I wondered who would now be my new boss but I didn't have too long to wait. The department announced that I would be appointed to the Nurse-in-Charge position. Delighted as I was, I doubted my abilities, but it appeared that the department did not share those fears. This was the starting point in my life to believe in my own self-worth and to stand up for my beliefs.

I walked through the entire length of the building. It was so quiet, no staff around, no patients and my partner well on her way to Ottawa, her home town. I was all alone. "What if ?" The question resounded in my brain. "I will manage", I told myself. I didn't have too long to wait before a second nurse was appointed, and who came complete with a public health diploma which was advantageous to the establishment. Unfortunately, not everyone is adapted to the isolation and rigours of the north, and this seemed to be the case with my new-found compatriot.

I recall an unpleasant occasion when I had been up all night having delivered a baby of a non-native woman and caring for the infant, who was having some neurological problems. It was decided that the new nurse would escort the mother and babe as soon as transport arrived. She was thrilled to be going on a trip south and busily prepared her suitcase for the occasion. It was hoped that this trip might have a more settling affect on her when she returned. Disaster descended when the radio operator from the Department of Transport called to inform me that the Zone Director from Churchill was about to land. He had been notified of our evacuation plans and being in a nearby settlement he decided to re-route his plane and escort the woman and baby to hospital.

I had made arrangements for the doctor and the pilot to have a meal at the transport canteen down the road from us. So often the nurses were left with the chore of cooking for the visiting personnel even though this was not part of our duties. Most times we didn't mind, but after being on duty a full twenty-four hours with concerns over a new-born baby and sporting a migraine, I did not feel inclined to start preparing meals. It was not long after receiving the call when the doctor appeared at the door along with the pilot. When I questioned him regarding his meal, he was offhand, stating,

"If you have food, we will eat and if you don't, we will do without." In the meantime, the pots and pans and cupboard doors in the kitchen were being assaulted by my colleague, who would no longer be going on the trip she had so much looked forward to. I blew my cool and snapped back at the doctor that we were not the local canteen. The consequences of this reaction would later be used against me. Still, I felt that under the circumstances, I was under a strain with the action around me, in pain and suffering from lack of sleep. I cannot remember now whether food was given to the unexpected guests. Perhaps I prefer to blur out the incident.

My colleague decided to resign after three months, which was unfortunate for me. She was a most agreeable person to work with as well as fun loving, a quality I had hoped would see her through her difficult times. In those isolated situations where two woman are thrown together to work and share accommodation, there is always the concern that there may be incompatibility. I had been thus far very fortunate with my associates.

This rapid departure left me alone once more. Had I known then that I would be without another nurse to share the workload and burdens that came my way for the next five months, I might have been inclined to board the same plane out along with my colleague. It became one of those situations where hope springs eternal with the promises from my superiors in headquarters that, "It should not take too long before we get a replacement to you." Such tales I believed whole-heartedly, but I dare say efforts were being made. Not everyone was jumping on the bandwagon to come north. I was able to maintain the workload, but being on call night and day for this period of time was quite exhausting and a little scary, when realising the responsibility of the community's health rests with you.

"I have a medical emergency and I need to commandeer the aircraft that is presently taking off." "Right away!", he answered. This was my communication to the radio operator. Just ten minutes before, an Inuit mother arrived distraught at the clinic door, with her six-year-old boy in her arms. He was unconscious. The mother did not speak much English, but certain words she used in her language were known to me, allowing me to understand that the onset of illness had come upon the boy the evening before in the form of a fever. It did not take long to diagnose meningitis with its recognizable signs. I was very unhappy with the arching of his back caused by this condition. I heard the familiar sound of an aeroplane as it taxied down the airstrip. I immediately contacted the Department of Transportation. It was a blessing to have a plane right there when I needed it. A considerable delay would have occurred while waiting for one to arrive from the nearest location, which may well have been from

Churchill. Such delays can be life threatening. The passengers had to return to their accommodation to allow me free access. As I was alone, I had to travel with my patient, and the interpreter had to be quickly notified of my departure. One prayed that no other emergency would occur in my absence. Fortunately there was a trained nurse in the community, should the need arise, although she was not currently employed. Antibiotics were commenced, an intravenous set up and sedation was given to the boy which helped to relax his state. With the mother by his side, it enabled me to pack medications needed for this trip, and prepare the stretcher.

Transport was already being organized to take the patient to the airstrip. The Zone Director had to be informed of the patient's condition and the proposed evacuation. The whole operation, with the help of so many, went very smoothly. Although the onus and medical responsibility lay entirely with the nurse on the scene, there were many willing hands to assist in other ways, and encouraging support from the Zone Director could always be relied on. Seats had been quickly removed from the plane to allow room for the stretcher on the floor. I climbed on board, made my small charge comfortable, fastened the seat belt and we were off. It was about four hundred miles in a twin otter to our destination which would take approximately three to four hours of flying time. The trip was an exhausting one, as I spent most of the time on the floor stooped over my patient taking vital signs and controlling his flailing arms and legs caused by the convulsions, so that no injury would occur. More medications had to be given to sedate him, and the intravenous had to be maintained, which under the circumstances was challenging. I was greatly relieved when the pilot announced our descent into Churchill, and on arrival an ambulance and doctor were waiting to receive the little boy. I spent the night there, sleeping in the nurses' residence this time. Even that short break away from the clinic had its merits. Just being able to have my meals in the dining hall, prepared by someone else, and communicating with other nursing colleagues, was a pleasant change. It was all too short. Duty called and I had to return. Before I left, I consulted with the boy's doctor with regards to his condition, so that I could bring this information to his parents and siblings. Although he was still very ill, she indicated he would recover and graciously credited my prompt initial treatment and action plan to the saving of his life. Praise apart, it was a glorious feeling just knowing he was alive. I looked in at him sleeping so peacefully and I felt a wave of satisfaction, acknowledging to myself that the work was worthwhile.

The Inuit were easy to be with, and not at all demanding, nor were they judgemental of us. Perhaps their show of stoicism evolved from their fatalistic philosophy of life which manifested itself so evidently over and over in times of death. They were tolerant of us, which says much for their race, as we came and intruded into their way of life, causing changes and disruption as was inevitable with the dominant attitude of our white ways.

One local resident told me that when she married, her first child, boy or girl, was spoken for. The grandmother wished to have this child to raise. Puzzled by this arrangement, I enquired further as to the rationale behind this. She explained that this was to ensure the child's grandmother would be looked after by the grandchild in her old age. She went on to say she could have more children later. Although the idea was foreign to my culture, it had its practical use, considering there were no nursing homes in this environment. With our increasingly aged population, maybe this is not at all a bad idea. Sometimes, too, this was a practical arrangement when a girl gave birth at a very young age and was considered to be too immature to raise a child.

Another white woman came to the clinic in early labour. Her water had broken earlier, and this was unexpected according to her due date, making the baby's arrival premature. There was no plane available, and she was progressing along fairly quickly. I had no alternative but to deliver her. How I hated to be alone at times like this when there was uncertainty of the outcome. At the time of delivery, I had to do an episiotomy on the mum-to-be, which in my training days was not done randomly and was not an encouraged procedure unless absolutely necessary. In my judgement I felt there was a need in this case. This procedure is done to enlarge the external opening. In a few hours she was safely delivered of a little boy. He was very healthy, and for the size of him he had a pretty lusty cry. Unfortunately, the mother retained the placenta. Rather than meddle too much with nature, I called a plane for a medical evacuation.

Sometimes we were lucky and hit the jackpot. In this case the Commissioner's plane was arriving with some dignitaries, including a doctor from Health and Welfare in Ottawa. He visited the Nursing Station and discussed my patient's case, agreeing that the woman should go to hospital. The baby was premature and would be better in a hospital setting. In the process of conversation he was quite amazed at how long I had been working on my own at the facility and urged me to stay overnight in Churchill.

The Commissioner's plane was made available to me, and in due course I was en route with the mother and baby to Churchill. Presumably due to with the varying air pressures of take off and landing, not to mention the bumpy ride, she delivered the placenta on the way to being admitted. When my patient was transferred into a bed, I could hear one of the nurses, standing behind the screen, remarking, "I don't know why she sent her to hospital, the placenta was right there". I smiled to myself and thought, how nice it would be to have this nurse for just a while in the north, and have her deal with a situation when far removed from a hospital and modern equipment.

I decided to return home right away, and once again travelled in the Commissioner's plane. By now it was dark and there was only a makeshift landing strip at Baker Lake. Not being a sophisticated airport, there was no proper lighting system in place. Rather, the runway was outlined with a series of flare pots. The plane was well into its descent with the wheels lowered at the ready. Then, as it touched down, I was thrown forward and the plane was suddenly airborne again. I did not realize at the time that in fact the plane had only touched down on one wheel and the pilot decided to make another attempt at a smoother landing.

Spring was drawing near. The lake was beginning to candle and therefore was not quite as safe to walk on. Some local people carried a long pole in front of them, across the chest. This would be useful if, when walking on a weakened part of ice it should give way. The pole would be useful to brace oneself. Going through ice could often prove to be fatal. Apart from the iciness of the water, one could become trapped underneath the ice and possibly drown. Quite a ghastly thought. The season would be a short one, and all of us had to make the best of it.

The advent of the impending warmer weather and open waters was enhanced for me by the arrival of a new nurse. She had not been too long out of training and had come from the Maritimes, New Brunswick, to be precise. At last someone could now share in the responsibilities and the on-call duties which were now becoming increasingly tiring. At least now, the nights I was not on call, I would be free to walk across the tundra without someone speeding towards me on a skidoo or an all-terrain vehicle, shouting and, with flailing arms beckoning me to return, to as someone was either having a baby, or was lacerated enough to require sutures. We were very compatible, as it turned out, and we both had a good sense of humour. I was able to pass on valuable information about the operation of the station, and, in a short time, when she was comfortable with the many aspects of the nursing life there, she became a valuable co-worker.

Within a few months we were both professionally challenged when an Inuk baby was brought in on a Saturday morning, and I happened to be the one on call. A young teenaged daughter accompanied her mother and young brother to the clinic. She would act as interpreter between the mother and myself. The little boy had been sick since the night before, but the mother felt she could cope by giving aspirin and tepid sponges for his fever. These people were so considerate of us and did not come rushing to the clinic unless the health condition of a family member became worse. It occurred to the mother that something was seriously wrong with her son when she could not waken him. On arrival the child was in a coma, his lips were cyanotic and his small body was burning hot with fever. I quickly unwrapped the bundled baby and administered oxygen while I listened to the medical history of events. On examination, again it did not take long to recognise the all too familiar signs and symptoms of meningitis. The child's temperature was almost 105 degrees Fahrenheit. I had to act fast, and I needed to get this fever down. He was wrapped in wet sheets, and I remember seeing the steam literally rising from him. An intravenous infusion was set up to counter his dehydration and antibiotics were administered quickly. The Zone Director was informed, and attempts to get a plane in to evacuate the child immediately were squashed due to a snow storm creating a "white-out" condition. No planes would take off under these circumstances, so there it was. We would have to utilise all our nursing skills and more. I called in my colleague for a second opinion, but all we could do was wait. With constant tepid sponging the fever did drop down to an acceptable level, but the child still did not respond. Again the Zone Director was contacted by radio. The signals were very poor due to the outside elements, and when the doctor spoke he was indistinct. Thankfully the radio operators, with their skills, were able to relay the messages. I found myself almost pleading with the doctor to send a plane. His voice was fading in and out, and, when barely audible, I heard his reply at the tail end of the conversation, "Nurse you have done everything humanly possible for the child and you will have to wait it out." The conversation ended, and only the crackling of the static could be heard.

We felt isolated and alone. We could not have felt any more so had we been on the moon. The child was dying under our very noses. The sense of helplessness was phenomenal. It was great that I had a colleague to share with, but this was especially hard for me to witness. This was the little boy I had delivered into the world in the first month of my arrival to the settlement. This fact created an extra bond between the little boy's family and myself. We sent the family home to rest. The evening dragged on into the night. We both stayed up to give him every ounce of loving care that we could provide. In the early morning the teenaged sister arrived back at the clinic. She stated, "My father says you must be very tired and you must rest. I will sit with my brother." It truly was an altruistic gesture. We were indeed exhausted, and fortunately there were no clinics scheduled on Sunday. We thanked her profoundly and told her the little boy could not been left without our care, so we would continue. Our vigil was soon drawing to a close. He lay there peacefully and only yawned. The breathing, which had become laboured, suddenly stopped and then there was stillness. Our little patient had left us to be with the angels. We had seen the inevitable and were able to contact the parents ahead of time. Our tiredness seemed unimportant compared to their loss, and again the thoughts, "If only this had been in the city and if only the weather had improved." It was so hard to say the words, "I am so sorry he is dead." At times like this, surely one's faith is sorely tested as to the existence of God. I wasn't quite prepared for what was to follow. The parents came forward and shook our hands, and in Inuktitut, the Inuit language, interpreted by the daughter, they said, "Thank you. You nurses did everything you could for our boy, but it was God's will." I was then offered money which, of course, was rejected. I had never before, or since, ever witnessed such a degree of acceptance and graciousness in the face of death. I had seen this little tyke into the world and out again in such a short space of time. When I witness the attitudes of many, but not all, of the younger generation in the white society today, where an egocentric attitude prevails, it is gratifying to look back on that unselfish act of the Inuit family and their gratitude, in spite of their loss.

Everyday life carried on at the clinic. As with any infectious disease there was always additional work to be carried out in finding all individuals who had been exposed to the disease and taking the usual precautionary measures deemed necessary.

"This is DOT calling. We have someone out on the land on the radio and a child has stopped breathing. Can you help regarding resuscitation?" "Roger", I replied, "Put him on!" This was yet another episode faced in the north. An aircraft happened to be in the area of a land camp. The mother of the child indicated to the pilot and passenger that her infant was very ill. They were about to take the baby back to the clinic and had it on board when its breathing had ceased, the cause being unknown at that point. Fortunately, being in the aircraft, they had the radio at their disposal and made this call to the DOT staff who forwarded it to us. Someone on board was attempting to revive the child, but was not sure of the procedure and required assistance. It is not the easiest thing to give instruction by radio when you cannot see the situation for yourself. I could hear the agitation in the voice at the other end, but the man made a gallant effort to resuscitate, continuing on during the flight back to Baker Lake. The estimated time of arrival was less than an hour which allowed us time to gather our equipment together such as oxygen, drugs and warm blankets to receive the child. The bombardier transportation took us to the dockside where the plane would land on floats. We waited inside the vehicle to keep warm until the plane touched down. The sound of the engines brought a number of curious residents. As soon as the aircraft opened its doors, we did a rapid transfer of the infant. The infant was dead on arrival. No one was at fault. It was merely the nature of things in these barren lands, with survival of the fittest. No autopsy was called for. The mother who had accompanied her baby was well aware that her babe had died. There was no fuss from her, just stoicism, but I am sure that she, like any mother, must have felt the loss acutely. We had to consider from the history of the illness that once again meningitis had struck and we acted accordingly with those in direct contact, especially with the man attempting to resuscitate. The child would be buried the next day, as was usual.

Before the ice broke up I would see from the Nursing Station window, heading out across the still frozen lake, the dog sleds loaded with equipment, and a canoe was included as part of the necessities. These were the hunters and some members of their families travelling for many miles from the settlement to set up camp and hunt the caribou. Some were still babies at the breast while others from toddler age to school children accompanied their parents. Here the children would get another form of education, that of survival on the land. This would help to keep alive their cultural inheritance which was being challenged even more by a greater influx of tourists. Our different ways enticed the Inuit away from their own simplistic heritage. Their travels would require the use of the canoe at times. With the crystal-like appearance of the lake at that time of year, there were often open areas of water appearing as large, gaping splits in the ice. In this event the canoes would enable them to cross until more solid ice could be reached. In these circumstances, the dogs would ride in the canoe until they were on strong ice again or on land. At the appropriate destination, tents would be erected and this would be home for the summer season. At a later time, I would travel to these encampments and see life on the tundra for myself.

I planned to go back to Rankin Inlet on another visit, but for a different reason this time. I was acquainted with one of the Scottish lads who was an employee of the Hudson's Bay Company, and he had been transferred there. Being a Scottish lass myself, there was a tendency to associate with one's own countrymen, not that we did not have other acquaintances. As it turned out, the Priest in Baker Lake also had a brother who was a Priest in Rankin Inlet. They each had a radio and were able to have frequent communications between the two settlements. The Priest, knowing my friend was no longer around Baker Lake, would set up an appointed time on the radio for me and, "I had to get to the church on time." Similarly the other Priest would make arrangements for my friend to be at the Rankin Inlet church radio, thus enabling us to have a chat. The Father's eyes would sparkle when he was able to do this kindness for us, and he would sometimes get involved in the friendly banter back and forth.

As I had quite a bit of overtime owing, I had made arrangements with the Zone Director for me to take a week's holiday. There was one snag. The RCMP plane was scheduled to arrive in one week with the Inspector on board. He would be visiting first Baker Lake then going on to Rankin Inlet, but the exact date was not known. As I had been given authority to travel on board the police plane, taking advantage of available transportation, I would have to be ready within a short time after notification. My superior in Churchill was agreeable to that arrangement, provided that everything was running smoothly at the clinic. It was with this understanding in mind that I made haste preparing for my journey on the scheduled day. I was unable to make direct contact with my superior prior to leaving, but I did leave a message in Churchill to explain that I was now en route to Rankin Inlet on my official vacation. The return trip would be on a regular flight of a DC aircraft one week later. Comfortably settled and chatting with the police officers, I was handed a message by the co-pilot which had just been received on the radio. It was "The Boss" demanding I return to the clinic immediately, without any explanation. The co-pilot asked if he should return to Baker Lake, but as we were half way there, I decided to carry on as planned. Of course this was a spiteful move on the part of the Zone Director. I had not been forgiven obviously for the episode earlier where there was an exchange of annoyances when he dropped in from the sky, unannounced, to escort a patient to Churchill. Now, I was in deep trouble!

I stayed at the Nursing Station in Rankin Inlet with my colleagues whom I had already met when they took over the clinic from me some months previously. I had to bunk down on the sitting room floor in a sleeping bag as the clinic beds were required for in-patients. The facility was a small mobile trailer. When you have been living in the fast lane, as I felt I had been at Baker Lake, it was the most wonderful feeling to relax and know that when the clinic doorbell rang it wasn't my problem. However, there were known occasions when a visiting nurse would have to pitch in, in the event of an emergency and staff shortages, but I wasn't too concerned about that. Because I knew I did not have to be alert during the night for bells and buzzers, the sleep was very deep and restful. I was awakened in the morning by a kitten who took advantage of my position on the floor. He had nestled down to sleep, using my head and hair as his bed. Still, that was a rather pleasant way to start the day.

I didn't do much in Rankin Inlet except walk and ride on a scooter with my Scottish friend, the week passing all too quickly. I felt well rested, and as I hadn't heard any more from the Zone Director, I assumed that everything was sorted out. The scheduled plane was due later that day, doing what is referred to as the "milk-run", stopping at each settlement. The skies had turned grey and foreboding and there was quite a wind blowing when I received the news that the scheduled aeroplane would not be coming because of the projected weather forecast. My heart sank, not that I minded an extra day or so of holidays. I did after all have more banked time owing, but I didn't want to create animosity with the good director by being absent longer than required. However, I rationalized that in the north these things cannot be prevented, and that he would understand. As luck would have it, a chartered aircraft belonging to a different company landed. After a brief stopover, the flight would proceed on to Chesterfield Inlet and finally to Baker Lake. Arrangements were made for me to travel on this flight. I was greatly relieved. On board, were the pilot, a co-pilot and three other men who were involved in some kind of community maintenance programme. They had to stop at the various settlements in the Keewatin District.

After leaving Rankin Inlet, their next stop was Chesterfield Inlet, a very small community lying inland from the northwest coast of the Hudson Bay. This inlet was first sighted by an Englishman by the name of Sir Thomas Button, in the 1700s. He was both an naval officer and explorer, but the inlet was named after Philip Stanhope, the 4th Earl of Chesterfield, England. He was an aristocrat and a politician, and while acting as ambassador in the Hague, Holland, he fathered an illegitimate son. When his child was five years old, he started writing letters to him, and the communications spanned thirty years. The Earl's letters were sold eventually and their publication in the 18th century made the Earl famous.

As was often the case, I acquired certain historical knowledge of people and place names at a later date from other researchers, and I knew little of the early explorers in the area. Also, unknown to me at that time, was the existence of Marble Island, which is situated about one hour's distance by boat from Rankin Inlet. Marble Island has great veins of quartzite running through it giving it an appearance of marble. In 1719, a fur trader by the name of James Knight, elderly though he was, set off with a small group of forty men to find precious metals. A previous earlier attempt by him to find the Northwest Passage failed and he returned to England four months later. This second challenge, however, proved to be his undoing as he and his crew, instead of finding the precious metals, perished on Marble Island. In 1989, when Professor Owen Beattie and John Geiger visited the island as part of an archaeological study, they found the remains of a crudely built house, pieces of clothing, a leather sole from a shoe and remnants of a coal pile, giving evidence of earlier human habitation. Their book "Dead Silence" gives a most interesting account.

The pilot instructed the men to act with speed as he wanted to get under way quickly due to the impending unfavourable weather. I remained on board with the pilots. Things did not exactly go according to Hoyle and some slight delay occurred. The pilot was a little annoyed, as by now the snowfall was becoming quite heavy. The men arrived back, task completed, and without further delay we set off to Baker Lake, but with the increase in the snowfall, visibility was becoming poor. We were not in the air more than half an hour when the pilot announced that we were going to descend and land on a small nearby lake which had open water. The pilot apparently had not flown in this area before, and without instrument rating and poor visibility he did not feel comfortable in continuing with the flight. There would be no problem landing on water as the plane was equipped with floats.

Once safely landed, we bobbed up and down on the lake. The men alighted from the plane and with a rope, anchored the plane to a rock on the shore. Exactly when we would fly again was not known. It was by now dusk, making it impossible to read. Conversation was limited. Had I not been the only female on board with five men, they might well have entertained themselves with risque' stories and jokes. When I asked the pilot if he would be radioing Rankin Inlet to inform them as to our position, he informed me that the radio was not functional. He assured me that in the light of day, the skies would be clearer and we would be able to take off. I found it all quite an adventure, spending the night on a small plane on a lake listening to the lapping of the water against the pontoons. Fortunately, I had my sleeping bag with me which was a warm arctic type. I slipped into it as I sat on the seat. The three men slept soundly, one stretched out comfortably on the floor. The pilot and his mate dozed off. Sleep eluded me. The loud orchestral sounds of snoring that surrounded me did not act as a lull-a-bye. A couple of boring hours passed with only idle thoughts of life in the north passing through my mind.

I never entertained the thought of danger. Now, I was faced with a serious dilemma. Mother nature had to be obeyed, and feeling somewhat awkward, I delayed the call and tried to distract myself. Eventually, feeling I could no longer contain the nature of my urgency, with temerity, I asked the pilot if there was any sort of facility on board which would offer relief of my predicament. I was fairly sure that on this small plane there was not a toilet. The pilot quickly responded to my question by saying, "No Nursey, the nearest one is off the pontoon." Fears of water had to take second place to my immediate need. Freeing myself from the warmth of the sleeping bag, I carefully made my way to the doorway, making sure as not to disturb the sleeping character on the floor. The pilot, in the meantime, had opened the door for me. The wind was briskly blowing, creating a little more vigorous bobbing motion of the plane. Tightly clutching the step rail I made my way down the metal rungs of the ladder, one, two, three and four. There, I was on the pontoons. Now, I just had to work out a system so that I could remain somehow attached to the rail, and at the same time remove the necessary apparel to carry out the function I had applied myself to do. As I crouched down, clinging with one hand to the rail, swaying gently with the movement of the pontoons, created by the water underneath, I cocked my head in an upwards glance to make sure that all inside were behaving in a gentlemanly manner. They indeed were, and with the coast all clear I proceeded to alleviate my suffering. At this point, hygienic hand washing was of zero importance. All neatly assembled, I made my way back to my seat. This type of situation was certainly an easier task for the male species.

It was getting light again and all were awake. I felt so hungry. I had no chocolate or raisins with me this time. The pilot explained that we could not touch the emergency rations as our stomachs first had to be allowed to shrink, thus requiring less food. Up to now, the adventure was okay, but when the hunger pangs set in, I felt a little different.

"Fasten your seat belts and we will be on our way", came the announcement from the cockpit. The visibility was still not very good, but our navigator decided to make an attempt. We travelled only a short distance when once again it was deemed necessary to come down and wait. This time we landed on a large lake. We were alongside the shore, and after the plane was secured, we were able to get off the aircraft to stretch our legs. Two hours later the visibility had cleared greatly, and another attempt to take off was tried. The sound of the throbbing engines seemed so loud in this tranquil setting, but we were not about to depart yet as planned. The pilot started to taxi on the water, but all around us were ice flows. The lake was in the process of breaking up, and large chunks of ice were beginning to surround the plane. For me it was an interesting sight, but the pilot was in quite a quandary. He was unable to get enough of a run on the water to enable him to get airborne. The other concern was that we could see the amount of ice on top of the water, but did not know how much lay beneath the surface. There was apparently a danger of damage to the pontoons. Once more it was back to the shore. We deplaned, and after some deliberations between the pilots, a conversation which we were not party too, it was decided that the co-pilot would walk to the Baker Lake settlement. Being already afloat on Baker Lake it was deemed that the community was nearby. The plan was to bring help in the form of boats to take us the rest of the way. At this point the emergency rations were opened and we enjoyed a brew of lukewarm tea, made on site to wash down sardines and graham crackers. It would not, under ideal circumstances, be my first choice of food, but it tasted good and helped to quell the rumblings of my stomach.

The co-pilot was well out of sight by now, and alone. Our appetites were somewhat sated, but he left before the rations were distributed. The navigator, meantime, had been watching the movement of the floating ice, and instructed us to climb aboard, announcing that there seemed to be enough of an opening in the lake for him to get a run. With bated breath, I sat, watched and listened intently as the plane taxied along the stretch of open water. We were off, up and away. This time we made it back to the settlement.

It was now the afternoon of the following day. We were given a royal welcome at the dock. I later found out that there had been concerns for our safety. Rumour had it that a plane was missing and presumed lost as there had been no radio communication from the pilot. Anxious questions had floated around.

"Who were the passengers?"

"Five men and a nurse!"

"Who was the nurse? What Nursing Station is she from?"

News had travelled fast.

We were back safe and sound and I had lived through yet another new experience which made this part of the world an exciting place for me to live. A nice warm bath and a meal were the order of the day, but what of the poor fellow out there that had been sent to get boats for our rescue? I phoned the Department of Transport to enquire about his well being. The staff member I talked with had no knowledge of the co-pilot, but promised to look into the matter right away. Shortly thereafter a plane was sent out to find him, and when they did locate him, the poor man was bitten by insects, somewhat exhausted, hungry and pleased to see his rescuers. If he had not been found, he would have been unable to reach Baker Lake, I am told, due to the swollen river which he could not cross. His efforts, however, were very gallant.

Two weeks after this event, the Nursing Supervisor arrived from Churchill. From time to time these visits were carried out to give help, advice and support pertaining to our work as required. It was in essence a form of a staff meeting that I welcomed. They were very in tune with the problems that we were confronted with, having themselves been in this same role at some point in their career. I wished at this visit to discuss with her the conflict I was having with the Zone Director. I felt he was rather caustic in his conversations on the telephone and in his letters to me since our encounter, which I have previously discussed. I very much wanted to meet with him and again enjoy the good rapport we had had before. Of course during the dialogue with the Supervisor, I had to bring in the episode of my vacation, his responses and the delay in returning to my station because of the weather conditions. At the end of my story she laughed and said, "We knew it was you on board, as the pilot later told me, and I'm glad you are being honest about all this." She agreed to arrange a meeting the following week with the director.

Waiting for this meeting made the week drag, and then suddenly he was sitting in front of me. We both had our say about the vacation arrangement and the patient evacuation episode which originally caused the bad vibes. To me, it was all nonsense, and I believed a misunderstanding came about due to cultural differences, my boss originating from India, and perhaps he was not used to a Caucasian woman asserting herself. At the end of the conversation he asked me, "Have you learned anything?" To which I replied, "Yes sir. From now on I won't say anything, I'll just think it." He became somewhat irritated with my remark and stated with great vehemence, "But that's no good, you are still thinking it!" I laughed and replied, "You, sir, do not control my thoughts, and you really don't know what I am thinking right now." Thankfully he saw the folly of his last remark and laughingly agreed I had a point. We became friends after this, which perhaps, was as well, he being in the more powerful position between the two of us.

I have been asked often whether or not I found life boring because of the lack of many of the modern amenities, and I would have to say I did not find it to be so, but then I was in a very demanding profession and my off-duty hours often became work hours too. An aspect of northern living that I do still miss is the people communication which existed. While in the north, there were no daily papers, no television, no direct phone lines and no shopping malls. We made do with shopping at the Hudson's Bay Company or through the catalogue. When the purchases of clothing arrived by plane, it was pleasant to receive the parcel. Basic needs were met, and sometimes one derived more pleasure from a simple life as opposed to all the frills and complications experienced in towns and cities.

There were local dances held in the community hall, which in itself was plain and small, but which served the purpose not only for dances but movie shows as well. In the adjoining room was the curling rink, curling being a popular sport there. On returning from my first visit to Rankin Inlet some dear soul placed my name on a list to take part in a Bonspiel. Little did they know I disliked the game and had no experience at all in this realm, but there was no backing out. As it turned out, after a few nights of play our team was declared the winner. A team cup was presented, which eventually had all our names engraved on it, and individual trophies were also given. I felt almost embarrassed to receive one of these, as winning was certainly through the skills of others, rather than with my efforts.

The snow was fairly well melted now and the lake was open. The sound of the skidoos were now replaced with the sounds of motor boat engines, and all of a sudden the settlement became alive. The illness rate was not so high, but more accident cases appeared, mostly lacerations requiring suturing and the removal of fish hooks caught in hands, faces and heads. Of course, babies arrived regardless of the season.

It was a relief to shed those heavy winter garments and don lighter clothing. Rubber boots were a must at break-up, because everything around was wet and muddy. The tundra, which just means a treeless grassy plain, had shed its white winter mantle and exposed mosses, lichens and an abundance of plant life. Underneath was permanently frozen soil, which remained so all year long and is referred to as permafrost. Walking was a very enjoyable activity in this landscape, and I spent as much time as possible doing just that. One could travel for miles and discover more small lakes, birds and if lucky, a caribou. There were arctic foxes out there on the land, judging by the amount of fox trim used on parkas, but I was not fortunate enough to see one in its natural state. I did come across a dead wolf, and I also stumbled across the remains of a husky dog. It had been tied to a post as evidenced by the short rope, and all that remained was the fur and skeleton. What had caused the animal's demise was an obvious guess, but why it had been tied there, so far from the community, I did not know. Perhaps it had been forgotten about and starved to death. Yes, it made me sad too, but sometimes as a white person it was better not to intrude on the ways of the culture. Being a government employee, it was always prudent to have a good rapport with those we served and not to seem to be meddling in their ways.

The summertime also brought additional people to the settlement for a variety of reasons other than the tourist fishing trips. Two helicopters flew in the area frequently. I had been told that geologists were looking for uranium. I was invited to experience a ride on two different types of these flying machines, but I cannot say I felt as comfortable on them as I did on an aeroplane, especially the bubble-shaped helicopters. Being surrounded by glass made me feel vulnerable, and I did not particularly enjoy the take off.

On the trip, I was taken to Aberdeen Lake and Shultz Lake further inland. The pilot flew low, giving me a good, bird's eye view of the landscape. He pointed out a caribou running across the tundra as though in fear of its life. The sound of machinery overhead must have been terrifying for the animal. On landing near the lakes, we found them to be crystal clear. The arctic cotton swayed gently in the breeze, while an arctic hare, disturbed from his hideaway, sped off across the wide open spaces. The birds along the shore line, unconcerned by our presence, carried on with their melodious singing. This was pure tranquillity and beauty. It was hard to believe how harsh the winter conditions had been.

The geologist had a mission, and that was to use his Geiger counter to detect uranium. Canada is a large producer of this silvery white metal, and is a major exporter in the Western World, particularly to the United States, where it was used to generate electricity. However, in the 1970s Baker Lake made National headlines when the residents contested the rights of companies to mine uranium in their land in a Native Law court case.

Visitors and pilots to the area were accommodated at the Department of Transportation quarters, and meals were available at the canteen. I was a little taken aback when, on answering the front doorbell of my residence one day, a burly fellow whom I did not know, stood before me. Lying by his feet on the doorstep, were his sleeping bag and personal effects. When I asked how I could assist him, he told me he was a pilot and had just arrived. He looked at me as though this statement should have conveyed something to me. He continued on, telling me he had need of accommodation. I directed him to the appropriate location along the road, but that was not quite what he had in mind. He informed me that he always stayed at the Nursing Station. I pointed out that new management had taken over, and that I was by no means a hotel, nor being a single woman did I feel it was a satisfactory arrangement. With that he picked up his gear and before disappearing into the blue horizon turned and said, "You are a real bitch!" His attitude and demeanour towards me was rather unexpected, but I shrugged it off and put it down to his ignorance.

The Nursing Station was a nucleus for activity within the settlement. Apart from being on call and working overtime, various medical personnel visited. In the evenings we socialised with them as well as entertaining our own friends and members of the community, but it was not a boarding house, as the gentleman at the door must have thought. It was our home and we also needed some private time.

The local graveyard stood in the distance overlooking the settlement. It was on a slight hill, and mounted thereon was a large, wooden cross. Sometimes I would walk out there. Even in the barren lands, the Roman Catholics were buried in one area and the Anglicans in another. This must have been perplexing to the Inuit. I wondered if God agreed with the separation? Were we not all his children? Did we need to have boundaries with religious beliefs in death also? We as a white race must have brought so much confusion and contradictions to these people.

Because of the permafrost, the digging of graves was not a viable option. Only a shallow grave could be scraped out, and sometimes even to accomplish this much, tires had to be burned to thaw the snow if a death had occurred in the winter months. The coffins, as I mentioned earlier, were a rough box. They were laid in the shallow hollow and stones were then placed around and over the box. This was to prevent wild animals ravaging the corpse. On one such visit to the graveyard, I observed that with the pressure of the snow and the winter conditions, one grave had partially caved in, exposing the skull and bones of the occupant. I mention this burial custom as a comparison to our own cultural ways, to depict the different practices that are shaped by the prevailing elements in our surroundings. The early pioneers to Canada would no doubt have been faced with a similar adaptation when death struck. The beloved newly departed are thought of in the same way as those commanding an elaborate burial in a solid oak coffin, the material worth being unimportant to the event. After death, the burial usually took place the following day. I did not attend the funerals, so the people's reaction at the graveside to grief was not known to me. I only witnessed the stoicism at the clinic when I discharged my duty to the family by informing them of the occurrence of someone's death. I had heard that sometimes a newborn was named after the deceased, with the belief that the dead person's soul entered into the baby, helping to guide him or her in life. Others in the community could also be named after the deceased.

The land was becoming drier and walking more pleasant. We now had twenty-four hours of daylight, and it seemed as though the children never slept. When I retired for the night I could hear their happy squeals of laughter as they played. I could not blame them wanting to take advantage of the long days when winter was so dismal and prolonged. It was during those summer months that a team from Edmonton, consisting of two x-ray technicians and one nurse, toured the various settlements, carrying out a tuberculosis prevention programme. The disease, being quite high amongst the Inuit and native Indian population, was taken very seriously. Each year when the team arrived, an attempt was made to chest x-ray each individual and to do as many tuberculin tests as was appropriate. Babes within six weeks of birth were given a vaccination against the disease, their young age making them very vulnerable. Some of the Inuit missed out on being x-rayed due to the fact that they were out on the land for the hunting season, but on their return we, the nurses, had to do the x-rays, as the team was no longer around. New cases of tuberculosis tended to appear from time to time, and, as previously indicated, were hospitalised.

Late in the summer the Royal Canadian Mounted Police aeroplane was due to arrive again. The purpose was for the constable from our community to visit the campsites at various locations in the tundra and immunize the husky dogs against rabies. The police carried out an immunization programme for all the dogs in the settlement but the dogs living on the land with the hunters had also to be included. At the same time the nurse was invited to join them on their mission in order to check the families on the land for any existing health problems that might have arisen, and to treat them accordingly. Being the senior nurse, I opted to make the journey along with the pilot, the constable and the Inuit health worker who would assist greatly with interpreting. It was a rather different experience conducting a clinic in the open tundra or inside a tent.

The aircraft was an amphibian type, and at one stop the pilot had difficulty getting close to shore because of the rocks. He decided we would have to make our own way to the shore from the aeroplane. For this we were each handed a pair of waders which were breast high. I made several attempts to wade to the shore flanked with the support of the "Mountie" on one side and the health care worker on the other. It was hopeless. The water was past my waistline and that feeling of buoyancy was too much for me. Because of my panicky state the pilot eventually manoeuvred the plane to the edge, allowing me to step onto stones and consequently on to land. It was a pleasant, warm day when we arrived, and we only had a short distance to walk to the first camp.

A woman in her early forties sat outside the tent. She was wearing a maroon coloured beret and her white cotton amauti. The amauti was an outer garment worn by the mother and which had to be pulled over her head. There was a large pouch at the back, like an extra large hood on a parka. This was where the baby or small child was carried. Around the waistline was a woven cord which, when tied, secured the position of the baby. In some cases I saw the babies carried in amautis made of caribou skin. They were decorated with beads around the shoulders and had large fringes around the lower end of the garb. The baby was naked inside the pouch where it was kept very warm. When feeding time came the mother had a knack of swivelling the baby around to the breast without taking the child out into the cold. As I approached the mother, I could see the bulge of the child underneath with only a tuft of hair showing at the top. This was her two- year-old son. This same little boy and mother I remembered quite well. He had been very ill at one time and I had him admitted to the Nursing Station. She would sit by his cot reading her Bible.

I carried with me my nurse's black bag with various items of the trade necessary for a physical examination. A second, larger bag contained ointments, already pre-packaged in tubes, while others were in large jars, and from them I could dispense the ointment into small cans which I also carried. In yet another bag were medicines such as antibiotics. I set about listening to the chests of all the children there, finding only one with a moderately severe respiratory infection. To be on the safe side, I treated her with antibiotics. We invited them to discuss any health concerns they might have, and after a congenial exchange of conversation, we took our leave. Out there they had no form of communication, so if severe illnesses were to occur they either depended on any local aircraft that might land or the husband might have to travel back to the settlement to get help.

The second camp we visited, some distance away, was similar to the first. Again, they were happy to see us. We followed the same protocol. Lying off to one side of the tent was a pile of old caribou rib cages, and a collection of antlers. The meat at some time had been stripped from the carcasses and would have lain in a nearby cache, covered by rocks to keep the meat cool and preserve it. The rocks also served as a protection against animal intrusion.

The third and last camp we arrived at was deserted except for the dog team. The main objective for the police visit was to ensure that all dogs were regularly given their anti-rabies vaccination. Somewhat disappointed, the "mountie" was ready to return home. I could well understand his feelings of wishing to carry out a comprehensive programme, thus ensuring the protection of the community. I felt the same way with regards to the human population. Normally the owner would hold the individual dog while the officer gave the injection. I suggested that I could vaccinate the dog if he held them fast and he gave me instructions as to where the needle should be inserted. The immunizing wasn't a problem, but some of these dogs were not friendly under the best of circumstances, let alone have us inflict some pain by injecting them. He was very pleased with the arrangement, and together we made a good team. He straddled each animal holding them tight while I did the job, and then I would quickly run before he let go. It had been a worthwhile trip.

During the year we had intermittent visits from various medical personnel. They were scheduled to be more frequent, but due to many unforeseen circumstances the visits were scant. Having new company to talk with and getting a news update, was very pleasant. At the Nursing Station, a logbook was kept of all patients we had concerns about and wished to have medically reviewed if the nature of the illness did not warrant an evacuation to hospital immediately.

One such visit was from a Jewish paediatrician. I met him at the plane and escorted him to the facility. As it was a short trip, he was happy to walk the distance. It was business right away as we chatted about one or two cases. He stayed a few days only, as he had a number of communities to serve, but I was glad he was there when the next case of meningitis arrived at two o'clock in the morning. I took the call, but as we were encouraged to utilize the medical expertise when available, I wakened the good doctor. He agreed with my diagnosis, but later chastised me for not reading the notes thoroughly first. I tried to explain that I had full knowledge of the child's medical history, he being a frequent visitor to the clinic. Although a little gruff, he did compliment me greatly by stating I would make a fine doctor. When the doctors did visit, we learned more about medical conditions, and although living in isolation, we were in fact receiving in-services, keeping us abreast with new medical knowledge.

On the Friday evening, I had invited the local priest to dinner before I knew of the doctor's arrival. Now I had a dilemma. I was entertaining a Jewish doctor and a Catholic priest, and my menu was not suited to their religious beliefs. I think that evening I served a hodgepodge of foods and somehow got by. I do remember the priest stating that this was the north and he would eat whatever was available. Situations like this made life more interesting.

During my stay at Baker Lake, we had separate visits from two dentists, each for one week. The first was an Englishman who was married with children. He did not want his visit to create any imposition for us, knowing full well of our rigorous life. He in fact tried to pamper us, and I still smile at the gentle tap on my bedroom door. With my permission to enter he brought in a steaming hot cup of tea. The first time it occurred, I was so stunned, having just been aroused from a deep sleep. Not knowing what was happening, I sat up in bed, with my hair in rollers looking like a porcupine, and my eyes appearing like slits. They were soon open wide and staring at the figure before me. This became a morning ritual, so I made sure that I would not be caught again with my curlers in my hair. He carried the pampering a stage further when he cooked a full dinner for us and served crepe suzettes for dessert. His kind deeds were completed when he did all the washing up. His actions were greatly appreciated. So often, after a hectic day in the clinic, the nurses had to cook for the visitors, and some would not raise a hand to help, as though the service was an expected part of their trip.

The second dentist and his wife arrived at a later date, and they also were pleasant company. Many tooth fillings were done, particularly on the children, with a few extractions. In between dental visits, part of our health programme was to teach oral hygiene and, as previously mentioned, do fluoride brushings on the children at school, thus affording some protection to their tooth enamel. Of course, with the gaps of time in between the dental visits, there were cases of severe toothaches, abscesses and decayed teeth that were beyond saving in some of the older generation. Those sometimes had to be taken care of by the nurse. I had no special training in the area of dental extractions, but I was called on two occasions to pull a tooth. I had to infiltrate the gum with the appropriate local anaesthetic before pulling the offending tooth. On one occasion, the Inuk caretaker had to take over when I did not have the strength to remove a tooth which had very strong roots. The patient indicated relief a day or so following the extraction.

The summer months saw the arrival of the sea lift. There were two vessels that came in with all our supplies. This was a large task, unpacking one year's supply of goods. The invoices had to be checked and finding space for everything was difficult now that the crawl space, located beneath the building, was out of bounds for storage. There was a hive of activity in the community as the other establishments also received their supplies. From my window, I could see the hulk of the ship anchored nearby.

By now, we had been granted a part-time secretary, which was a godsend, for the paper work was becoming an increasing load unto itself. The policeman's wife, whom I already knew as a friend in the Yukon Territory, was qualified for the position and proved to be highly efficient.

The summer season was so short, and gradually the evenings became cooler, just to remind us that fall and winter were not too far behind, but I was still able to enjoy a few more long walks. Soon the lakes would freeze and the tundra would be covered in white with only the Inuksuit standing like stark sentinels in the snow-clad land. These were stones assembled in a formation resembling that of a human figure, which the Inuit had built as land markers.

The planes left to pick up the children at the land camps and bring them back for the opening of the school in September. The parents, toddlers and infants stayed on the land a little longer for the hunting, to ensure they had an adequate food stock for their larder. Once school was open, our workload increased. Physical examinations were carried out on the school children to detect health problems and appropriate referrals were made to the parents. Immunizations were given and tuberculin testing done. Staff were also encouraged to participate in this program, as well as the different agencies in the community. Hearing and visual tests were done also.

Winter had now settled upon us. The nights were dark and the temperatures had dropped. One of the ships unloading the sea lift did not manage to get out on time, and as the lake froze the ship was trapped. The icebreaker arrived to lend assistance, but it too became ice-bound and was unable to break free. They would remain there for the duration of the winter. The frozen lake once more became our playground. Amusement had to be sought for the winter season and what better way than to walk across the ice in the daytime, and in the evening enjoy skidoo races. Our clinic was supplied with a skidoo. These were mechanised machines on skis. Its use was solely for the purpose of carrying out home visits to patients, and on no account to be used for pleasure. I am sure that the department specified the use of the skidoo for the purpose of legalities, and having advised us about the rules, they could not be held responsible in the event of injury after hours. In so stating, I believe a blind eye was turned to its extracurricular uses. This was well demonstrated when we asked the Nursing Officer, visiting at the time, if we could take out the skidoo. Her reply was to remind us of the rules and regulations governing such an action, but with a twinkle in her eyes, she simply said, "I didn't hear the question!" That's all the encouragement we needed. Of course when no government personnel were present we made our own "sensible" rules. The teachers and Hudson's Bay staff had their own machines, and we would race alongside of them, the marker point being the trapped ice bound ships. Following the races, we often met back at our home for hot chocolate. At other times, we would go tobogganing, usually on a Saturday afternoon, using one of the small hills nearby. If a sled wasn't available, then heavy cardboard was used as a substitute.

We were too young to be cooped up inside for the duration of the long season, and socialization with laughter kept a healthy mental and emotional balance. Perhaps in each of us, there still remains a little bit of the child. This northern environment allowed us to be in touch with that part of our being and to break free from the learned constraints instilled in us, namely that at a certain age one should behave in a specific way. Many a good belly laugh was enjoyed with our activities.

We weren't long into winter when another emergency case appeared at the clinic. A white woman, whom I had seen throughout pregnancy, had delivered her baby safely in Churchill. She had just arrived back into the community, and newly off the plane, she wanted to discuss a concern she had en route home. The babe, she explained, was spitting up small amounts of brownish coloured material, and she wanted to know why. I examined the baby and as part of this examination I observed him feeding, particularly watching the abdomen. As he fed hungrily I observed the telltale signs of peristaltic waves which are like ripples seen on the abdomen, and I was able to confirm my diagnosis. The baby had an condition called pyloric stenosis, which causes the baby to have forceful, projectile vomiting and regurgitation. Sometimes the amounts brought up are copious which would not only lead to starvation but rapid dehydration of the infant. Because of my paediatric training, I had seen many of these cases and basically knew what to do. The plane had already left the settlement. With nightfall approaching, and a change in the wind velocity and direction, we were unlikely to get another one before daybreak for the medical evacuation. I admitted the baby to the clinic following a discussion with the parents who were very anxious. It was unfortunate that this had not manifested itself sooner when mother and baby were still in the hospital. This problem only begins to show at two or three weeks of age.

I had to pass a tube into the baby's stomach through the nose, and every two hours I had to aspirate the contents. The main nourishment was given by means of a subcutaneous drip solution. The needles were inserted into the fatty layer of skin in the thighs and after a time the sites used had to be changed. This drip infusion had to be given very slowly. As if this was not enough to contend with, an elderly Inuk woman was also admitted to the ward, very ill with pneumonia. Fortunately the relatives took up a bedside vigil with their respective family members, thus allowing us some much needed shut-eye.

The weather was promising at daybreak, thankfully, and a plane had been dispatched to evacuate our patients. By midday, they were on their way, with my colleague acting as nurse escort, first stopping in Churchill with the elderly woman. Arrangements were in place for the mother and baby to be transferred on to a larger centre in Winnipeg. This baby would require surgical intervention to be performed at the Children's Hospital, to relieve his condition.

When the baby eventually returned home following his surgery, he was brought to the clinic for a follow-up visit. The mother was very grateful for the treatment received previously. The surgeon had sent me a message, via the mother, to say the baby was so well hydrated and cared for that he was able to have immediate surgery. The successes were wonderful but we did at times lose a few battles. The elderly lady died a few days later, but at least we took comfort in knowing that we had given her a fighting chance by getting her to hospital. There is a time to live and a time to die, and we had to accept that life's end was not in our control.

All admissions and discharges from the Nursing Station were entered on a form which had to be sent to the Vital Statistics Unit, in Ottawa, at the end of each month. There was accountability for patient admissions and the duration of their stay, and this had to match with the diagnosis. That is to say, a "runny nose" would not be a justifiable reason to admit someone to the facility. I was chastised by the Statistics Office some time later, for admitting the Inuk lady with pneumonia. As it turned out she also developed congestive heart failure. They felt she could have been nursed at home. People in the cities had little concept of living conditions in the Arctic and all modern conveniences were not available in the average Inuit home, nor was telephone communication in place for a quick update on the patient. I found it frustrating when I was in the situation and better able to assess the needs of my clients than those far removed. Needless to say, I fired off a letter in response, advising them that due to the nature of her illness, she was now deceased. No apology from them was forthcoming.

The sky was a little dark this particular Saturday morning, so I hastened to take my customary walk before the snow fell. I decided to walk across the frozen lake only as far as the ice-bound ships. When I happened to look back towards the settlement, I was dismayed to find that the buildings were barely distinguishable from my position. I made tracks quickly for home, travelling in a straight line towards the Department of Transport buildings first. Having reached them, all out of breath with hurrying against the wind and swirling snow, I headed for the weather station a little further on. Luckily two men were on duty. After catching my breath, I called my colleague at the station on their radio telephone and asked her to drape a cloth or something bright outside so that I could identify the building. The men agreed I had better hurry, as visibility was pretty low. I hadn't gone very far when I could no longer see anything. The sky, the ground and all my surroundings were as one. I was totally disorientated. I was caught in a white-out, which is no laughing matter, nor an experience I would care to go through again. I just stood there transfixed, when muffled in the distance, I heard the sound of a skidoo approaching. I stood engulfed in what looked like a heavy blanket of fog and yelled, "Over here, I'm over here!" As mysteriously as the sound appeared it disappeared and once again I was alone. I could feel the panic mounting in me.

I had heard tales in the Yukon that people did not lock their doors so that if a traveller lost his way in a white-out storm they could enter the home. The stories also related how men were found frozen to death very near to the shelter of a home without even knowing it. These eerie tales pervaded my thoughts, causing me to imagine my own demise. I started to walk in some direction feeling very chilled. Fortunately the swirling snow slowed down at intervals giving me just enough vision to see a few steps ahead. Suddenly, I heard the sweet but muffled voice of my buddy. We called back and forth so that I could head in the direction towards the house through her voice contact. I was making progress. Her voice was becoming clearer, and then I saw the red rag. Phew! I was home! A nice mug of hot tea soon put me right. The important lesson learned from this experience was that I should have paid heed to the skies or made contact with the weather station.

Speaking of the weather station, the staff would send a helium balloon into the air attached to a small instrument box which recorded and relayed back to the station information about the atmospheric conditions. Unexpectedly, one little box did not do exactly what it was supposed to do. Whilst working in the clinic, I heard a loud clatter above me. I ran outside to see if my roof was collapsing. When I looked up, I saw the weather instrument box sitting there on the roof. I was very glad that the helium did not escape from the balloon or there would have been a number of individuals including myself walking around with rather squeaky, high-pitched voices.

Christmas was fast approaching. Tree decorating and preparations for the festivities were in full swing. We had an artificial tree, as we would not have found one in the Baker Lake tundra. Shopping was hassle free, as gifts either had to be home made, purchased through the catalogue or bought at the Hudson's Bay store. Sometime earlier in November we received black plastic bags full of children's gifts. No instruction was given as to what we had to do with these, as they had been donated by an organization in the south. My colleague and I put our heads together and decided to play Santa Claus. A red skidoo suit that hung on a peg within our home was seized upon. I was too tall for it, so it was decided that my co-worker would be Mrs. Santa Claus. I would drive the skidoo, and we would hitch the Qamutik to the back in order to carry all the toys. Before embarking on our trip, we had to sort all the presents into male and female categories according to age. We set off after supper to catch the children before they went to their beds. We had a bell to ring and with a "Ho, Ho, Ho, Merry Christmas everyone", we made our rounds to every home in the settlement. There were a few startled but happy little faces. I don't know if this had ever been done before in quite the same manner, but it was as much pleasure for us as it was for them.

While on home visits, I made arrangements with one of the hunters and his son to take me on a trip with them across the lake by dog team, to try a spot of ice fishing. They agreed to this, and it was decided that on Saturday, all being well with the weather, we would go. Although this was the Arctic, we had some beautiful sunny days when the sky was so blue and the snow and ice glistened giving off the colours of the rainbow. It was on a day such as this, well dressed for warmth, I went to meet the hunters. When I arrived at their home they were busily hitching up the dog team. I was so impressed with their dress attire, I asked to photograph them. Worn was the traditional outfit made of caribou furs which comprised a jacket, with an attached hood pulled over the head, and the pants. The Kamiits or boots were made from seal skin. The clothing looked cumbersome but very warm.

The Qamutik that the dogs would pull with us on board was ready to go, loaded with the necessary tackle for fishing. They showed me how to sit side-saddle on the sled beside them, but I found it uncomfortable once we were under way. The dogs, who had been straining at their harnesses and yelping loudly, were now given the command to start. The fan hitch consisted of a team of five or six dogs, so called because of the fanned-out formation the dogs travelled in. Within each dog team there is a lead dog whose qualities include dominance and leadership. They were wearing little hide boots to protect their paws from being cut by the sharp pieces of ice.

The motion of the travel was agreeable and the air bracing. We did not go too far before we reached the first hole in the ice where nets had been left previously. Some chiselling of the ice was required, followed by scooping out some surface ice that had partially filled in the hole. The son bent over and hauled in his catch of three handsome arctic char. We proceeded on a little further, and this time, they wanted to set a fishing net. I was allowed to help on this occasion. A series of holes, in a straight line, were chopped out and scooped free of loose ice until the water level was reached. At this time of year the ice was not at its thickest, perhaps, I guess, about two feet thick. An apparatus, which consisted of a long piece of wood, threaded the net first through one hole and on through the others to the far end where it was anchored. Through the various holes one could observe the unobstructed journey of the net from one end to the other. The net would be left in place and would be checked several days later. It was an enjoyable experience, but I think that I preferred the comfort of shopping at the fishmonger's for my meal.

This same man later did a traditional drum dance at the community hall. This drum was a large round wooden hoop with a handle. Stretched across the circumference was a hide skin. The drummer moved around the room twisting and beating the drum rhythmically with a wooden stick while the Inuit ladies sang and recounted tales of hunting. This was still very much a part of the culture. A long time ago these drum dances were performed on various occasions such as births, marriages and deaths.

He was an active and traditional man, also participating in a yearly competition in building an igloo. The men competed to see who could build the largest in the shortest space of time. The event was held in front of the Nursing Station, on the shoreline of the still frozen lake. We watched as the Inuit good-heartedly applied their skills and worked feverishly to become the winner. The only part not given detail to was the sealing-off of any cracks which would have been done, were it to be lived in. A few of us wanted to lay claim to having slept in a real igloo. That very night, the two of us from the clinic and some of the Hudson's Bay men decided to spend one night in one. There we were, about six of us all together, arranging our sleeping bags on top of the ice floor. We crawled into them complete with parkas, scarves, wind pants and Kamiits in order to be warm. There was a great deal of laughter before we attempted to sleep. I say attempted, because a few of us never did settle. A couple of the lads were snoring loudly quite oblivious to us. A few hours of tossing and feeling cold was enough, so we nurses headed back to a real bed and the comfort of a warm room. Apparently we were wearing too many articles of clothing and would have been warmer with less constriction.

There really was not a dull moment in our Arctic living. Every now and again we would have a party at our home with our friends from the other agencies. We always invited the priest and he always came. He enjoyed a cigarette, a beer and a chat.

At times too, the caretaker, his wife and some other Inuit that we knew well would come to our residence and bring along an accordion. We rolled up the carpet in the living room and had a dance on a small scale. Other times the Bay boys would bring regular movies, and we, having a projector on site at our disposal, were able to enjoy the movie show in comfort. As always, one of us had to be on call, and this made for a good arrangement, being available in the building, but at the same time enjoying some leisure in a congenial way. When we knew they were coming, we would always try to bake some treats.

I received a letter from friends in Yellowknife sometime in November, inviting me to travel through Europe with them. I was in somewhat of a dilemma. I loved my life and work, but at the same time I felt a strong pull to do something different as long as I was young and free from the bonds of matrimony. The three of us had talked previously about travelling, and their offer enthused me. I decided to go for it, but I had to resign, as the travel time would span four months.

Each time I moved it became harder to pack, because by now I was collecting many mementos. The latest were Inuit carvings of soapstone and they were quite heavy, their fragility requiring piles of packing material to protect them against breakage. Then there was the amauti that I had one of the ladies sew for me, as well as a colourful one for a child. I found the innovative idea of the garment very practical, keeping the babe in close contact with the mother and letting the mother's hands be free for taking the hand of a toddler. I carried a child home in this way.

A farewell party was held for me at the local community hall. The walls were decorated with pictures of newborns and toddlers that I had been involved with, either in the prenatal phase, delivery room or at the immunization clinics. The usual speech and presentation was made which always brings forth the emotions. One Inuit lady gave me a pair of hand-embroidered caribou skin boots. She thanked me, and through the interpreter she said if I had not been there when she had delivered her premature baby, it would not be alive today. The baby, who was very tiny, actually was delivered on the land, but was quickly brought to the station. I had it transported in an incubator to the hospital.

Departure day came and the farewells were over. With all my possessions I waited on the frozen lake for the arrival of my transport. Then the news was broken to me that the aircraft was not coming in and I would have to wait another two days until the next scheduled flight arrival. However a small plane did arrive while I waited, with a very important person on board. It was Prime Minister Pierre Trudeau, accompanied by Mr. Chretien who was at that time the Minister of Indian Affairs and Northern Development. At the time of formulating this book, Mr. Chretien had recently been Prime Minister of Canada. Accompanying them was the Commissioner of the Northwest Territories, Mr Stuart Hodgson. Their stay was brief. In their honour, an Inuit dance was held at the local community hall. After supper I decided to listen to a speech from Mr Trudeau and join in the activities. I was a little late in arriving, and the hall was crowded. I managed to get a peek at the Prime Minister, who had a captive audience. While he spoke, an interpreter translated into Inuktitut. There was a small space available on the stage next to the dignitaries and at the feet of Mr. Trudeau. The Commissioner signalled to me to come forward and occupy the space, which I did. Following the speeches and presentation of gifts from the people to the Prime Minister, the announcement of the dance was made. To my surprise an Inuk man whom I knew well, came forward and asked me to be his partner. It was a type of Scottish reel where we all stood in a circle. As the dance progressed, partners were changed from time to time. I was even more surprised when I stood alongside Mr. Trudeau and we exchanged a few words regarding the length of the dance, and, shortly thereafter, I did a little twirl with him. The news media, of course, were there to follow the Prime Minister's Arctic trip, and I was quite unaware that the cameras were recording the dance.

The next day I was informed that the Lear-jet waiting on the ice was going back to Churchill and on to Winnipeg. They were taking the films of Mr Trudeau's visit to be edited and shown on the news. There was a spare seat on the plane and I was invited to ride as far as Churchill, where I had to overnight and attend to some final business with the department. I was grateful for the ride as my overseas flights were already booked and I had a strict schedule to keep. My trunks had to follow on the regular flight and be placed in storage in Winnipeg where all the arrangements had been made. Once again, I waited on the ice in readiness to board.

The aircraft was very compact, seating the pilot and co-pilot in front. Behind the cockpit was a double seat and another double one behind that. Further back yet was an area that accommodated gear such as sleeping bags. We were airborne in no time, and from above I got a good view of the layout of the settlement. From the vantage point, the community seemed so small and insignificant in comparison to the vast expanses of terrain that were covered in snow and ice. Were it not for the various forms of communication and transportation available to us, we would have been utterly isolated. It made me realize the hardships the Inuit had, compared to our world.

As we journeyed, the time passed slowly for me. We enjoyed an exchange in conversation and the co-pilot served coffee from his flask in a disposable cup. I passed one to the only other passenger, an older gentleman, sitting behind me. The co-pilot came well prepared, and there were several small refills along the way. However, the law of nature that governs, dictates that fluid going in must also be fluid going out. Once again I found myself surrounded by men. In this modern little plane one, of course, would assume there would be a toilet facility. Wrong thinking! I sat silently saying nothing for a very long time. My bladder had reached full capacity when I was informed we would touch down soon at Eskimo Point coastal community. I requested a toilet, but alas! there was no pity. The plane would refuel and go on to its scheduled destination. The village, being located some distance from our landing, would have taken away valuable time in order to reach it. It was important that Mr Trudeau's film get to its destination by a certain time, and as I was getting a free lift, I had no voice in the matter. On the ground my discomfort was tolerable, but once airborne I sat in agony. To make matters worse the gentleman behind me, bless him, understood my predicament. With a light tap on my shoulder he announced, "I always carry this for emergencies." As he spoke he produced from a deep briefcase an empty plastic bottle which had once contained bleach and which had the top neatly cut off. He went on to say, "Maybe you could go right to the back and use it." My mouth just fell open as I looked at him not sure how to respond. He had the kindest intentions in the world but I started to laugh, thinking of my slim chance of success. The laughing only increased my problem.

Thank God! We were on our descent into Churchill. When the doors of the plane opened I made haste, yes, to the nearest one!

I spent the night in the nurses' residence. As I walked the corridor that evening, I heard on the radio the song "Supercallafragilistic Expealadotios". I stopped to listen. This was the Baker Lake choir of which I had been a member. As the choir sang, I listened carefully to hear if my own voice was discernible. Previous to my leaving, there had been a talent contest, and due to lack of participants, the choir were asked to fill in with this song.

I arrived in Winnipeg from Churchill the next day. By taxi, I made my way to the hotel where I would spent one night before making the necessary connections to Amsterdam, Holland, my first European stop. After I checked in, and while unpacking, I turned on the television set for background noise. The news was on. "What was that? Prime Minister Pierre Trudeau and Baker Lake." I couldn't believe my eyes. There was a small portion of film showing Mr Trudeau dancing, and there I was swinging with him. Being young and impressionable I felt very excited, so much so that I wanted to run down the hallway and shout, "That is me on the telly with the Prime Minister." However not wanting anyone to think I was some crazy woman who should be locked-up in an institution, I had to sit there and muse over the event on my own.

I winged my way to Amsterdam where I spent four days on my own. From there I flew to Zurich, Switzerland, to meet my friends. I spent a week in the beautiful city until the last travelling companion arrived. Three glorious months were spent visiting Germany, Italy, Yugoslavia, Spain and Greece. It was a good feeling to relax after the long winter months I had spent in the Arctic and away from the heavy workload with all the attached responsibilities. At the end of the European trip, two friends returned to Canada while two of us toured Ireland for a month. We entered Northern Ireland and only saw a little of Belfast. This was 1970 and due to the bombings, we were advised it would be safer to travel in the southern part of the country. Having just spent a part of my life in isolation in the Arctic, where there were very few minor offences, this was a cultural shock to be in an area of violence, and have the guards on the train we travelled on, look under our seat for bombs.

CHAPTER EIGHT
SIOUX LOOKOUT

Touring and relaxing were very pleasant pastimes, but eventually all good things come to an end, and the inevitability of having to earn a living loomed nearer. From my parents' home in Scotland, I sent off resumes to Canada. I had a map given to me by Health and Welfare, Canada, which identified all the Health Centres, Hospitals and Nursing Station locations throughout Canada. The Federal Government was responsible for all the Indian and Inuit medical care as previously mentioned. I really desired work in another Nursing Station in isolation, having such positive feelings from my past experience at Baker Lake, but there was not a vacancy at that time. My next choice was the hospital at Sioux Lookout, in the province of Ontario, which was clearly marked on the map. I addressed my letter to the General Hospital, and back came the offer of a job to commence work immediately. Gathering, my worldly possessions once again, I headed back to Canada.

At my appointed destination, the Director of Nursing, an Englishman, gave me a tour of the hospital. We visited each room to acquaint me with the facility and staff, but at the end of the rounds, I was somewhat perplexed. Nowhere had I seen evidence of Indian patients, which I considered to be unusual. I voiced this observation to this likeable, portly gentleman who now was my employer. He laughed and said, "Oh the Indian hospital is located over there", pointing in another direction. "Oh!", I said, "I've come to the wrong hospital." What I did not realise was that in this small community there were two hospitals, and I had addressed the envelope as General Hospital in error, believing it to be the Indian one. He was very kind, and offered to release me from any commitment there. I decided I would stay, having already unpacked and been welcomed into the residence. However, the understanding was, that as soon as a Nursing Station became available in the Northwest Territories, I could leave and rejoin Health and Welfare.

I settled in nicely. The workload was not at all heavy, leaving me with plenty of energy for recreational activities, including finding out about Sioux Lookout's origins.

In 1912, the township of Sioux Lookout was incorporated, but it had an interesting history before that. In days gone by, Indian tribes lived in the area. Later, men from the Hudson's Bay Company arrived in search of fur pelts, such as beaver. The town came into being when the Canadian National Railway was built in the early 1900s. The railway played an important part in the economy of the town. In the 1960s, the population was around three thousand. The hospital that I worked in was relatively new, having been opened in 1951. The top floor became the nurses' residence, and my home for a few short months.

To the west of the town there is a mountain that gives Sioux Lookout its name. It was used as a lookout spot by the Ojibwa Indians to watch for their enemy, the Sioux Warriors. A tribal battle was fought over a century and a half ago. The Sioux were very savage, and were known to plunder and kill the women and children of other tribes or take them prisoner. Legend has it that one day an Ojibwa scout, looking down from the mountain, spotted the Sioux below in their canoes. The scout made haste to warn his camp. The Ojibwa elders held council and the braves prepared for war. The ploy to be used was to gather the women and children, all their valuables and load them into canoes. For safety they were hidden on Squaw Island. To create the impression that the main camp was occupied, fires were built while the old men busied themselves at the waterside with their fishing snares. Meantime the warriors retreated up the hillside making a semi circle. The Sioux leapt from their canoes and went swiftly into action, ignoring the old fishermen. The Sioux women invariably accompanied their men-folk on these raids, but remained in the canoes. At once the Ojibwa elders went into action, overturning the boats and drowning all the women, and afterwards encircled the Sioux. The Ojibwa rose victorious, having slain their opponents. It is said that one small Sioux boy was saved by an Ojibwa woman from being killed with a hatchet. He was adopted into the Ojibwa tribe and became a respected chieftain. Some earlier settlers claimed that on certain misty June mornings, the figure of an Indian could be seen standing on the Lookout. That Indian, they claim, is the little Sioux boy who was saved.

I had been in the community for three months and was anxious to go further north. It was a lovely, friendly little town, but working in a hospital seemed so mundane after the life in a Nursing Station. I worked on all three shifts on the general ward and took a turn also on the maternity wing. One evening while I was on duty, a set of twins was delivered by the Scottish doctor. Within the week, a set of triplets was born, assisted by the same physician. Given the size of the population, twins and triplets were not an everyday occurrence. Following the delivery the doctor turned to me and jokingly declared, "Nurse, perhaps you and I better not work together anymore, it might be quads next time". We never did work together again.

As it was, I had applied for the Nurse-in-Charge position on the evening shift and was appointed. This was much more to my liking. I needed more responsibility, and felt I was a good organiser in a team setting. The shift was a busy one, with myself as the only registered nurse in the general ward area along with three assistant nurses. It was on one of these evenings that I overheard a comment uttered by an assistant nurse to an elderly male patient. The nurse was changing the patient's bed linen which, from the comment, he obviously had wet. As I passed by I heard her berate the man by exclaiming loudly, "You dirty old man, you have wet the bed again!" In a flash, I dealt with her very severely for her despicable remark. I was so enraged that a human being was treated in such a manner for something that was outside of his control. Thirty years later I can still hear the sting from those words she spoke. The elderly gentleman succumbed a few days later from his illness. I only hope that he was not able to recall the incident. From time to time one does hear about abuse in one form or another of the very young or the elderly in care, and perhaps frustration leads to this, but it cannot be ignored. We have to protect those in care who do not have a voice.

I had not realised how small the world was becoming with our global interconnections. I was sitting in the hairdresser's salon in Sioux Lookout, idly looking through a magazine. The door opened and in walked another customer. I looked up from my book for a brief moment to be inquisitive, and I am sure my mouth dropped open, if for only a second. About to pass by me was a nurse from my old training school in Scotland. We were both students at the Sick Children's Hospital some ten years before. We had never worked together, nor were we friends at that time, only nodding acquaintances. Now she was standing in front of me, and we both registered instant recognition. When you are an immigrant it is always pleasant to meet someone from your own country. It gives one a warm glow and it is pleasant to talk about our grass roots. Briefly, we exchanged information about our work locations, only to find that we were both at the same hospital. She had just arrived from working in a Nursing Station further north. I was soon to leave this small township and would not be able to get further acquainted.

Another coincidence occurred that day. When I went across the road to the coffee shop, I recognized a male customer. He, it turned out, was the pilot with whom I had flown in the Northwest Territories and with whom I shared the emergency rations on the way back to Baker Lake. He was now back flying in his home turf.

Even stranger, at a later time in my life, and on a return visit to Scotland, I visited this Scottish nurse from Sioux Lookout who had returned to live there. It was revealed in conversation that she had resumed her career and was supporting a small son. The father of the boy was the pilot from the Arctic that I had met in Sioux Lookout. Fate has a strange way of bringing people together. I visit with her still, and have done so over the years, being able to share stories of the north.

The Bowes-Lyon family had some distant connection to Sioux Lookout through a young man by the name of Frederick Vaughan Lyon, who came to the area in the late 1800s. He was the third cousin to the 14th Earl of Strathmore, whose ancestral home was Glamis Castle, near Brechin, Scotland. I am acquainted with this castle, having paid some visits to it during my childhood and adult life. After exploring the country around Sioux Lookout, he married and settled at Lake Minnitaki. There he ran a trading post for the Indians, a hostel and also a livery stable for the teamsters and horses. He passed away in 1933, following an accident at home. He had refused to seek professional help, and when he eventually was hospitalised, he was in a weakened state, hastening his demise.

At some point I went over to the Indian Hospital on a visit and was introduced to a Nursing Officer. Although she was already with Health and Welfare, she too had an application in place for a position in the north. It was shortly after this meeting that I received a call from the Northwest Territories, in Frobisher Bay. They had received a copy of my resume and were now offering me a posting at Resolute Bay as the second nurse. I of course, informed my new friend from the Indian Hospital of the new development in my career, and her immediate response was that she wanted that position, and speculated that because of the similarity of our names, headquarters had made a mistake. I felt a little downcast and thought this theory was probably accurate, because she did at that time hold a more senior position than I. I called Frobisher Bay the next day and asked to speak with the Supervisor. I went on to say, "You must have made a mistake when you hired me. The Nursing Officer at the Indian Hospital believes that our names have been confused and that the position was most likely hers." "Not at all", came back the reply, "It is you we want." I was delighted, although afterwards, I did feel a little awkward when the matter arose at our next social encounter.

Now I had the task of resigning and I felt somewhat abashed at the inconvenience to my boss who had made my stay a very pleasant one for the past six months. He didn't seem to mind, as he had encountered these situations before. I felt perfectly at ease with the job, but I needed a little more spice to my work life, and I certainly would find it at Resolute Bay. I did not feel any deep attachment to the immediate community for that short time period. I certainly had no way of knowing that in 1991, I would again set foot in Sioux Lookout, en route to Fort Hope.

It is said that when one door closes, another opens. Our lives are very much like a book with each new chapter bringing forth new experiences, and at the same time maintaining a thread of connection to our past roots, making the character within us adaptable and interesting. All of us have the makings of a book within us, I am told, because life is always in perpetual motion. My chosen paths have been satisfying to me and the journeys have made my life richer.

Home visits by skidoo

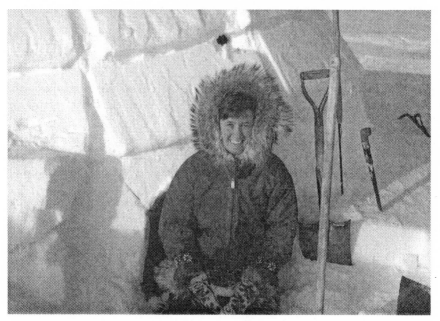

Outside igloo

Bombadier, local transport

Ice fishing, Baker Lake

Ticanogan (Cradle Board) for carrying papoose

Visit to land camps by RCMP plane

Dog team, Somerset Island

Stern Wheeler, Yukon

CHAPTER NINE
RESOLUTE BAY

I travelled by plane from Montreal to Iqaluit, known to me then as Frobisher Bay, so named after an Englishman, Sir Martin Frobisher, a mariner and explorer in search of the Northwest Passage during the sixteenth century.

I saw very little of this community, which is the largest on Baffin Island. I had the customary two days' stay for business purposes, and it was at that time I learned I would be the new Nurse-in-Charge at Resolute Bay. I was perplexed with the new arrangement, as the indications were that a senior nurse was already in place. In answer to my puzzled expression, I was assured that the present nurse would still be on staff in spite of her demotion. For some prudent government reason she was being asked to step down from her current status. She was at that point unaware of the decision, but this fact was about to be revealed to her, prior to my arrival.

An emergency flight to Lake Harbour arose the following day, giving me an opportunity to see a different community in that district. I accompanied the doctor and escorted a baby back to Frobisher Bay General Hospital. The baby was quite ill, having been diagnosed with meningitis.

It was April when I flew into Resolute Bay, a small community located approximately about one thousand miles from Montreal, Quebec. Looking from the porthole window on board the Nordair aircraft, I saw below a very barren, desolate landscape that was not at all welcoming, but that was not surprising, considering Resolute Bay was located approximately nine hundred and thirty nautical miles from the North Pole.

Resolute Bay is situated on the southern tip of Cornwallis Island, which was named after Sir William Cornwallis, an explorer. The island had been discovered by Sir William Parry, who in the eighteenth century, went in search of the Northwest Passage.

After the last war, a joint American and Canadian airfield and weather station installation was put in place. There were also scattered locations across North America of an early warning defence system known as the

Dew Line. There existed, I am told, military fears of foreign air-strikes and missile attacks.

The Government devised a plan. The Inuit from Port Harrison, in the Province of Quebec, were selected for relocation to the high Arctic, some fourteen hundred miles north of their homeland. The Inuit in Port Harrison traded in furs with the Hudson's Bay Company and earned a living by doing so. Eventually the price of fox furs dropped, and with less income, tough times lay ahead. The Government at first offered relief payments to them and the bureaucracy, in its infinite wisdom, selected seven families for that relocation process to Resolute Bay, advising the people that there would be good hunting and fishing which would make them independent again. The Government would no longer be required to give financial support to these Inuit. According to the film "Broken Promises", inhumane treatment was shown to the Port Harrison Inuit, and indications were that there may have been an ulterior motive, that being to maintain the sovereign rights to the Arctic regions of North America.

Louis St Laurent, the Canadian Prime Minister at that time, sanctioned the move, so in 1953 this small band of people said good-bye to family and friends to embark on an unknown journey, filled with promises that they may return after two years if they did not like the location. They were, according to the film, deposited on a barren landscape and given only tents to sleep in. Buffalo rugs were also distributed, and these they used on the tent walls to insulate themselves from the cold. The only warmth came from a seal oil lamp, called a Qulliq. They endured three months of total darkness in this Arctic region, which was a new experience for them. The hunting that was promised had depleted numbers of caribou and musk-ox. Orders came from Ottawa that only one caribou per family could be killed per year. According to those interviewed in the film and who experienced this event, they found it too cold and too dark even to hunt and fish.

Later, other families were dispersed to Grise Fiord which today is the most northerly situated community. The promises of returning to Port Harrison after two years were not honoured and it was suggested that if they so desired to return to their homeland they would be responsible for their own costs.

Had this political move not taken place in the fifties, I would not have been winging my way to Resolute Bay as the Nurse-in-Charge of the health programme nor would I have been able to lay claim to being Canada's most northerly appointed nurse in 1970/1971. I did not know at the time I arrived, in the very early seventies, that the Inuit were not native to that area. It would be twenty years later that I would be enlightened through the efforts of other people's investigative studies as to the many injustices handed out to the First People of Canada.

This small hamlet on Cornwallis Island, a part of the Arctic archipelago, had a population of two hundred Inuit living comfortably in heated homes, but they did not have all the modern conveniences that we would take for granted.

In conversation with the former Nurse-in-Charge, it was obvious that the information as to her recent demotion had not yet been imparted to her, as in discussing certain duties, she was of the belief that she was still in the senior position. I was angry at the administration for not affording either of us the courtesy of informing her. Not only was I angry, but somewhat embarrassed at having to break the news to her. Her mouth literally dropped open, having had no hint of dissension between her and the department. I must say that when she recovered from the shock and embarrassment, she treated me very admirably and without animosity. Although I was an innocent bystander to this event, it could have been a situation which allowed a colleague to harbour hostility. At that point of discovery, I assured her that her input would be invaluable to me and that we would be working as a team, and rank did not need to be pulled.

The Nursing Station comprised three metal mobile trailer units, all interconnecting and painted dark green on the outside. The colour, along with the large Health and Welfare logo above the door, made them a landmark, easily distinguishable to any new visitor to the settlement, or during a white out. Inside, it was very comfortable and warm. There was a sitting room, dining kitchen, two bedrooms and a bathroom, complete with a bathtub and toilet.

Adjoining was the second trailer, which contained medical equipment and all the medical supplies arranged in rows on metal shelves. At the far end was the third trailer. This was the main clinical area. Each Nursing Station was basically set up in a similar manner so that a nurse could be fairly functional if sent in to help in an emergency. There was an examination couch, x-ray machine, oxygen, suction machine, a desk with a typewriter and a telephone. The cupboards were filled with medication supplies, bandages and splints. All in all, well equipped. Further down the hallway was a small darkroom that was used for developing the x-ray films which we did as part of our duties from time to time. Beyond this were two small furnished rooms held in readiness for any sick patients requiring admission. A small cot and an incubator were also on hand in the event that a premature baby was delivered. Again, like at Baker Lake, we relied on sea lift to bring our medical supplies.

I have to smile when I say that we had a toilet. This was an indoor facility for which I felt grateful, but it was not the usual flush type that I was used to. At first glance, it seemed like a regular "loo", but on lifting the lid, there was a black plastic bag liner which emitted a strong odour of disinfectant. Having worked in hospitals, I was well used to disinfectant odours, but this was overpowering, and I am sure that not one tiny organism could have survived in there. If the solution didn't do the trick then the fumes would have. When the bag became full it had to be removed, tied and placed on the snow outside the clinic near to the roadway, ready for collection whenever it was possible. It was not an uncommon event for the bag contents to seep or burst before collection. The bag was emptied during working hours by the caretaker, but in the event of company visiting in the evening, or on weekends, particularly those enjoying a beer or two, the little black bag reached its capacity rather quickly, and so we would have to remove the offensive matter ourselves and replace it with a new bag. I didn't mind this too much, but my biggest fear was that en route to the exterior of the building, the bag might suddenly give way. However, my fears were always unfounded. I am sure Glad Bags extra strength, as advertised now, were not available in those days. The plastic bags were affectionately called "honey bags" and the disposal truck known as the "honey wagon", just like at Baker Lake. One soon caught on to the various slogans and songs depicting our primitive toilet system of the seventies. It was not unusual at a party to have a rendition of this subject put to music and with a guitar accompaniment.

We did have running water of a sort that came through a tap. However, we had a holding tank located in the kitchen next to the sink, and this tank was filled twice a week from a water truck. This service was provided by the base camp five miles up the road from the settlement. During bad weather, it was not unusual to receive a telephone call, which was a modern convenience we did have, advising us to conserve our water supply as the truck would not be able to reach us perhaps for a few days.

We had a second tank, the other being located in the clinic area. When the water supplies were low, daily bathing had to be curtailed. Other times we would augment the meagre hot water in the tub by loading buckets of snow and using that as a means to cool the bath water. There were times as well when snow was melted for tea or cooking needs, and if you have ever tried to melt snow when camping, you'd know that a pot full of snow does not equate to a full pot of water. It wasn't so bad, but it did give an insight into the hard work and conditions previous generations had to cope with, compared to the modern facilities now available. There was always, of course, a reminder not to use "the yellow snow", the dogs having contributed to this colour.

There was also a large tank of water situated near to the Nursing Station where the residents filled their buckets. This tank of water required chlorination, to render it safe for community consumption. It fell upon the nurses, on one occasion only, to carry out this task. We were quite clueless about this procedure, which normally would not be under the umbrella of nursing duties. We were given an approximate capacity of the holding tank and had to figure out how much bleach to add to give satisfactory purification of the contained supply. With the calculation completed, we had to haul bottles of bleach up the metal rung ladder, which was several feet high, and add the solution. At the bottom of this tank one could just see a pair of skates. How long they had been there was anyone's guess, but we were not about to volunteer to retrieve them.

Each move I had made called for adaptation, both to the environment and to protocol. No two communities functioned in the same manner, even though we were all under the auspices of Health and Welfare. What would work in one community would not necessarily be an appropriate method in another, and it was important not to push new ideas on to the populace. After all, the staff would come and go, but the Inuit remained, having to both tolerate and live with the changes, positive or negative.

The dialect was different in Resolute Bay, and therefore I did not recognize words that had been familiar to my ears previously.

I had arrived at a good time of year with summer to look forward to. According to the census, there were about two hundred Inuit residents of varying ages and a few Caucasians who worked at the local school as teachers. I did not find the clinics quite so busy. However, we were also responsible for the population five miles away at the air base, as well as the many transients that passed through for a variety of reasons. They did have a first aid post, manned by one male attendant, but anything of a more serious nature was brought to our facility.

Having a deep love of animals, I was delighted when my co-worker was approached to look after five husky pups aged three months. The Game and Wildlife Officer in the settlement had been given these puppies to use eventually as a dog team for his travels. He had previous commitments which meant he had to leave Resolute Bay for a week. He asked if we minded caring for them in the interim. Minded!! We had those dogs at the Nursing Station within the hour, fussing over them. We made a small make-shift shelter for them from a plywood crate and tied them up at the back of our clinic. It was tempting to allow them inside, but we decided it was not in their best interests, given that their home would always be outdoors. Every morning we got up early, before work, to feed the animals and clean up their living area. My colleague usually had the porridge on cooking for them before I came to life. Then the two of us, sporting old slacks and gum boots, filled five little bowls and watched them guzzle down the contents, tails wagging incessantly. They would look up as if to ask for more, smacking their lips and licking off the porridge still stuck to their whiskers and nose. Those five black and white fur bundles were a joy to look after.

From the kitchen window in our trailer home, we overlooked the open water in the bay. We were fortunate to see, at times, schools of beluga whales coming close to shore. It was a spectacular sight. Sometimes the first indications that the beluga whales were nearby would be from the sound of a rifle being fired and someone shouting "Kilaluak!, kilaluak!" I hated to know that the whales were being killed, but one had to keep in mind, that hunting was how the Inuit lived for centuries and the meat would be eaten. They were not wantonly killed for sport. I ventured down to the shore once the shooting was over. There were many dead whales lying on the shore and it was not a pretty sight. The women went about the chore of cutting the carcass into strips and chunks. It was suggested we give some maktaaq, which is the whale blubber, to the pups. I had an ulu which I had purchased at Baker Lake. This was a semi-circular, flat, smooth piece of sharp metal with an attached handle made from caribou bone, centrally and perpendicularly placed. The Inuit used this for cutting meat and scraping the skins of seal, caribou and polar bears. I fetched my ulu and cut tiny pieces of blubber from a carcass already being butchered. We thought the pups would enjoy this, but their milk teeth were unable to chew through the thickness.

It was then I was invited to try cooking and eating maktaaq. I was a little reticent at first, but eventually I boiled some and added lemon juice as instructed by the local women. I could only describe the morsel I ate as tasteless and did not find it at all palatable.

Clinic life went smoothly and only the occasional case of meningitis was encountered, with the patients being transported to Frobisher Bay Hospital. During one of the morning clinics there was a commotion outside in the waiting room. Before we could check it out, the clinic door was thrown open and a young Inuk male entered accompanied by a friend.

He was shouting, and in an agitated state blurted out that he had taken LSD and other stuff. We tried to quieten him down as he implored us not to call the police, whose offices were located five miles away from us. Just at that precise moment, there was a knock on the interior clinic door and two police officers entered. Obviously, someone had called for their intervention. All this happened within a few minutes. The young man, feeling a sense of betrayal, grabbed me by the lapels of my white uniform and pulled me towards him yelling, "I told you not to call the police!" I started to laugh as I tried to explain to him that I hadn't moved my position since he came through the doorway. The police then took control. In their presence, before any questions were asked of the Inuk, he announced the names of the drugs he had taken. There was such a potpourri, we were uncertain as to the accuracy of his claims. The hospital was contacted for advice as to the appropriate medication we could safely administer to him to calm him down and one that would not cause a bad interaction with the supposed intake of the other non-medical drugs. Having received the information, medication was given by injection and he went off quietly with the police. We heard no more of the incident.

One evening when my friend was out visiting and I was on call, another young Inuk male came to the clinic clutching his side, "I've been cut", he moaned, pointing to his side. When I examined him, there was no evidence of bleeding. All that I could detect was a clean small circular wound in the proximity of the stomach. When I proceeded to take a case history, he insisted that someone, whom he would not name, had hit him with a beer bottle when they were drinking. I said, "Young man, this is not a cut, but a bullet wound." There was no way he would admit to this fact. I x-rayed him using the portable machine, on the suggestion of my cohort who had just returned home. I called her to look at the x-rays with me. We were not trained to read x-rays, but could discern some shadows. On the advice from the doctor in Frobisher Bay, a medical evacuation to the hospital was arranged. We found out later that indeed there were several fragments located near to the spine, so near that they were left, surgery being considered too precarious.

The working arrangements with my colleague went well over the months, but unfortunately I had to pull rank on her because of a number of incidents that had occurred. She was engaged to a worker, stationed at the base camp. He did not have independent transportation. Wishing to see his betrothed on a regular basis, he required assistance from his friends to take him the five miles to the settlement and later return for him. As it turned out, those friends believed that for their act of hospitality, it gave them special access privileges to our residence. On a few occasions when they arrived to transport the boyfriend home, they were invited in for a night cap by my colleague. At the residence, we did not have live television programming, but did receive the occasional video film from the department. These young men, perhaps a little the worse of drink, would play these tapes, turning up the volume very loud, usually causing me to awaken. I never complained initially, but I would hear my colleague begging them to keep the noise down. It fell on deaf ears as they continued to take over.

When I was asleep one night, one of the men opened my bedroom door, which had no lock on it, and ordered me to get up to have a drink and to be sociable. To me, midnight or later was not a time to start socializing, nor were these men my friends. In fact, I quite disliked them from the beginning. Being on call could be very exhausting and I made sure I had a good night's rest whenever possible. I asked him to leave. He was utterly defiant at first, but eventually he went back to join the others. I was unable to sleep now, feeling somewhat angry at being the subject of this man's sheer ignorance. Not wishing to be involved with them, I got up, dressed and I went to the clinic at the far end to catch up on some paper work. In a short time the offensive ignoramus followed me there and stood over me as I typed. I ordered him to leave. It wasn't enough for him to disturb my sleep in my home, he now became impertinent. Grabbing a jacket, I left for a friend's house where I remained until I could see them leave. As there was no one now to antagonize, they did not stay around. Because the accommodation was shared, I allowed the matter to drop for the sake of compatibility, but perhaps I should have laid a charge against him. The arrogance continued on different evenings.

There was one more episode that brought the matter to culmination. I was awakened by Rita, who was obviously very upset. She said, "You better get up as I've called the police!" Barely able to get my eyes open and focused, she proceeded in a wavering, half sobbing voice, to give an account of the circumstances which had just transpired, leading to an angry outburst in the other room. Once again, the same group were being entertained, with liquor being served. My colleague, before retiring to bed, enjoyed a drink as a nightcap and she always left the bottles displayed on the counter for all to see. One of her guests was drinking the last drop in the bottle of her favourite drink. Rita reprimanded him for doing so. In return, he threw what remained in his glass over her and a battle of words ensued. I ran to the telephone in an attempt to intercept the policeman's visit, but he was already at the door. I asked him to allow us to handle our own internal affairs as there was no violence involved, but rather a dispute. He willingly conceded. Over coffee and in a civilized manner everyone had their say in the presence of the police officer, whom I asked to remain should these men refuse to leave. I advised them that they could not return to the facility anymore.

Our Nursing Officer, already in the vicinity at a neighbouring community, was due to give us an official visit. I decided to give a full report to him and use my position advantageously to eradicate the problem from our midst. To my surprise, Rita was in full agreement. I believe she felt badly about the disturbances and was feeling a little awkward about saying too much to the offenders, who were on friendly terms with her fiance'.

At the meeting with the "boss", I voiced my opinions, adamantly stating how I wanted the situation dealt with. It was simply that the Nursing Station, being my home, had been intruded upon, invading my right to privacy. I continued on to say that the behaviour of the visitors was grossly inappropriate and unacceptable. My request was for a cooling off period regarding the visits of the fiance' with a total ban of the other characters in question, from entering our home again. Any violations of this rule would lead to my laying charges against them on the grounds of trespassing. The Nursing Officer gave me full support.

I was glad that my colleague saw wisdom and was supportive of my decision. Everything settled down and in due course her fiance' was allowed to visit again. When he first appeared, I was showered with humble apologies. I accepted them in good grace. I did, however, remind him that an engagement to a member of staff did not afford him a privileged status in our home, and as a guest he would behave accordingly.

It was summertime, but chilly. The thermometer registered sixty degrees Fahrenheit. Sea lift was underway, but not without some casualties. A first-aid person was on board the ship, but any suspected fractures or serious accidents would be brought to us. We would be required to do x-rays and send any injured party to hospital. Fortunately we seldom saw anything too serious except one man sustained a broken and dislocated ankle. After we attended to him he was flown out for treatment.

As a token of appreciation, the Captain of the ship invited us to dine on board. The dinner was arranged for the following evening and the helicopter from the ship landed outside the Nursing Station, ready to transport us to the vessel. The helicopter was a bubble-shaped one, and it was thrilling to see it land ever so precisely on the ground, stirring up loose soil and creating a bit of a dust storm. I am not sure whether we felt important or a little embarrassed as we boarded the craft, in full view of community members, only to be flown a very short distance to the deck of the ship. We descended the steps of the helicopter and were directed to climb the metal rungs in the direction of the Captain's quarters. We did so amid stares from the crewmen. Safely up the ladder, we were met by the First Mate who in turn introduced us to the Captain and the Purser. These three gentlemen were our dining companions for the evening. Following the enjoyable meeting and meal, we were ferried back to land in the flying machine.

Rita by now had decided on a wedding date and resigned her position. I was sad to see her go. In spite of our ups and downs, she was a very competent nurse and I would miss her medical knowledge and high-spirited, fun-loving nature.

Shortly before leaving, she brought a dog to the clinic with a possible fracture to its front leg. An x-ray was taken by her and a break was obvious. She decided to apply a plaster cast to the limb and I found myself helping with the task. The poor dog hobbled around on three good legs and one in a plaster cast. The x-ray was kept, and the next poor, unsuspecting visiting young doctor was asked for a medical opinion on the fractured limb. To add a little spice to life, we did not tell him it was that of a dog, but pretended it was a young child's. He quickly clued in to our mischief, but took it in good humour.

"Goodbye and don't forget to write", I yelled, as Rita boarded her plane and headed to England. The familiar feeling came over me when I returned to an empty house. The same little nagging doubts were beginning to come back again. Now, I would wait for an undetermined period of time for a replacement. I found out, a long time later, that the positions were not advertised until the person had physically left, which would account for the time lapse between those departing and new recruits appearing. The logic had to do, I was told, with an occasional employee changing their mind at the last moment and not leaving.

Now that the snow had left for a duration of three months, it felt good to walk out on the tundra again. It was cool, but I enjoyed the long days. I would go to bed at night, and because of the twenty-four hours of daylight, sleep often eluded me. Tin foil was frequently attached to the window to darken my bedroom. It was effective, if one did not mind the rustling sound when the wind blew. The other factor was that I could hear the children playing about in the extended daylight hours. I was well aware of their daring antics that could possibly end with my forfeiting a night's rest whilst attending to their injuries.

The next settlements to me, in the Baffin region, were Arctic Bay and Pond Inlet. When they needed to airlift any patients from their community, they often came to Resolute Bay first. Sometimes that meant for the patient, an overnight stay with me before continuing their trip onwards. The nurses were inclined to drop off their clients and then head back to their respective locations. At times this was justifiable if they were alone at the station and if we were fully staffed. Many times this was not so. It took me a long time to find out that they were responsible for the care of their own clients and should have stayed with them. This matter came up for discussion when a baby, suffering from a bad respiratory infection, was flown in one evening from Arctic Bay. It was not always possible to medically transfer a patient out immediately, with weather a consideration. If the medical condition would allow, it was preferable to wait until morning. In this instance it fell on me to care for the baby. Given the child's condition, I set the clock every two hours to check that the baby was comfortable and to give it fluids. First thing in the morning, the babe would be sent out with a nurse escort, provided by the hospital. This was a practice when we were short staffed.

I was bathing the very irritable and sick baby in preparation for her trip. In the midst of this I received a telephone call. On the other end was a male shouting excitedly, "There has been a bad accident nurse, involving five men, and they are on their way down to your clinic!" "Dear Lord", I murmured, "Not now!" I returned to the care of the child and completed the task of bathing her. The doorbell rang and the elderly caretaker came scurrying down the hallway to get me, beckoning me to hurry. I instructed him to dress the baby and feed it. Bless his heart, he called for his wife and she came over and did the essentials. Fortunately the paperwork had been completed with a progress update report on the infant.

There was much ado in the clinic area as I approached, with a significant number of workers trying to assist. As I tried to get a sense of what was happening, it seemed everyone wished to give me their version of the accident. I quickly assessed the situation and found three of the men to have non-threatening injuries, but they were quite shaken. Some type of heavy grader machinery had, while parked on a slope, rolled backwards out of control and, as a result, five people were knocked down. One man, who was fairly severely injured had all the symptoms of a heart attack as well. It had to be assumed that he had until proven otherwise. I did not have the means to determine that conclusively.

Intravenous therapy was started, oxygen given to this man, as well as a narcotic injection. Wounds had to be cleaned, suturing, bandaging and splinting where necessary for the different injuries. Files had to be compiled. There was not a secretary to do this task. A proper medical history and accurate details of the accident and a patient's condition were essential. Nurses were sometimes subpoenaed to appear in court and present the medical records, especially in the event of an unexpected death. Vital signs had to be checked frequently. Arrangements were under way to have two of the men airlifted as quickly as possible to Frobisher Bay Hospital with the already available nurse escort and aeroplane. One would be a stretcher case. The nurse would have her hands full checking this man and attending to the baby. The Zone Director, as always, had to be notified and arrangements for an ambulance at the other end would be made by him. The patients would be reassessed at Frobisher Bay and it would be determined as to whether transfer to a major centre was necessary. The remaining injured were treated and allowed to go home.

Meantime, out-patients had gathered in the waiting room to be seen at the morning clinic. They realized that an emergency had occurred and waited patiently, some going home of their own volition. Those that remained were the very sick and I saw them as quickly as possible.

It is quite a task dealing with several injured people at one time, more so when attempting this feat single-handed, trying to provide the services of a hospital emergency room. One has just to look at the activities within a hospital and see all the different types of professionals required for that care-giving service in order to appreciate the role nurses play in the north. We had to be a "Jack of all Trades", At the end of a hectic day, it was possible to be up all night too.

The base, located five miles away, had at least a couple of hundred men for whom we were medically responsible. These men worked for the oil exploration companies in the airport terminal, as mechanics for aircraft maintenance and heavy duty operators, and some were researchers. The Royal Canadian Mounted Police were also based there. Resolute Bay was an incoming and outgoing terminal. Some crews worked further north at Ellesmere Island, and others were with the Dew Line.

Supplies, including food, had to be flown into these areas and were assembled at the storage depot in Resolute Bay. The company that supplied our food was Tower Foundation. Each month, I typed out my list of requirements and presented it to them in person. Although we paid a minimal amount for food and shelter, we lived well, being able to get fresh fruit and vegetables flown in.

The male Nursing Officer, a Scotsman, arrived at Resolute Bay on one of his visits. We were kept abreast of any operational changes, and he in turn made sure our work was being performed to standard as well as giving us support in our endeavours. It was usually quite informal and I looked forward to these visits, especially as he was from my home city in Scotland. It just added a personal touch between the boss and employee. When he arrived he was having a problem with his stomach ulcer. In the evening he asked if I had any milk that he could have to quell the burning sensation he was experiencing in his gut. I instructed him to help himself. I had quite a bit of fresh milk on hand, only it was in a frozen state to preserve it. When he went to retrieve the milk, he had a look at all the different cuts of meat that were in the freezer, neatly wrapped in brown waxed paper and the contents identified. He made some sort of utterance and when he returned he held up a long meat package which contained filet mignon. He exploded, "Twenty-one pounds of filet mignon, that is bloody ridiculous Nora!" I started to laugh as I explained, but he didn't find me amusing. I was a very amateur typist and when I had ordered the filet mignon, I had requested two pounds (2lbs). Whoever read the order mistook my typing and so the two pounds became twenty-one pounds. Having once received this choice cut of meat, I thought it quite a shame to return it, and decided, as it was already billed as twenty-one pounds, I would keep the order, my rationale being it would last that much longer. After all, there were different medical, dental and nursing personnel visiting off and on, all requiring a good meal.

I remained good friends with my supervisor for a number of years after he left the north, later staying on numerous occasions at his home with his wife and children, in British Columbia. .

Still there was no sign of a replacement. How much longer would I have to wait, I wondered. Nurses were not exactly jumping up and down to come to the Barren Lands. Mostly they were from the United Kingdom or Australia. Still, I was managing, being kept busy with the daytime clinics, home visits and being on call twenty-four hours a day. Shelves had to be replenished. Bottles of pills were pre-packaged by the nurse at the clinic with the appropriate instructions printed on the labels in both English and syllabics. Filling prescriptions and labelling the bottles was time-consuming during a busy morning clinic, making it advantageous to have these at the ready. The developer for the x-rays, contained in tanks, had to be cleaned at times, which was an additional duty. Just as at Baker

Lake, we were required to do a number of x-rays on the men who returned from their hunting trips, who were missed by the visiting team. We also did x-rays on various ill persons.

There was always some unusual happening that helped to keep the spice in life. One such event occurred when the Game Officer brought back two polar bear cubs from the tundra, each weighing a few hundred pounds. The mother bear had been killed previously and there was concern that the cubs were not yet able to fend adequately for themselves. Two oil drums had to be welded together to contain and transport each bear, who were also tranquillized for the aeroplane ride. The officer in charge was sending them to a zoo. Until this could be organized, he built a fenced compound, next door to his own house. The structure was reinforced with some steel bars, to ensure their confinement.

At a later time, I received a frantic call from the Game Officer's wife. Her husband was out of town hunting, as were many of the men. The bears, she said, were lunging at the fence causing some of the mesh wiring to separate from the ground posts. She needed to get them sedated and asked if I could help. What did I know about sedating bears? I ran down the road with some tranquillizers in my pocket. I found the bears indeed were in a very agitated state as one would expect, with their abnormal containment. They would rear up on their hind legs. As they came down, and in a thrusting motion, used their front paws and body weight to lunge against the metal bars and screening. This caused the paw of one bear to bleed. Although cubs, they were still large animals and did possess great strength.

The officer's wife was prodding at them with a metal bar each time they started a new assault. Nearby lay a rifle belonging to her husband which, if necessary, she may have used. When I arrived she ran indoors quickly and brought back chunks of meat. We placed capsules of the tranquillizing drug inside the meat and then threw it to the bears. In the meantime she had made radio contact with her husband to action his prompt return to the settlement. At most, he would get back in a couple of hours. We ordered all the adults and children, who were curiously watching the activities, to stay indoors in the event that the bears did break out. I certainly did not need to contend with a bear mauling. The sedatives that laced the meat may have dropped out before being consumed or there may have been an insufficient dosage of the drug to have any effect on the animals. I was unable to judge, this not being my area of expertise. For whatever reason, the bears did quieten down, but perhaps they were tired from their own actions.

It was late in the afternoon when I went to answer the front doorbell of the clinic. Before me stood two military gentleman. Removing their caps, they shook my hand and proceeded to introduce themselves, one as a Major and the other as Captain. I invited them in and found the purpose of their visit was to check out our Health facility and to seek my co-operation, should any of their soldiers become ill or severely injured. At the end of the visit, the Major, who was Danish, took a photograph of me.

Located at the base were military personnel involved in their Arctic training. These Canadian troops were being readied to defend the Northern Territories should any unthinkable invasion occur. It was considered that if an attack were inevitable, the operation would require the establishment of an air head. Thus began the training of the newly-formed Canadian Airborne Regiment. The Mobile Command exercises saw the entire Regiment dropping at Resolute Bay in December.

The military camped in tents at a location a few miles away affectionately known as Crystal City. At night, I could hear in the distance the "ack-ack" sound of mock gunfire and the drone of engines from aeroplanes flying a few miles away. From these planes, the men practised parachute assault exercises at night. During the daytime on one occasion, I observed a group of army men, totally clad in white uniforms and boots, running across the snow-covered terrain near the Nursing Station, with rifles slung over their shoulders. These exercises were also carried out at Frobisher Bay and christened "Exercise Patrouille Nocturne."

Although in an isolated region, I never really felt alone. If anything, I met more interesting characters there than I would have done living in a city.

At one o'clock in the morning, I was awakened by the door buzzer. It had a very distinctive and ghastly sound to it, one that could almost have awakened the dead. Slipping on my dressing gown, I hastened to answer the door, knowing that there would be a medical problem on the other side. A young Inuk male greeted me. He had his arms draped around an older man in a supportive manner. As I ushered them into the clinic, he proceeded to tell me how he had found his uncle lying on the kitchen floor, bleeding from a leg wound and feeling very cold to touch. It was obvious that the injured man was in shock. I got him onto the examination couch and quickly assessed his injury, the wound still oozing blood. Judging by its depth, the bleeding must have been quite profuse at first. I wrapped him in some blankets for warmth before darting off to put on some respectable attire. Having dressed, I was ready to tackle the problem in hand. The laceration was deep and long, running down the outer side of the leg from the knee towards the ankle. On questioning the young man, who acted as interpreter, it appeared that there had been a family altercation, ending when the son pulled a knife on his father, thus inflicting the wound. I was relieved it was not an abdominal injury, as the situation would have been more serious.

Drinking had been involved, with the patient still showing some effects from the alcohol. He was more concerned about sleep than anything else. I started an intravenous on him first, letting the solution of glucose and saline water infuse him, to combat his shock. I set about cleaning the laceration, infiltrating the area afterwards with local anaesthetic in preparation for suturing. The wound was deeper than I had anticipated, requiring some muscle suturing with catgut, before stitching the skin. In all, he required twenty-seven stitches. It took some time to perform as I had not actually stitched muscle before. Sterile dressings were applied and I started him on antibiotics. On completion, I stayed with him while he slept, but for me it was one more night without sleep. Regardless, clinic duties would resume as normal in the daytime.

At eight o'clock in the morning, satisfied that my patient had recovered from his ordeal, all vital signs showing normality, I discharged him. During the process of cleaning the clinic, I had just gone outside to hang two blankets on the washing line to air. It was a cool, crisp morning, and as I was returning indoors a cheery voice said, "Good morning!" I turned to acknowledge the greeting, only to see an older, tall gentleman standing at the edge of the road. As I walked towards him he extended a welcoming hand and at the same time stating, "I am the High Commissioner of England." With a firm hand-shake I replied, "I am Nurse Philip, from Aberdeen, Scotland." The meeting was but a brief encounter and not long enough for me to find out what his mission was at Resolute Bay. He was joined by other members of his party.

There was not a great deal to do socially. The local bar, five miles up the road, was never an attraction for me. Had it not been for the after-hours work that required to be done, I might not have survived there. Because some of the men were injured in the workplace, I often had to fill out and submit forms to the Worker's Compensation Board. There were reports at the first, intermediate and final levels required to be filled in, all having to be typed for clarity. There was usually not enough time during the normal work day to do this.

Nurses, at that time, gave many, many hours of their own time, and certainly the one day a month extra holiday time given to us did little to compensate for the extra hours worked. I don't believe nurses made a measurement of their time, nor made too many demands with regards to this. It was accepted as part of the job. Fortunately, the unions saw the matter in a different vein, and today overtime is paid for hours worked beyond the regular shift. In some quarters, nurses are still looked upon as "angels of mercy", and many times unreasonable expectations are placed on them, the public often impinging on their time. I do believe that nurses on the whole are very giving creatures, but at some point they have to learn to say "No", and without guilt. Many, including myself, eventually burned out from the unending demands on and off duty.

Various research studies were carried out in the Arctic. I am able to recall meeting two biologists at the Nursing Station. Their assignment was to study the ecology and behaviour of the musk-ox at a location called Polar Bear Pass, north of Resolute Bay, and centrally positioned on Bathurst Island. The National Museums Field Camp began their studies in 1968. The two men welcomed the opportunity of spending winter in the Arctic conditions so as to observe the animals in their frozen habitat. Included in their supplies brought in were two Parcoll Huts, which comprised aluminium frames covered with an insulating material for warmth. A diesel oil stove used for cooking sat on the wooden floor. A Coleman lamp was used for light.

I am sure that Providence played a part in guiding me to ultimately write about my Arctic experiences at the right time. Who would have believed that in the community of Canmore, Alberta, so far removed from the frozen wastelands of the north, that I would meet an Inuk female from Rankin Inlet. She had worked as a dental therapist and had stayed with me. Through her, I met another Inuk lady from Pangnirtung to whom I was able to turn to for clarification on some information points. It was in this setting that I also came across one of the two men who had been on the musk-ox project in the Arctic. They had been invited to dine with us at the Resolute Bay Nursing Station. It was convenient to be able to talk again about the northern studies and listen more attentively. It seemed strange to hear tales of how they lived in the winter conditions, where three months of darkness prevailed, and to remember these stories some twenty five years later, as though they had just recently happened. They were apparently kept busy with their schedule of animal observations, weather reporting, cooking and entertaining themselves by carving soapstone or playing guitar.

I am sure that anyone who has experienced the northern elements, will treasure the memories forever as I do, for the adventure it was.

There were rumblings of a new nurse replacement being imminent. I was a little tired again, and felt it would be good to have a companion.

There was a definite chill in the air and the nights were much shorter. It was time to think about parkas once more. I made myself one, and had a local Inuk woman stitch applique' of igloos and hunter figures around the hem. The only thing left to do was to acquire some fur to be placed around the hood for warmth. I would very much have liked artificial fur, but it was not obtainable there. It almost seemed that real fur would not be obtainable either. I talked at the clinic with an elderly patient, and asked where I might purchase some fur. She assured me that in due course she would be able to get some for me. I asked on a few occasions how her search was going, and she would say, "Not yet." This same lady had two husky dogs tied up in front of her house. I frequently fed my table scraps to these dogs. One day I didn't see them around and assumed they had gone hunting with the men. About the same time, my benefactor produced the much-needed fur. I asked if it was a wolf fur and with that she went into great guffaws of laughter and would not answer me. Suddenly, I had this ghastly thought that this might be the fur belonging to the dogs. Until the day I left, I never found out the origins of the fur, but chose to decline the offer. I could not bear the thought that, just perhaps, these were the animals I loved and fed. To the sensitive reader, again I point out that there are cultural differences and practices that occur with regard to the animal kingdom, which we may find offensive, but are part of life in such a harsh environment.

"We have a new nurse for you, and she will be arriving at Resolute Bay on Monday at noon. Please avail yourself to meet the aeroplane", came the telephone message. "Yippee!", I cried aloud to an empty clinic. I scurried around the entire facility over the weekend, making sure everything was ship-shape for the new arrival.

In the midst of preparations, a call came from the RCMP barracks. The constable on duty mentioned something about an air crash. He was coming to see me at the clinic. Apparently a small aircraft had taken off in the early morning and within a short time had crashed into the side of Brown Mountain. The pilot, a six-foot Texan, had been flying solo at the time. The policeman arrived and imparted this information to me, mentioning that the sight was not a pretty one, the corpse being very badly charred. Blood samples were required to be taken and he volunteered to draw the blood from the deceased pilot so that I did not have to witness the unpleasantness.

I was very grateful for his consideration, especially as the aviator was known to me. Of course, at that time, there still had to be an official positive identification made. It was later confirmed to be the Texan.

I had flown sometime earlier with him in a Hercules aeroplane to Eureka, three hundred and eighty nautical miles further north and a mere five hundred and fifty nautical miles from the North Pole. Drilling for gas and oil had taken place at Eureka, and now all the equipment had been removed. An inspector was flying in there to check that the land had been left in proper order. It was then I had the opportunity to fly with the pilot, now deceased, to see a new landscape. I was saddened by the man's demise and at the same time felt a shiver down my spine. It was a great sense of relief for me that I had not been on board the downed aircraft.

I felt privileged to have flown as far as Eureka, but at the same time, I wished that I had been able to reach the North Pole and land there. From history, I remembered reading about Frederick A. Cook and Robert Peary, the two Americans who reached this barren land as explorers in the early 1900s, each claiming to be the first one there.

It was a cool, blustery day as the plane from Edmonton made its landing and taxied along the length of the runway. I felt very exuberant about the anticipated meeting of my nursing partner-to-be. As the aircraft doors opened, I found myself peering into the distance, balancing on my toes to gain better vision. Others in the community were also eager to identify the incomer, craning their necks to see. As most of the passengers deplaning were men, one quickly knew on sight which one was the nurse. I stepped forward to greet her. The Inuit looked curiously at her, and she being Chinese, made them perhaps wonder if she were of their race, the similarities being obvious. The trip back to the settlement was filled with female chatter as we got acquainted.

Lee had never worked in an nursing outpost before, nor even in the north, so there was much to educate her about regarding the environment and the work duties. As with any new employee, it takes time to find one's way around and know where precisely everything is kept before being completely functional.

I had a busy clinic the next day, but found time to give the necessary orientation to Lee. As the work day drew to a close, I received a telephone call. The voice, that of a white female talking at the other end, was high pitched and somewhat hysterical. The call was being made from a research site four miles from the clinic. "You better come quick, there has been an accident, and bring the police with you!" she blurted out. I enquired as to the nature of the accident and how many were involved and at the same time telling her to ring the police from her home. By now she was yelling down the telephone, "Hurry up, the man's head is off !" I asked her to calm down and give me all the details, and assured her that if the victim had been decapitated, he was beyond anyone's help. She was very angry and demanded to know where I was hiding the police! To recall, the police were located five miles away and were nearer to the scene of the accident than I was. I mentally assessed the situation and ascertained that they had a stretcher and some extra men to help. Having confirmed this for me I instructed her to have several men help lift the injured man onto the stretcher. They were to keep him straight, immobilize his head and neck, keep him warm and bring him to me immediately. The reasoning behind the decision was that I did not have available transportation. The site where the accident occurred had a bombardier. The temperature was zero, and valuable time would have been wasted while I dressed warmly and organized a vehicle to take me there. Meantime a shocked patient was being exposed to a long, cold wait. In this case, with a new nurse, I deemed it more appropriate to prepare for the patient's arrival. The oxygen tank was wheeled into the room, an intravenous readied, bandages and sterile dressing packs assembled. A narcotic drug was removed from the locked cupboard in preparation to administer should his injuries be very severe. All of this took time.

Upon arrival, the patient was brought into the examining room amidst much clamour, everyone directing everyone. The injured person, a male from the settlement, was in a deep coma, and his head, I must say, was very much still attached. His airway was checked for obstruction, and oxygen was quickly given, his colour being a purplish hue. An intravenous was started and the patient thoroughly examined for hidden injuries. There was heavy bleeding from the left thigh. Two major problems were evident. The entire left leg was mangled and a small vessel was spouting blood. I had to try and clamp this at once which was very difficult. He had a compound fracture of two ribs which had to be immobilized. Fortunately, an army doctor happened to be in Resolute Bay, and when he heard of the accident he came straight to the clinic to assist. In such a situation, I had to concede to a superior and follow any directions he might give. He supported my efforts and arranged for an army Hercules aircraft that was currently in the area, to fly the man out immediately. He would act as the escort. The situation was grave and I was thankful for the professional help the doctor offered. He was better equipped medically to deal with the lacerated limb. No time could be wasted for fear of inclement weather.

I gave a sigh of relief when the patient was taken to the airport, knowing his only chance of survival was in getting him quickly to a hospital and into surgery. We busied ourselves when he left. The clinic room looked as though a cyclone had passed through. Blood, swabs, masks and instruments were strewn everywhere. Within this unit we did have an autoclave in which all instruments and dressing trays could be properly sterilized. The examining table had to be disinfected from top to bottom and the floors washed. In the middle of this, there was another telephone call. It was a relayed message from the Department of Transport, stating simply that the patient had died en route and they were on their way back.

Professionals involved in life-saving situations and including family members know what a wrench this is. In spite of our efforts he had not survived. There were no guarantees that he would have recovered, even with the medical attention in hospital. It was thought that, had he lived, he probably would have had his leg amputated. We now had the painful task of informing his family.

On that sad meeting with his next of kin, his wife told me he had had a few drinks at the bar. He apparently told her he felt very happy that day after quitting his job. On the way home he was riding his skidoo when the collision occurred with a vehicle, driven by a non-Inuit. I never found out who was to blame, but the other driver was not injured.

The deceased was left in a Quon-set hut, at the base overnight, until funeral arrangements could be made. The doctor and police dismantled the medical equipment.

I attended the funeral. Many from the community came and the small church, located across the road from the clinic, was filled to its capacity. I was amused when, shortly after the service commenced and in the solemnity of the occasion, the church door opened and a late comer noisily stepped in. He just happened to be one of the sons. He took the funeral in a very matter-of-fact way.

The day after the funeral, I decided to meet with the husband of the woman who had advised me initially of the accident. She was out to malign me and had it in her head that it was my fault the patient died. She concluded erroneously that his death was due to my absence at the scene of the accident, and seemed to have it fixed in her mind that I was hiding the police. The nature of the victim's injuries and the limitations we had within our community seemed to have gone unnoticed by her. After meeting with her husband, I was glad to hear that he did not share his wife's hysterical point of view.

Some time later, the police officer presented me with a subpoena to appear in court. The purpose was to give the medical evidence as to the cause of death. I protested, saying that a doctor had also been present, and asked why he would not be called. The answer was that I had been the main care giver in attendance, and therefore deemed the most appropriate person to call. The officer was unable to say when this would take place and this concerned me. I indicated that I would be going on vacation in the fall, and that the flight was already booked. I was naive about such proceedings, although I was aware that in an accident causing death, it was normal procedure to hold an inquest. He instructed me that if necessary, I would have to cancel my flight should my departure coincide with the court date. I never knew whether or not the officer was joking.

As it turned out, the inquest was heard well in advance of my anticipated trip. A classroom in the local school was improvised as the courtroom. I never liked attention focused on me, and I hated to talk in front of people. The very idea of taking the stand gave me goose bumps and my heart raced as I waited to be called. Although the policeman was a friend, it did not make it any easier. My heart skipped a beat when he announced my name. I entered, but at that moment, warmth did not emanate from the classroom that I had visited often before. It took on a coldness and felt very much like a courtroom. I took my place and, as instructed, raised my right hand while placing my left hand on the Bible, swearing to tell the whole truth. I was not very long on the stand, but was simply asked to explain to the court the cause of death. Having given the medical terminology, I was then asked by the judge to reiterate in layman's terms. It was over in ten minutes, making my worries seem futile.

Sunday was usually a quiet day, except for any unforeseen emergencies. It was a time to write letters and generally catch up on personal matters. It was also a good time to show Lee around the settlement. As we walked and talked, we passed the husky dog teams lying in a row, attached to their tracers. Lee pointed to one pup which she thought to be sick. On looking closer, it did seem very lethargic. We decided to call the owner who came promptly. After unhitching the dog, he carried it into the house. When we examined the dog, we saw what appeared to be tooth marks in both groins, but there was no bleeding. The owner indicated he would keep the dog in the house, and we would visit the dog again in the evening.

We carried out our promise, revisiting the animal. As we entered, using sign language, the owner beckoned us to look at the marks in the groin. Lo and behold, the skin in the lower abdominal area was sloughing off and exposing what we thought was muscle. He made a gesture with his hands, indicating he would shoot the animal, but had waited as a courtesy to show us the new development. By now one of his school-aged children had come in and we promptly used her to act as interpreter. "No!", I said to him, "Don't shoot the pup. Let me take it to the clinic and treat it." I advised him I had never given a dog antibiotics and that it might have a reaction or die as a result of its wounds. If it were to recover I established that he would take the dog back. He agreed, but I am sure he thought the dog would die.

He carried the dog the short distance to the clinic and left at once. By now, the dog was very weak and I had to apply human medical logic to the sick animal's care. I placed him on a blanket on the floor of the clinic. I just hoped that no patients would arrive whilst I was tending the dog. He was conscious and I wanted to get him drinking fluids, so I offered him some beef broth, hoping the salt would in due course make him thirsty. The dog being too weak to lap the liquid, I scooped handfuls to his lips, and surprisingly, he drank all of it. Next, I gave him an intra-muscular injection of an antibiotic. I allowed him to rest, checking on him frequently in order to give him water to drink. My colleague looked on, amused at my fussing over the animal. The pup fell into a deep sleep. Later, when I approached to give him his midnight antibiotic injection, he looked up at me in recognition. I moved him to the porch onto a comfortable bed of old blankets, with disposable under-pads beneath him, as there was now leakage from his wounds. I cleaned the raw areas before leaving him for the night.

I had to rise much earlier in the morning, in order to attend to the needs of my little furry friend. I bounded down the hallway before breakfast to see if he was still alive. I held my breath as I gently opened the door to peek inside. A cute little face peered back at me, appearing a bit perkier than the night before. I gave him his third injection of medication. He took it without a whimper, as though he sensed I was trying to help him. I fed him a little porridge which he ate hungrily, licking his lips when finished. Unfortunately the wound area was gaping more now, but at least the antibiotics would soon attack the infection and then I would hopefully see signs of improvement.

The protocol of injections, feeding small amounts of food and giving adequate fluids continued throughout the day, as well as keeping his under-carriage clean. He could not stay in the clinic area indefinitely, so at the end of the workday a new location was prepared. The chosen site was behind the clinic, utilizing the same location that once accommodated the five husky pups. The same plywood box was used as a kennel. The outside of it was packed with snow to provide further insulation. Another piece of plywood, strategically placed, acted as a door. It was left ajar and anchored, so that the pup could access the outside to relieve himself, but still keep him warm and sheltered from the wind. Old blankets were placed inside the makeshift kennel with under-pads on top for easy changing. After a short life in the outdoors, this shelter would have been very comfortable.

As the days rolled past, our furry friend improved. When he was able to tolerate a full solid diet I stopped the injections and completed the course of medication by mouth. The abdominal wound, which I believed was gangrenous, remained the same for a few weeks and then the formation of new skin growth became evident.

About the same time, a visiting dentist and doctor had appeared on the scene, on one of their Nursing Station rounds. On being shown the dog, their opinion was that the animal would never be able to walk normally. They surmised that the formation of scar tissue in the groin area would inhibit movement when the dog ran or walked.

With a good, nourishing, high protein diet, the dog was recovering in leaps and bounds. As he made progress he left the snug abode, opting to spend more time outdoors. At intervals during the day, I would untie him and make him chase me, a little at a time. I would hide from him behind a snow bank, and he would scramble over the icy mound to reach me, lavishing me with kisses from his long wet tongue when he found me. The exercise was a form of physiotherapy to avoid any contractures, as well as giving an enjoyable playtime for him. He progressed so very well that I decided, reluctantly, to relinquish this ball of fun back to the owner. He was as happy as I was sad. I am sure if I had wanted to keep the dog, there would not have been any objections on his part. I was still of a mind to travel, and I felt it would be unfair to own an animal for that reason. I was gratified when I learned that the dog, in due course, became a lead dog. Unknown to me at that time, I would, at a later date, have a chance encounter with him.

This episode brings to mind another doggy tale. I was busy after my day's work, preparing my evening meal. The meat was sizzling in the pan. The wafting of the pleasant aroma was indeed making my mouth water, and made me feel even hungrier, when I heard a gentle knocking on my house door and wondered who it could be. Normally the clinic bell would ring if it were a patient to be seen. When I opened the door, a group of children were standing there and seemingly all at once, excitedly said, "Aanniasiuqti!, aanniasiuqti!, come quick!" This was the Inuit name for nurses in that region. "The dog had a puppy but it is dead." They had such a pleading look in their eyes and such a sincere desire for me to come to their home that I shut down my kitchen operations and left with them. The house was only a short distance away and upon arrival there, I saw a dog, part Husky, sitting on the ice. She was in labour. Only one pup was evident at that stage and the mother had her paw over it as though she had rejected it. There was no sign of life, which left me to conclude that the pup was either dead or near to death. The voices again implored me to help the puppy. Managing to get it away from the mother, I took its lifeless body inside. Placing it on my knee, I blew a few breaths into its mouth and at the same time massaged its chest. In a short time one paw twitched to life, then another, and it started to breathe.

Meantime, the small group that had been surrounding me, their eyes as big as saucers, let out squeals of joy. One little girl ventured to say, "aanniasiuqti you make it live again." They truly believed that a miracle had been performed. That perhaps was advantageous for the position I held within the community. I took the puppy home and fed him with milk through a dropper. To keep him warm, I placed him in a shoe box with a covered hot water bottle. Amazingly, he did survive, and in a few days, when he was responding well, I took him back to the children. Presumably the mother dog accepted him back. The dog grew and it always amused me that when I did home visits to this family the dog would scurry behind the wood stove. From his safe haven he would bark at me until I left. I would say to him, "Stop barking at me, don't you know I revived you!" He was functional, but whether he was brain damaged I was not sure. I noticed he always held his head to one side. A year later he was run over by a skidoo.

A brand new mobile home was delivered to us and it was positioned behind the Nursing Station. This was to serve as an accommodation unit for visiting personnel and it came fully furnished. I envied the transients that would use this modern unit with its beautiful kitchen, especially knowing that most of the time it would sit empty.

The first person to have the opportunity to use it was the new Nursing Officer, from Frobisher Bay. She was familiar to me, having known her from Sioux Lookout. She was not so inclined to use the new trailer, preferring to stay in our home. As there were only two bedrooms in our living quarters, and both were occupied, she had to settle for sleeping in the area designated for patients. Had those beds been needed, she would have been required to move. It was during this visit that she had a rather rude awakening. It was standard practice not to lock our doors in the north, a practice that was about to change. Three or four young boys entered the building in the early hours of the morning, at a time when we had twenty-four hours of daylight. They sneaked into the living area unknown to Lee or myself and from a cupboard had removed liquor that had been left behind by the previous nurse. On their way out, they went into the patient area, probably accidentally when looking for the exit. The first that we knew of the intruders was on hearing a commotion and yelling coming from the distal end of the trailer. The Nursing Officer awoke suddenly, to see these faces peering down at her. Startled, she let rip with her vocal cords. By then, we were all fully awake, ready for action. The young boys made off in a hurry. After a quick look around the premises, we noticed the cupboard door was open and realized there had been alcohol pilfered. The two of us went in pursuit, but they had had ample time to disappear by the time we got dressed. We did find, in an old abandoned building, some broken glass and fresh blood, but never found the culprits, nor did we have anyone in mind as suspects.

When morning came, we were admonished by the supervisor for leaving our door open and cautioned to keep it locked at all times from thereon in. The open door policy existed in many places I had lived in the north, and although reticent about this arrangement at first, I accepted this just as those before me had. I had considered it safe with the low crime rate.

The visiting person was very fussy. It was an annoyance to us when she arrived on the scene. It was just a matter of time until she moved chairs in the living room, even a few inches, to where she felt was a better position. As we paid the rent, we objected silently, moving them back again when she was not around. In turn, she would move them again, reprimanding us. We really wished that she would use the provided new accommodation. There she could move every piece of furniture all day long, if she so desired.

We invariably had people dropping in for coffee in the evening. Sometimes I would knit and on this occasion I was busily making a parka for myself and anxious to complete the project. The local "Mountie" was there and one other male. We had served them coffee and cake, and I sewed as we talked. The fellows seemed interested in what I was doing, asking a few questions. When I looked up, the supervisor was discreetly shaking her head, drawing her eyebrows together in an attempt to give me a signal. When I went to replenish the coffee mugs, she quickly followed me to the stove, muttering that I should not be sewing when guests were present. I carried on, not agreeing with her thought. She failed to recognize that I was off-duty, in my home, performing a recreational activity. If I had stopped every time someone decided to drop in unannounced, I would have achieved little. My artistic endeavours were my relaxation.

Life at Resolute Bay had its up and downs, with intervals of relative quiet, always a pleasant respite from the more gruelling times. The team had arrived with the portable machine to carry out chest x-rays and a tuberculin testing programme. It was like a meeting of old friends, having known the team members from my days at Baker Lake. The nursing colleague who accompanied them stayed with us. It wasn't long before she found herself being a participant at our clinic. The men in the crew occupied the new trailer.

Approximately one hundred and twenty miles northeast of Resolute Bay, at the southern tip of Ellesmere Island, lies the small community of Grise Fiord. It is just north of the 76th parallel and close to the North Pole. How, I asked myself, could anyone live in this barren, desolate landscape? Nevertheless, a small group of ninety Inuit eked out a living in such adverse conditions. There was a small school and one policeman. For what purpose he was located there, I am not sure. Being such a small community it was unlikely that crime would ever occur. Then, of course, there was a grocery store where staples could be bought to augment their diet of fish, seal meat and caribou.

There was a mobile home unit at Grise Fiord in which to carry out clinical procedures. A female Inuk acted as lay dispenser, serving the health needs of the people. Anything of a more serious nature was taken care of by the nurse at Resolute Bay. I had made this trip a short time before, and I would have to admit that although it was very isolated, it had great beauty. I visited during the twenty-four hours of daylight period and I marvelled at seeing the sun at two o'clock in the morning. The calm sea reflected the surrounding mountains like a giant mirror. Here and there, chunks of ice floated past. The birds chirped, and from time to time I was made aware of activities in the water. The seals would surface, and every so often I could hear the splashing sounds made by the fish jumping and see the wide circle of ripples left behind. As I walked along the shore, there was evidence of previous seal and walrus hunts. The head of one walrus was missing, the remaining carcass left to rot. Probably the ivory tusks were used for carvings, which ultimately would be sold in shops far removed from its origins. Enjoying the beauty of their purchase the buyer would never witness the gory remains of the animal. With the sale funds, the carver would have bought food staples and more ammunition for his rifle for the next hunting trip. Enjoying the tranquillity of my surroundings made me feel once more that in spite of the harshness of the winters, the

Inuit had something special here, a peace that so often can be envied when compared to the noise, traffic congestion and air pollution in our cities.

A medical student was spending the summer at Grise Fiord, and it was from him I received a call for assistance. A patient was quite ill, and required airlifting. I flew in there to lend support to the student and to escort the client back to Resolute Bay. From there the patient would be flown to the hospital at Frobisher Bay, escorted by a nurse that had been sent in. Every detail had been coordinated and the transfer went without a hitch.

With the patient safely on board the aircraft and on his way now to hospital, I headed back home. It was late afternoon, and I was ready to relax. However, at the clinic, the x-ray team nurse was overjoyed to see me. There had been another emergency in my absence and Lee, my nursing colleague, had taken off in a hurry. My friend, during her brief stay there, had been left to man the clinic. She abhorred this type of work. Not everyone was cut out for this way of life, and I could appreciate her fears.

Lee did not have a pleasant experience on her trip. Apparently there was a young man who, I believe, worked on the Dew Line and was on his own. We understood later that he had been feeling depressed with the isolation, although there may have been other contributing factors, unknown to us. He had made radio communication with the base. An aeroplane would have been sent in to take him out, but due to poor visibility the pilot was unable to take off. At some point there was no further radio contact, and the communicators feared the worst. When the weather had cleared, Lee flew out to the destination, only to find that the fellow had shot himself and was found lying outside. According to the report given to me, it appeared as though part of one leg had been gnawed at. The assumption was that this had been done by a polar bear.

I came in contact, at the clinic from time to time, with men from the base. Some were having marital problems. They worked long hours without a great deal of diversion through other activities when work was done. In these empty moments, one did come face to face with one's self and all the realities of life. If people had hoped to run away from their problematic lives they had left behind, they were sadly mistaken, as the north was not a panacea for all ails.

Lee was given the opportunity of going on a seal hunt with the Inuit. I would not have relished that experience. On her return she told us that the fresh liver of the newly killed seal was offered to her. It was considered a delicacy and an honour to be given this. I felt a little bilious at the very thought, and had it been offered to me, I may well have insulted my host by refusing to sample.

There were numerous reprieves from the work routine, entertaining our friends with a meal being one. Thanks to the generous food allowance given to us by the government, we were able to provide sumptuous meals without further out-of-pocket expenditure. Fresh shrimp was often on the menu as a starter, followed by Cornish hens and wild rice. Of course one cannot forget the filet mignon. Lee, being from Hong Kong, taught me how to make wanton soup. We would sit at the kitchen table, patiently folding meat into the wanton wrappers which she had brought with her. Next, I learned how to make a good chicken fried rice.

As well as cooking skills to be learned, I was called upon to do haircuts of some male friends. I had become adept at using a razor comb, having to keep my own hair trimmed in the absence of a hairdresser. At least, I felt I was adept until I went to a beauty parlour when out on a patient escort trip. The hairdresser said in a dismayed tone "Who cut your hair? What a mess!" Sheepishly, I had to admit that it was me.

Looking back on those years, it was a busy life, full of the unexpected, demanding in every way, but very fulfilling. We shared a camaraderie, both in the workplace and in our home.

As it started to turn colder, I was challenged to sleep out on the tundra, in a sleeping bag all night. I surprised myself when I agreed, as I had never really been a camper or girl guide. With a male friend, I walked a short distance from the Nursing Station where we set up our sleeping bags. Both of us had the Arctic down type. We brought along a Coleman stove in order to make tea to wash down the sandwiches we had packed with us. Under the open sky and fresh air I slept very well. At least I could lay claim to having slept under the stars in the Arctic.

Back at my home base the next night, I had to admit I much preferred the comfort of my own bed to sleep in, and without disturbance, but that was too much to hope for. Duty called and this time an Inuk lady came to the clinic acting rather frightened, seeking refuge from her husband. He was, she said, chasing her with a gun, and had been drinking. I took her inside and made tea. Being a Scottish lass I believed a cup of tea to be great in many of those circumstances. There were no further developments and after a while she ventured home, the whole episode ending quietly. The Inuit in Resolute Bay, unlike their counterparts at Baker Lake, allowed alcohol into the settlement. It was also readily available at the base camp bar.

The winter days had now set in and the subzero temperatures were back again. Summer, it seemed, was gone in a flash. We had three months of darkness to face, beginning in November, and we would not see the sun come up again until February. Keeping busy helped the time to pass, but the nature of our work gave us no other option. I did enjoy a good storm once in a while, when the winds would blow and the soft snow drifted higher and higher, making small hills. The metal roof on the mobile home would flap and rattle. The outside conditions were an indicator that business would be slow except for urgent matters. No one wanted to stir outside, which meant an extra half hour in bed for us. On occasion, we would not be able to open our door, due to the drifting snow packing tightly against it. Someone would have to dig us out from the other side by making a tunnel to our door. In the distance were the huskies, huddled down in the snow with their noses tucked under their tails to keep warm. From time to time they would stretch and shake off the layer of snow covering their coats.

One afternoon, an older gentlemen from the base was brought in with severe chest pain. I had known him as a friend for some time, and he had been a guest at the Nursing Station for a meal on occasion. A heart attack seemed to be the obvious diagnosis, but without the back-up of blood work and an electrocardiogram, one could not be one hundred percent certain. We did not take chances and decided to airlift him. It was Lee's turn for escort duty, but the gentleman insisted that I accompany him, as he felt more secure with someone he knew.

Arrangements were promptly made. Getting an aircraft for medical purposes was easier in Resolute Bay than it had been at Baker Lake. This was due to us having an airport and planes in the hangars. A pilot was invariably available at short notice. The same procedures were in effect, taking a sleeping bag, food and dressing very warmly. It was essential to pay attention to these details and not run off with inadequate equipment, believing the pilot will get you there safely. Weather elements had to be acknowledged.

The aeroplane would not be going to Frobisher Bay due to inclement weather, but instead would land at Yellowknife. We came down en route, at Cambridge Bay, for refuelling and to take another patient on board. The nurses were at the landing strip and I was able to at least confer with them with regard to my client's condition. When there is concern for a human life, another colleague's input is very encouraging. My friend was in great pain, requiring more morphine in transit. Although he was on oxygen, his colour remained poor, and he became increasingly restless.

Many thoughts pass through the mind when travelling on a plane, accompanying someone so sick. Where one thought ends, a new one quickly takes over. Will the patient make it to the hospital? Will he survive after, and what if he dies now before my eyes? There was a feeling of helplessness, knowing that at several thousand feet in the air, with only basic equipment available, the chances of successful resuscitation were negligible. You are alone because the pilot has his own concerns navigating his craft. Very seldom was there a co-pilot on board. You look down on the bleak landscape with only snow and more snow on the horizon. The barrenness is never ending, and you try to imagine what you would do if you came down in the middle of nowhere due to a storm or mechanical failure. Logic passes through your mind. You would build a snow house and radio for help, and you envision the pilot as your saviour, because he must know what to do. The emergency rations on board will, you hope, sustain all until help arrives. You do not see a hopeless scene, nor believe you would not survive in the event of a crash. Perhaps, if the human mind did not focus in this way we would never have had the courage to fly, sail or set foot on any mechanized vehicle, or indeed, embark on any type of adventure.

To my relief, the trip came to an end. I safely discharged my client into the care of the hospital personnel. I stayed overnight at the residence and in the morning I visited my friend before flying home. The staff confirmed he had suffered a bad heart attack but had a comfortable night and would survive.

A similar route from Spence Bay to Yellowknife was taken on the fateful night of November 8th 1972, by Nurse Judith Ann Hill. She was escorting patients to the same hospital. Judy had in her care an Inuk teenager, suspected of having an appendicitis, and a pregnant Inuk woman. Sadly, they never made it.

Judith Hill was a British, trained nurse who served the Inuit community at Spence Bay, on the Boothia Pensulia, in the Arctic. Two patients required hospitalisation and were first flown from Spence Bay to Cambridge Bay with the intent to carry on to the Stanton Hospital in Yellowknife. The first leg of the journey completed, the patients were taken to Cambridge Bay Nursing Station until further arrangements could be made. Norman Hartwell was to be the pilot for the medical evacuation, his aircraft being the faster out of a choice of two. The aeroplane crashed in the darkness and Judy was killed. Some time later, I understood, the pregnant woman also died. The young Inuk boy survived a while, but unfortunately died before rescue came. The pilot was the lone survivor. News flashed around the world of the event and his survival, with particular focus on the fact that he had eaten part of the nurse's body in order to live during the thirty-two days. It must have been a gruesome sight for the rescuers to embrace. From my time in the Yukon Territory and at Baker Lake, I knew one of the police constables who was designated to accompany the bodies to Edmonton for autopsies.

Much has been written about this air crash by people with more knowledge of the complete circumstances and it is not my intent to expound on this matter, nor to make judgement. The point I wish to illustrate is that aeroplane crashes have occurred, taking the lives of patients, nurses and pilots. Perhaps not enough praise and recognition is given to those who are faced with the decision-making process when dealing with human life in these northern hemispheres, and the personal risks involved.

Although the plane crash did not take place until two months after my departure from the Arctic, it has always struck a cord within me. I had travelled a similar route to Judy, only I came from Resolute Bay which was further away, escorting my patient to Yellowknife, not so long before her demise. On hearing of the crash, I thought, "There, but for the grace of God go I."

The aspect of cannibalism was quite a topic in many quarters, with some people feeling revulsion. I have always felt that none of us really knows what we would do when faced with a need for survival. In the comfort of a centrally-heated home, a full belly and people all around, it is not easy to surmise the abject misery that must befall the victims of a downed aircraft, facing cold, darkness, hunger and despair, not knowing if they will ever be rescued. That unknown factor must have been a mental torment.

I found myself once more in the presence of my supervisor, visiting at Resolute Bay. The moving around of my furniture was, this time, the least of my concerns. My "boss" had other plans. Immunizations were high on the priority list with my employers. Being a treatment centre, there was not always an opportunity to carry this out, time being utilized to full capacity in many other ways. Try telling that to the bureaucracy in Ottawa who, in my opinion, were not in touch with the reality of our circumstances. It is so easy to sit at a desk, pushing paper, where all around you is normality as we know it, with a seven-and-a-half hour workday schedule, coffee breaks and lunch on time. Low statistics on a report that showed a number of clients not fully immunized, are easily remedied. Send a memo to the Zones, directing a greater thrust in that area of health. Of course, at the Nursing Station the workday routine can be easily disrupted by emergencies. At these times, intense work is involved. Nurses know well the crumpled look, dark shadows under the eyes, pale face, all remnants of make-up beautification long faded away, hair in much need of a brushing. There is a need for some food, because you have worked through the whole day, evening and night, with time only to snatch a coffee. Some of these clinics had meals prepared, but I was not so fortunate. They say you cannot teach an old dog new tricks, but if ever I should return to the north, this old dog would gravitate to new and easier ways. Perhaps with age comes knowledge.

An example of unorthodox workings occurred when my supervisor heard that a family were out on the land and the two young children, not yet school aged, were in need of immunization. She found out where their geographical location was, and then decided that if they could not come to us then we would go to them. With that in mind, a journey across the sea ice was planned to take the clinic to the family. Being the senior nurse I was the one chosen to go with her.

Plans were under way. My job was to prepare my little black bag with the necessary vaccines, needles, syringes, medicines for fever, skin medications, antibiotics and the like. As there was no communication with the family, we did not know what state of health we would find those individuals in. The supervisor made travel arrangements with the caretaker of our facility, an older man, and also a younger man from the village. Both were hunters and knowledgeable about travel on the land. We packed canned food rations and the caretaker's wife baked bannock for us. Some extra clothing was essential, should any articles become wet. The trip would not be with the traditional dog team, but rather by a skidoo pulling a Qamutik, passengers and equipment. The travel time was set for two days later.

I stepped outside to test the temperature. It was cool and the skies were overcast, but then it was still June in the Arctic. The journey could not be delayed, as in the near future the break up of the sea ice would occur. I asked repeatedly, "Is the ice safe?" "Yes, yes!", was the reply from the Inuit guides, while laughing at my worried look. I hastened back inside to dress for the occasion. I left nothing to chance. First the "long johns", then slacks and on top a pair of heavy wind pants. For the top attire, a polo necked sweater, then a heavy wool sweater that I had knitted for living in those climes. Finally, a heavy parka made of duffel material and covered with an outer shell of cotton and polyester to keep out the icy wind. I couldn't forget my warm furry bonnet, which when donned, made me look like a member of a Scottish pipe band. Lastly, a pair of duffel gloves, also covered with an outer shell. I wore sunglasses, the glare from the snow being quite irritating to the eyes. After a generous application of an emollient to my face and lips, I was ready. Well, at least, I thought I was ready for this trip into the unknown horizon. I really shudder now, when I think about the venture, but youth knows no restraints and seldom envisions a catastrophic situation.

The arrangements for travel were that I would accompany the young hunter, his wife and newborn baby on their Qamutik, while my boss would travel with the caretaker on another. The Qamutiks each had a box built and secured on top of the sled, in which we sat. This was a comfortable arrangement for the long journey. The box was lined with caribou furs for warmth. We set off to Somerset Island, situated in the region of forty nautical miles or more southeast of Resolute Bay.

The landscape was miles and miles of -snow and ice-covered land and sea. At times the two skidoo parties were far apart, each driver choosing his own path. The sun began to shine through, giving a sense of warmth and well being. The frozen crystals beneath us glinted like diamonds. Here and there were footprints in the snow of the arctic fox and later, we saw the indented tracks of the polar bear. I hoped, on the one hand, to see this animal in all its majesty within its own domain, but at the same time, I felt a little apprehensive over our safety, should a confrontation occur. The men were armed with rifles and would not have hesitated to fire should we be endangered. There was a high density of polar bears near to Beechey Island.

We made our first stop and reluctantly, we all extricated ourselves from the warmth of the fur-lined box in order to enjoy a mug of tea. The men had a small primus stove to boil the water we carried. We stood around on the ice, making friendly conversation in between sips of the brew and eating the bannock. Our guide's wife had gone to great pains to provide us with an ample supply of the bannock to eat. It was neatly done in coils and had been deep-fried, giving it a lovely flavour. It was an easy food to pack for travelling. Without further ado, everything was packed away. Those requiring relief did so, with each of us turning our heads in respect of privacy.

The monotonous sound of the skidoo engine, accompanied by the swishing sound of the sled runners, was hypnotic. No other sounds were heard. No conversations, just silence, with each of us deep in our own thoughts. Suddenly, a shout breaks the silence. What can the matter be? There was some open water ahead, a large crack in the ice creating a channel, and a seal had just been observed at the surface. The machines were stopped. The men proceeded forward with their rifles at the ready. They waited in anticipation for the seal to surface again, as surely he would. I prayed that the seal would hurry away and not return. They waited patiently. Without warning, the sound from a discharging gun was heard. It is was all over for this beautiful seal. I did not want to know of the deed but this was their way of life, and it was the responsibility of the hunter to sustain his family with food in the traditional way, handed down over the centuries. I didn't want to witness any of it, but how could I not? The bright red blood on the white virgin snow was very obvious, particularly as the carcass had to be loaded onto the sled. Thankfully, it was not placed on the one I occupied.

A large long gap in the ice had to be navigated around. To me, it was an impossible and scary feat. I was all for going home. To the Inuit, this was not a major problem. Undaunted, they first unhitched the skidoos from the Qamutik. We had to lighten the load by removing ourselves. Individually, the men brought the skidoos around behind the sleds, and with a fully revved motor, they nudged the sleds forward so as to suspend them across the gap. We were instructed to climb back into the Qamutik from the rear, and in this manner, we were ferried across the gap. As we sat there I could not bear to look down at the hole beneath us. From a distance, to get momentum, the skidoos, in full throttle, charged like mad bulls, flying across the gap and landing safely. Next, the skidoos were hitched again to the front and as the drivers drove forward, the Qamutik followed. All on board again and we were off. I was feeling a little unhinged with that episode and concerned should we encounter more gaps that might be wider and deeper, especially on the return journey. Another day or so would allow the ice to disintegrate more.

How these men were able to navigate in this desolation, without maps or compasses, remains a mystery to me, as the land and sea mass all appeared the same. As we continued on our way, I was startled to see, looming before us, a large mound of reddish brown rock which appeared circular in shape from our vantage point. The rock face had many convoluted contours and seemed to emanate from the sea. I asked my guide to slow down so that I could photograph it. This rock mass was to have significance for me later. After a tiring eight hours of travel in a cramped, but warm box, we finally reached our destination.

A male in his thirties came forward to greet us with a questioning look on his face at our appearance at his camp. He was quickly joined by his wife. We were led to their tent and made very welcome. The children were lying asleep on caribou furs, quite unaware that soon they would be disturbed unceremoniously, to have a needle given, to ward off diphtheria, whooping cough and tetanus. One couldn't help but wonder, if we had left them alone, whether they would have been perfectly alright. There, in the middle of nowhere, in a tent, was a Singers hand operated sewing machine, which the woman was using to repair a tent. She was making good use of her time on the land. Outside was a child's modern tricycle and some toys. It was hard to comprehend the meshing of the two cultural ways in a nomadic setting. On the one hand living primitively with hardships, and on the other with some modern conveniences.

The men set about putting together the nurses' tent. The guides and the other family would all share the larger one. While they did this, I was instructed to carry out the immunizations right away. It was two o'clock in the morning, and all I wanted to do was to have some sleep. I wondered what this poor mother must have thought about this intrusion. I look back at some situations, and I think, "What a nerve we had, to intrude into their lives in this manner and uninvited". It must have appeared to the Inuit to be a thoughtless action, even although done in the name of health care. In the zealous attempts to provide care and protection against disease, there was such a thin boundary line that could be overstepped. Their lives and culture had been changed, although they did not ask for it to be so. Now that their lifestyle had been altered, it would be difficult to go back entirely to the old ways.

The children now had their injections given, with only a whimper as the sharp needle pierced the skin. A cuddle, some reassurance and soon they were back in slumber-land. Our mission was completed. All in the camp seemed to be in good health.

I trudged off to the tent, where my boss had a pot of soup heating on the primus stove. That, along with cheese and crackers, was very welcome. Feeling sated, I climbed into my sleeping bag for only a few hours of sleep. I spent a restless night and before I knew it, it was time to eat a small bowl of porridge with a lukewarm beverage before returning homeward.

I stuck my head out of the tent door to get a gulp of pure fresh air. Close by was the dog team and every so often, individually and collectively, they would give the husky howl. I approached the dogs cautiously in order to pet them, some being friendlier than others. At the head of the trace line, one husky was leaping about, wagging his tail in excitement. I guess he recognized my scent or voice because this was the dog that I had nursed back to health. It truly gave me an inner warm feeling to know he was safe, well and the lead animal. I hugged him over and over as he licked my face in affection. As I turned to leave, he gave me a long throaty howl, as though to say he was sad at our parting. The owner was not the original one I had known.

At what point of Somerset Island we were located, I did not know. We meandered across the ice, sticking to areas which were thicker, so that the distance might have been greater than I realized. By not travelling in a direct line, we positioned ourselves close to nearby Devon Island. It was not as though we were bound for a specific point on a map other than our final destination. It was to me the middle of no man's land. The Island was named after Somerset County, in England, by yet another British naval explorer, William Edward Parry, who discovered it in the 1800s.

At first I was not sure about this intended trip, but when I look back, I am eternally gratefully for the opportunity I was given, and for having the good sense to accept. This was the land where famous explorers had ventured. One of the most well known of these explorers was Sir John Franklin, who was born in Lincolnshire, England, on April 16th, 1786. He enrolled at age fourteen in the navy and in 1805, he served in the Battle of Trafalgar. Much has been documented about this rear admiral/explorer whose aim was to find the Northwest Passage. Many before him had tried and failed to find the seaway connection between the Atlantic and Pacific Oceans, thus accessing the Orient in a more expedient manner. At the age of fifty-nine he led an ill-fated expedition into the icy waters of the Arctic, in May, 1845. The expedition consisted of two ships, each made of sturdy timbers, thought to be able to sustain the elements of the subzero Arctic weather and the dangers of crushing ice. Franklin captained the ship Erubus and Captain Crozier was at the helm of the ship, Terror. There was a total of one hundred and twenty eight men and officers aboard the ships. It must have been an awesome adventure for most of those men, to leave their loved ones and set sail from the shores of England and all that was familiar to them. They were voyaging into a distant continent, where previously, failures to navigate a passage had been experienced.

On reaching the Arctic waters at Baffin Bay, Franklin entered into Lancaster Sound where his ship was last sighted by a Scottish whaler in July 1845, never to be seen again. He circumvented Cornwallis Island and reached Beechey Island where he and his crew wintered. Three of the crew died there. In 1986, Dr Owen Beattie lead an anthropological team to the Arctic and exhumed the bodies of the same three seamen. Specimen sampling, x-rays and autopsies were performed to establish the cause of death in those individuals, who at that time had been dead for one hundred and forty years. The conclusion was that the lead used to seal the cans, containing their food supply, had undoubtedly contributed to their demise, by weakening them, making the men susceptible to the ensuing tuberculosis. Dr Beattie and John Geigor give an enlightened account of their findings in their book and video tape documentary, "Frozen In Time."

Reading about the Franklin expedition created a stirring within me to consider putting down on paper an account of my life as an northern nurse. Although I was never interested in writing about my Arctic experiences, my brother believed that I had something to contribute. He was the catalyst that spurred me on in my writing endeavours. However, the more I read about the many explorers of the Northern Hemispheres, the more I realized that I was one of the few women privileged to have travelled in areas which had been explored in earlier centuries, with the place names entered into the annals of history.

My excitement mounted as I followed Franklin's journey on the map. I was stationed at Resolute Bay on Cornwallis Island, and as I went southeast to Somerset Island, crossing Barrow Strait on the way, I had not been aware that the mound of red rock I had snapped a picture of was Cape Riley, on Devon Island. I learned later that I had been approximately within a mile or so of Franklin's winter camp and the graves of the three crew members at Beechey Island nearby. Had I known of the existence of the burial ground, I would have diverted the journey to view this historical site. My travel there took place in 1971.

Franklin and his crew travelled southwest to King William Island. It was there that Sir John Franklin and twenty-four of his crew met their deaths, in 1847. The remainder of the crew continued on. In due course, they too died. It is written that cannibalism was resorted to by the starving men and the site where they died is aptly named Starvation Cove.

As there were no survivors nor a documented account relating all the facts, we have to rely on historians and anthropologists to piece together the saga. We can individually allow ourselves to imagine the plight of these men, far from home, cold, facing the severity of the Arctic climate, and suffering hunger pangs that ultimately drove them to eat their shipmates. The sickness that pervaded their bodies perhaps caused them to hope death would come quickly.

History tells us that Franklin's second wife sent a search mission in 1847 to find out what had happened to her husband and his crew. For twelve years, search expeditions were launched to find out what became of them, but to no avail.

The return journey to Resolute Bay was similar, except more water was showing on the top of the ice and a few more gaps were evident. The guides were able to steer around these and to avoid crossing them as before. We met a caravan of twelve travellers, also on skidoos, heading in a different direction. Some were Inuit while others were white men from our community. We made a brief stop to greet one another and then continued homeward.

Vacation time was rolling around again, and I had to make a decision whether to stay in Resolute Bay or move on. I really enjoyed the life, but to some degree the work and the landscape were confining. In July, I handed in my resignation, the termination effective in September. Following my holiday I would seek a posting in another location, less isolated, but remaining with Health and Welfare.

CHAPTER TEN
BELLA BELLA

I was ready for a change in nursing duties when I was offered a new posting with a different concept. Nursing Station life was rewarding, dramatic, even scary at times, especially with the lack of other supporting medical staff. It was then I decided to try a Health Centre which was more orientated to promoting wellness to the inhabitants of the community, as opposed to treating sickness.

My submission for such a transfer brought me to the small community of Bella Bella, on the west coast of British Columbia. Having made my way to Campbell River, on Vancouver Island, I boarded an aeroplane to take me the ninety-six nautical miles to my destination. There was a brief stopover at Port Hardy, allowing just enough time to switch to an amphibian aircraft. There were no roads into the community and access was by air or sea. At that time there was no airport and so our landing would be on the water. There were four other passengers, one of them being my male Nursing Supervisor, accompanying me.

During the trip, which passed very quickly, he reinforced the fact that my accommodation would be for me only, and any visiting Health and Welfare personnel would be accommodated at the hospital or nurses' residence when the need arose. This was very important to me. I had considered the fact that I was now into my fifteenth year of nursing, and apart from one brief interlude, I had always lived in residential institutes, having to share space with others. It was now time to have a private life. His reassurances were based on the emphasis I had placed on this matter at headquarters before departure. I was by no means antisocial, but at times it had become tedious at the Nursing Station to accommodate and be expected to cater to medical and nursing personnel on their visits, especially after an extra heavy day at work, and having to be on call.

Small aircraft flew lower than the large commercial ones, and from the small windows I could clearly see the mountains all around and, below, a vast expanse of sea. It was now the month of October. Looking down one could see the whitecaps on the water. It was very windy outside and every so often we would experience turbulence. Close to shore and extending way beyond were the magnificent evergreen forests. As the plane started to gradually drop in altitude in preparation for landing, I felt excitement ripple through my body. Lower and lower we went, and as we slowly approached the dock I could see many small fishing vessels tied up alongside, all painted in different colours.

As I deplaned I saw a small group of Natives standing on the dock. It was not a welcoming committee for me, but rather curious bystanders with time on their hands watching idly the comings and goings from the village. The community were aware that a new nurse was due and I could sense the subtle scrutiny on my arrival.

My trunks with most of my belongings were to arrive by boat later that week, as were my meat and basic groceries supplies from Vancouver. Before departure and as instructed by the department, I had selected cuts of meat, fresh vegetables and the like from a major grocery store on the mainland. They would, for a price, see to the shipping. This was one aspect that differed from my Arctic living. Many food items could not be purchased locally, nor was there as much selection for individual tastes. Those available were often costly and it was considered worthwhile paying the shipping freight charges.

Carrying the two suitcases containing my immediate needs, we walked a short distance from the dock towards my new home. Attached was the clinic, office and waiting room. My boss pointed to the building as we got nearer and I was immediately impressed. It was a very large, old, wooden-style building two storeys high, leaning towards a Victorian design, with a bay window in the living quarters and dormer windows upstairs. It was painted white with a dark green trim around the windows and on the door. I chuckled inwardly with delight when I first glimpsed it, and thought to myself that I had really hit the jackpot this time, and it was all mine for the duration of my stay, which was as long as I or the Native people wanted.

There was a long ramp from the roadway leading to the front door and just as we made our way up it, a young man with long blond hair, metal rimmed glasses and a bashed looking hat on his head hurried past us, pushing his lightweight motorbike down the ramp. On this passing encounter, the thought struck me that he looked like the singer, John Denver. We meekly stood aside to let him pass with neither party uttering a word.

Once inside the door, we found ourselves in the waiting room area with, oddly enough, several people sitting there. I was a little perplexed as I hadn't planned to hold clinics for at least several days in order to get settled. A few more steps forward and we entered the office. As I looked around I noticed a large television set sitting on top of the filing cabinet. The power was on but only a white snowy effect was showing on the screen with background sounds of static electricity. My instant reaction was that I would not have television, or if I did, the reception was going to be awful. My eyes then lighted on metal containers strewn about the desk top, stuffed full of what appeared to be medical records. Still silent, we entered the adjoining sitting room. At an instant glance it was obvious that a great deal of cleaning would be required. In the corner stood an empty table which was obviously meant for the television, judging from the way the surrounding dust formed a square. On the coffee table, covering the entire surface, were brochures of a religious nature. Through the adjoining door we stepped into the kitchen. It was vast and typical of the old farmhouse style. As I entered the room, my jaw dropped in amazement, for there in front of me and all around me were denture moulds. Dotted here and there were already completed denture sets, flashing pearly white teeth set in artificially-made pink gums. They seemed to be grinning in a mocking manner in my direction. A gentleman, obviously the sculptor of these essential food masticators, hastily left the room without a word. Almost simultaneously a heavy-set woman came from another room. Smiling, she said she had just thrown in some laundry to wash. I pushed the door open and saw that both the washing machine and the dryer were in full operation. It was evident by the giant-sized box of washing powder and numerous plastic bags, which I presumed were full of soiled clothing, that she was washing for several people.

By now I could feel the blood vessels in my head and neck pulsating strongly. I was about to erupt! Trying to keep a lid on my feelings, I turned to speak to my boss who looked equally bewildered. "You said I could have this place to myself! What Is going on?", I asked in a voice quavering with emotion. Sheepishly he replied that it was a mystery to him also. Because the previous nurse had been gone several months, he had assumed the place was empty.

Our attention was turned to a drilling sound. Following in that direction, we entered a small room which I learned would be the clinic area where I would conduct immunizations. In front of us a patient sat upright in a dental chair, mouth gaping and all the paraphernalia arranged around him for the necessary work in hand. Between drilling sounds and those of the patient's mouth being suctioned, the dentist introduced himself, mentioning by way of interest that he was a Seventh Day Adventist dentist. He stated that he and his family, as well as the denturist and his wife, were occupying the upstairs. He went on to say that I could have the downstairs bedroom which was directly across from the clinic room where he was working. The bedroom could be accessed either through this clinic door or by one leading off the sitting room. I vaguely heard him say that he also worked on Saturdays. This, of course, would be on my day off and I would be awakened to the accompaniment of his dental drills, ghastly suctioning sounds and no doubt the shrieks of some terrified client.

I had heard enough! That was the last straw! I was an employee of the government, paying the rent for this house, with a promise of me being the sole occupant. This individual, a private practitioner from the United States, in the field of dentistry, was now allocating me my room. Irate and disgusted, I left the clinic room with my boss in hot pursuit. "That's it! I am leaving on the next plane", I announced. I was very angry at the invasion of my privacy and what I perceived as being hoodwinked. I had no intention of letting the bureaucracy off with this. It was bad enough having to share my dwelling unexpectedly, but to have all this religious literature scattered throughout the living quarters and office was too much. Freedom of religious beliefs was one thing, but living surrounded by it was quite another matter. Who else would have been expected to pay rent, sharing not only with these families but with the patients too, amidst noise and debris, particularly on a day off?

My supervisor could see my distress and related to it, whereupon he immediately contacted a higher level of authority within our department. When his telephone conversation ended he looked well satisfied, with the ensuing outcome fully supporting my sentiments. It was simply one of those situations where, due to lack of communication, the right hand did not know what the left one was doing. The facility had been without a health nurse for seven months. Someone in the higher echelons knowing this, gave sanction for the use of the centre to the dental team.

The verdict from the telephone conversation was that the team had to leave the following day. They were none too pleased with this decision and after my boss left to settle into his accommodation at the hospital, the dentist asked me tersely where I thought he should go. Understanding the question fully, I was sorely tempted at that point to tell him precisely where! Having a proper upbringing prevented me from doing so.

I had done Public Health Nursing duties at the Nursing Stations but on a much smaller scale, and now I had to set about scheduling and implementing the various programmes as set down by the Health and Welfare guidelines. It could have been simplified if the previous nurse were there to discuss and guide me in this new setting. A gap of seven months between the staff was a considerable loss to the community, in terms of immunizations lagging behind. Other related preventative services were also at a disadvantage. With all the clutter in the office space, clinic area and living quarters it seemed like a huge and insurmountable task at first.

My boss left the next day, as did the dental team, never bothering to clean the facility after their usage. They had managed to gain space at the local school for their dental practice, acquiring an empty teacher's house for accommodation.

There was some criticism within the community, particularly from the school Principal, believing that I had wronged the dental crew by not allowing them to stay with me. Not long after, I began receiving sympathetic acknowledgement from him and other individuals, whose lives became disrupted by the dentist and his occupation of their facilities, which were to be on a long-term basis.

The sequel to this scenario occurred quite some time later. I had a visit from the Royal Canadian Mounted Police, who were located in a place called Ocean Falls. They wanted some information about the dentist using the Health Centre. I thought it odd as the matter was an internal one and had been resolved.

It was explained to me that the dentist had brought his boat from the United States and it was to be used as his accommodation and his dental office. It had to do with the boat usage and applied taxes. He obviously was not using it as intended.

Living nearby was a native woman, hired by the previous nurse to do the cleaning of the Health Centre. I promptly called upon her to thoroughly clean the place while I set about organizing the office and medical files. I had an appointment to meet with the Chief and Band Council that afternoon so that I could introduce myself to them. This was the politically correct thing to do and their support in the delivery of health programmes was paramount to the success. Accompanying me to the meeting was the Community Health Representative, a jolly native lady with whom I would be working closely. In the ensuing months, she helped me greatly, both in my duties and to settle in, carrying out at the same time her own programmes that she was trained to do. Without her help my progress would have been slow. Being from that area she toured me around the village, introducing me to clients and advising me of their various health problems.

The meeting was short and congenial. It allowed me to ask for their support, reinforcing my need for cooperation from the community in delivering the programmes. I also gained knowledge from them with regards to different aspects of the community that would involve me, which included a breakdown of the population ages, housing, location of the water source, sewage and garbage disposal, and the various maintenance crews whose services I might require.

My first week went past very quickly. I did not hold clinics immediately but rather was further familiarized with my environment and introduced to the school staff, students, doctor and hospital staff, local Tribal Police and numerous other individuals.

When it came to the nurses in the residence, I was distressed at the cold treatment I was given. Only one nurse visited me and became a close friend. As time passed there was a gradual and distinct thawing in their relationship with me. I found out later that their reservation towards me stemmed from their intense dislike of the previous Health Nurse. It was as though I was expected to prove my worthiness. Fortunately, as time passed, I was well accepted. They became a big part of my social life, even though I lived in a separate home from them. They were employed by the United Church.

The ship had arrived at the dock on Saturday morning and I scurried down to claim my meat supply and personal effects. One of the natives at the dock kindly loaded my trunks onto his truck and delivered them to my home. The rest of the weekend was taken up with unpacking my treasured possessions. With a few pictures on the walls, an ornament placed here and there, it became home, a far cry from the way it had initially looked.

In arranging my schedule, I decided to make the school children the first priority. I would have to bring their immunizations up to date. Each file had to be gone through systematically and the appropriate vaccines had to be ordered.

The population of the community at that time was around twelve hundred, but as well as serving Bella Bella I was also responsible for visits to the lighthouses and two other villages, all being accessible only by plane or boat. I settled in well to the community life and very much enjoyed the independence and scope of the job. I had the flexibility to order a plane and travel to the different communities when I felt there was a need, which became a monthly ritual.

Once things were in order at Bella Bella, I decided to visit Klemtu. This was the home of the Kitasoo Band. I had to fly into this remote settlement, located approximately thirty-eight nautical miles further north and which had two hundred and fifty residents. For this first trip, it was arranged that the local doctor and I would travel together, sharing the aircraft. I attended to public health matters while he held a clinic for the sick.

The air travel was relatively short. Being in a small aircraft we flew fairly low, which enabled us to view the landscapes and seascapes below us. At times I found that when flying over the treetops it was a little bumpy with all the up draughts and down draughts, but passing over the water was less so. It was exciting when the pilot pointed out a school of sperm whales below us. The pilot indicated that landing at Klemtu could be tricky at times depending on weather conditions. The small fishing village lay protected by an island shaped similar to that of a Chinese hat. From the wooden dock we climbed quite a few steps and then followed a long, meandering boardwalk all the way to the Health Centre. Waiting there for us was the Community Health Worker. In these remote areas they acted as lay dispensers in the absence of a doctor or nurse, carrying out a basic health programme.

There was a gathering that night at the Health Worker's home to which we were invited to attend, giving me an opportunity to meet the local residents. Sandwiches were served in abundance with tea and coffee. Each time they brought the tray of food around I would decline, having eaten my fill. I noticed that the others beside me were loading their plates to full capacity. I was a little perplexed by this, believing them to be a bit greedy. As time passed, and I gained knowledge of customs within these communities, I learned that I should not offend my hostess by refusing her hospitality, but rather I should take the sandwiches home. Not understanding the cultural difference, inadvertently I must have offended her, although nothing was said.

This was an overnight trip and I stayed at the Health Centre. The building was a modern, modular structure and situated at the end of the reserve, a little isolated from other homes. On subsequent visits I never cared to stay there alone because of this fact. It had a large living room that doubled as the clinic, two bedrooms, kitchen and bathroom. The furnishings were sparse but adequate for the purpose intended.

The following day we left Klemtu. I had not accomplished much on this trip but the next one would be very different. I had at least familiarized myself as to its geographic position, the layout of the community and what exactly my duties would be.

We arrived at the dock in Bella Bella at suppertime. On the roadway home, we were greeted by a playful young dog. She had the build and markings of a collie with perhaps the influence of some other breed in her genes. I did not realize at first that she belonged to the doctor. He, I learned, had not been a willing owner, but rather had inherited the animal from a previous resident who intended to return for her but never did. This little dog would eventually play a role in my life.

Within a week I made a journey to Rivers Inlet, accompanied this time by the Community Health Worker. This small village, with a population of fifty people, was located south of Bella Bella. The flying distance was a little longer than going to Klemtu. These primary inspections were useful to me in order to meet the lay dispenser, community members, and carry out an inventory of supplies requiring replenishment. Having no nurse for several months meant that many of the items were now depleted. On the flight home we stopped at three lighthouses. It was more of a social visit, finding all the clients healthy and well. No children or pregnant mums were living there that would require my services. Some time later these visits were eliminated as an unnecessary part of my programme.

It was very hard to get patients to attend clinics for prenatal and immunization and most of the work had to be done within the homes. The natives on the different reserves where I worked, over a period of many years, saw the comings and goings of white people and one could not blame them for harbouring mistrust. Often by the time that trust was gained, the nurse moved on. The indigenous people, however, had to start all over again, making the acquaintance of the new personnel and having to accept whoever was sent to them. Nurses, too, came in different packaging, bringing their cultural ways, opinions and training standards. When I look back, perhaps we expected too much of the natives, in asking them to accept our cultural ideologies without putting energy into understanding theirs.

I was informed one evening that some children were at home on their own. With a hospital nursing friend who was visiting me at the time, we went to check out the situation. Indeed, we did find three children, all under the age of six, by themselves. I succeeded in finding the parents, but they were very intoxicated. Leaving the parents to sober up, the two of us went to feed the children. All that we could find in the cupboard was macaroni and cheese, and that is what we prepared for them. I asked the local doctor to let the children stay overnight at the hospital until I could reason with the parents in the morning. He agreed, but only if we attended to the children and did not overload the busy nurses. It was settled. We would bath and tuck them into their cots. Those sweet urchin faces with their big wide brown eyes made me feel sad at the disruption and insecurities they must have felt. Often these young children had to adopt an adult role of caring for younger siblings. When the parents were handed back their children they were neither happy nor grateful for our efforts. The abandonment of their children and the legal consequences were spelled out to them, but I found that the warning fell on deaf ears. The need for a Social Worker was essential and eventually one was employed.

Three miles across the water from us was a small group of non-native people who were involved with the fish cannery business. Not being native they were not my responsibility. The community was called Shearwater, so named after the Royal Naval ship which served on the British Columbia coast in the early 1900s. I was approached by a community member, asking if I would agree to immunize their children as they did not have this service provided by anyone else. I agreed readily and it added only a small percentage to my total population. In order to get there, a barge had to transport me. The man at the helm was a Scotsman and the short trip across was enjoyable, particularly having a fellow countryman to converse with. Each month I made telephone contact with him and arranged a time for pick up and return. I would be waiting at the dock with my little black bag and other necessities, and this rather large, flat-bottomed boat docked long enough to let me hop on board. I enjoyed these excursions, meeting yet another Scottish family living there. They were always my last port of call. Duties done, I would take my leave of them but not before being handed a large piece of smoked British Columbian salmon, wrapped in tin foil. I had to make my way along a rugged trail of bushes to the dock. While waiting for the boat to take me home, I would nibble on this tasty morsel.

After several months I felt well established in my job and comfortable in my home. The house was located on the reservation, with the native people as my neighbours. From my bedroom window on the main floor, I overlooked the United Church and to the left of the window, the local doctor's residence. A little further up the road was the office and home of the tribal policeman, who was the brother of my companion worker. Further along the road was the local school and staff residences. Looking from the front bay window of my house I could see the small hospital which was run by the United Church and across from the hospital was the nurses' home. My other immediate neighbours, who were non-native, consisted of the United Church minister and his wife, a charming and warm hearted couple. There was a second doctor's house nearby but the occupants were occasional locums who came in the absence of the regular doctor. At the far end of the community was a small store and a Pentecostal Church.

Bella Bella was a small island and the inhabited area could easily be walked. The road was a rough, gravel one and only a handful of vehicles were seen. There were rows and rows of little wooden houses, some situated by the water while others were on higher ground. I did not have a vehicle, but with my little black bag in one hand and an insulated one containing vaccines in the other, I made my visitations on foot. At these visits I tried very hard to coax the residents to attend the clinic. Some days went better than others. I worked hard at the job and believed strongly in the health mandate that I had to present to the public and enjoyed immensely the freedom to get on and do the job I was hired to do. The government had to trust in our honesty to carry out our functional role and accept that our monthly report submissions indicating our accomplishments, were correct.

Soon it would be Christmas and before closing down business for the customary two days I flew in once more to Klemtu and Rivers Inlet to hold clinics. Another surprise awaited me at Klemtu. I would be on my own at the clinic this time, or so I thought. Instead of an empty facility, lo and behold the Seventh Day Adventist denture maker, his wife, and one or two others were occupying the place. I gave a quiet inner groan. I decided not to fuss, and perhaps that was just as well as they informed me they would be moving on. I stayed overnight and at six o'clock in the morning, which to me is an ungodly hour to be up, at least for my biological clock, I was awakened by the sound of the vacuum cleaner running over tiled floors. I got up and planned my day. At lunch, as I prepared my sandwich, I was invited to join them. It was hospitable of them, but I didn't relish the soya products on the menu. I returned home the following day.

The festivities were now upon us. The outside of the houses were decorated with lights. Through the windows, from the outside, I could see the trees all lit up and adorned with ornaments and tinsel. Like anywhere else, Christmas was greatly enjoyed. I went out carolling for the first time ever with the minister and a few of the nurses. With flashlights and sheets of music in our hands and wrapped up warmly, our merry little band went from door to door. The village people invited us in here and there and offered donations for the church.

I, along with some of the nurses, had Christmas dinner with the Reverend and his good wife. Afterwards he played the piano and a sing-song ensued. He was a beautiful pianist, and later when I showed an interest in the piano he said that he would willingly teach me to play. I truly did try to be a good student, but somehow at the piano keys, my left hand seemed to want to disassociate from my right hand.

It was during the winter nights that I learned of the terminal illness of one lighthouse keeper's wife. I had not been to visit there for some time. I heard that the hospital nurses were taking turns on their days off to stay with the lady during the night, administering the necessary narcotics and providing the nursing care. Each day the family members were kept busy with her terminal care management and needed some respite from this rigorous task. One night there was a staff shortage and I offered my services.

As arranged, about ten o'clock in the evening, the woman's husband arrived at my home, ready to ferry me across in his boat to the lighthouse. This landmark that was seen as a beacon of light for the ships, to me, this night, appeared dismal and isolated. This was another trip across a body of water I am unlikely to forget. The night was very dark, with no moon and not a star to be seen. Not only was there darkness, but the wind was gusting.

The husband escorted me to the dock where the boat was tied up and I could see it bobbing up and down like a cork. It was made of aluminium and was fitted with an outboard motor. I put on my life-jacket and went on board. I cannot recall the distance to the lighthouse, but perhaps it was three miles. As we made our way across, I heard the waves of the murky water lapping against the boat, interspersed with the sounds of the motor. I put my hand in to feel the water temperature and it was mighty cold. Forward and back, side to side, we rocked in motion. I was quite anxious and feared, with the strong wind, that we might capsize. In the darkness I felt I was in a void with no sense of direction. It seemed like an eternity to our destination. That same fear of water lurked in my mind and perhaps it was as well I could not see the swell clearly. Finally we reached the dock, more than a trifle wet from the spray. The next difficulty encountered was getting out of the boat once docked. It seemed each time I attempted to make the stride onto the floating dock it would part company from the moored boat. Unable to swim, I felt I might lose my footing and disappear into the dark depths never to be recovered. Practically on my hands and knees I made it and I remember thinking I would prefer to stay at the lighthouse all week if I had to, rather than travel on a choppy sea again in such a small vessel.

My patient was very frail, drifting in and out of consciousness. The main thrust of care was to keep her comfortable and free from the awful pain which had wracked her fragile body so often. She had reached a point in her illness that death would be a welcome release for her. Each time I gave her the necessary morphine, I cringed when I inserted the needle into this lifeless body where practically only skin and bone remained. To turn her scrawny frame and see the pain felt by her, was hard to watch. In the morning I bathed her, changed her night attire and repositioned her. With a kiss on her forehead and a gentle squeeze of her bony, limp hand, I took my leave. Her time left would not be long and I did not expect to see her again, even although I was willing to volunteer my time.

Before leaving I spent some time with the daughter who was the main caregiver. So often there is a tendency to forget it is not only the sick person that is suffering. The family dynamics become very disrupted with feelings of guilt, loneliness and despair setting in. She needed to cry with someone other than a family member, and with a nurse the barriers could be let down. Instead of having to put on a stoic front, a show of kindness and understanding allowed the flood gates to open and let the repressed feelings flow out. It was the start of coming to terms with the inevitable loss of her mother. For her, it was more poignant as she was there constantly, while other members came and went from time to time, allowing them to emotionally distance themselves a little from the daily reality of their mother's fragility.

At the time of writing this story there is a great debate as to whether we have the right to end our own abject misery through controlled euthanasia when an illness becomes unbearable. Being in the caring profession, I have reflected many times on this subject. I feel I would not want to be part of finalizing someone's life but I also see beyond. I have witnessed many times the suffering of those individuals with a terminal illness. Their pain is emotional as well as physical, and as yet I cannot draw any definite conclusions other than it becomes a personal issue, each case with its own merits. I do not agree with religious or other strong-voiced groups having the right, particularly when they are not afflicted, to foist their beliefs and judgements on others and indirectly influence the lawmakers. By doing so they criminalize the desires and actions of a sick person. It is a dilemma many of us might face with our own mortality. I have never been a proponent of the belief that God gives us only as much pain as we can bear. For those that support this philosophy, then presumably they would not require the intervention of pain medications but rather, would tolerate that which has been placed on them by a higher power.

The water was calm when I made my way back to the Health Centre and I was ready to get some sleep, the first in twenty-four hours. I learned a day or so later that the lady died but I was glad that I also had been able to give her some comfort.

There were many deaths within the community over the two years I spent there. Some were from natural causes and others from accidents, often alcohol induced. The local pub was located across at Shearwater, which meant that after an evening of pleasurable drinking some natives and Caucasians would return home by boat. Just as my trip was in complete darkness when going to the lighthouse, so often was theirs, with varying sea conditions. Feeling happy after a pleasant social evening would have broken down any sense of caution. Some were not capable of driving a boat with their level of intoxication and accidents resulted. I can recall one such tragedy where three men on their way home collided with a tug boat, resulting in their drowning. After several days the sea gave up its dead and the relatives came to lay claim to the bodies of their loved ones. Because of various family interconnections, the village was thrown into deep mourning at the loss. The husband of my Health Worker was one of the men drowned.

At Bella Bella there were many cultural beliefs surrounding death and customs that were adhered to. As in the Arctic, there were no morticians for embalming a body. A local woman or women previously selected, cared for the body at the time of death. The body was washed and dressed in clothing, sometimes sending to the mainland for a new pair of shoes or jacket. A wake was held which could last two, three or more days, waiting for a casket to arrive. I never attended one of these personally, but had others describe the scenario. However I had decided to attend a wake one evening, but as I reached the door I hesitated to go in. I had to admit to myself that I was going more for curiosity and considered my presence an intrusion on the grieving family. I turned back and went home.

Any entertainment that was scheduled to take place in the village was called off when someone died, in deference to the family. I had known of several deaths occurring in succession, with activities shutting down each time, giving one a sense of isolation with the deathly stillness in the village. Relatives and others like myself in the community made sandwiches for those attending the wake and gave monetary donations to assist with the funeral expenses.

A short time after the funeral, a Potlatch was given by the family. This was a feast which often was held at a time of major life events. Those individuals who had given their services to the family at the time of death were invited to partake. I was privileged to attend such a feast. I had offered to look after the two children belonging to my co-worker and I had them in my care for three days.

As told to me, in observance of their culture, the mother of these children, after hearing of the death of her husband, remained in the same clothing until the day of the funeral. With her baby girl in my care, I asked the mother to bring a change of vest and clothing for her but I was advised not to change the vest until the day of the service.

On the day of the funeral the woman bathed and all clothing was changed, as were the vestments of the children. The clothing was then burned by an elder on behalf of the immediate family. An elder in the community, who could be a relative, also gave guidance and told the woman how long her official mourning period should be, which for her was to be six months. The belief was that the spirit of the dead lingers around for a time. If a widow was to weep too much for the loss of a loved one, she might be advised by the elder not to cry so much as this would make it hard for the spirit to go elsewhere. There existed, I believe, a practical attitude for the living, regardless of cultural belief.

Having readied the baby, I offered the hairbrush to the mother when she came to pick the child up for the funeral, so that she might arrange the child's hair as she liked. She declined and explained as part of the cultural belief she was not allowed, during her mourning time, to touch any sharp objects such as knives, scissors, forks, combs or brushes. The explanation I was given was, that by touching anything sharp would be like taking their loved ones by the scruff of the neck or killing them.

Within two days or so a burning sacrament took place. Household articles that had been used and shared with her spouse were burned. These included kitchen wares, bedding and the like. As part of this ceremony, clothing to be passed on to relatives was smoked, thus giving a blessing.

On the first or second day after the death, the favourite food of the deceased was cooked for his/her spirit and, as part of this ritual, prayers would be offered by the elder. This was done in this particular case at the beach at high tide, due to the fact that death was by drowning. A second time it was done at the graveside. When and where this was done depended on the family.

When I attended the Potlatch, I really did not understand their custom. All three widows were there. The feast was held in a hall where long tables in rows were set attractively for a meal. In another part of the room were gifts for the widows. The settlement feast was given by the in-laws of the widows, usually about two days after the funeral, depending on the wishes of the family. Following the meal, usually of stew meat, each widow stood up and welcomed and thanked everyone for their support and talked about the deceased. The Yilistis group sang a song of mourning. There were many tears shed that day and one could not help being caught up in the emotional atmosphere. The gifts that were given and presented to them were replacement items for the home since many shared items were by now burnt. It almost seemed to me like a wedding shower and a new beginning. The giving was a two-way street, because after receiving their gifts they then called upon various members to come forward to receive a monetary gift from them for services rendered. I was sitting next to a non-native nurse, who by marriage, was a family member of one of the deceased. She whispered to me that I would be called to receive a gift for caring for the children. I whispered back that I didn't want anything. I had only done this as a kindness as anyone would have done. She told me that I had to accept this as refusing would be very offensive to them. In due course my name was called. After a few words of gratitude were expressed to me, I was handed a gift of money from the widow. As it was presented to me she requested that I buy something with the money that would be lasting, and would remind me always of the deceased. With this money I bought a set of good quality stainless steel cutlery which I still have thirty years later and, sure enough, each time I use them I do think of the family. If someone new dines at my table I tell them how I came to be in possession of the attractive cutlery.

At a later date, a potlatch supper is given by the widow as a memorial to the deceased. She chooses the time which, to some degree, revolves around economics. More gifts are presented. I had left the community before this took place, but had I remained, apparently I would have received a lace tablecloth.

To give an in-depth account of the meaning behind the potlatch feast would be too complicated and I do not possess enough knowledge to do the presentation justice. According to one native writer, the word "potlatch" was used by the early Europeans and possibly derived from the Nootka verb Pa-chitle or Pa-chuck, a noun that meant "article to be given." These words were used when articles were given at a public feast. Blankets were used as units of value, as was copper and I observe today that natives in other regions, when having celebrations, often give away blankets.

This sorrowing within the community when deaths occurred, seemed to be brought home to me more so when, in the morning, I opened the bedroom curtains and my view was of the church. In the long window of the church I could see the coffin resting. After funeral services were over the coffin would be borne on the shoulders of men and a long procession of mourners followed, passing closely to the clinic and in front of my sitting room window. The sad entourage slowly made their way to the dock whereupon the body would be taken for burial at Grave Island, a short boat trip away. In the distance I could see the vessel taking the deceased, known to me also, to their final resting place.

There were many happy times and occasionally I went to the local beer dance. It was very lively and as the name would imply, only beer was served, along with sandwiches. I got to know the local doctor well and we would attend this function together but he always managed to be cajoled into taking his turn serving at the bar which usually ended up being for the whole evening. Everyone danced well into the night but I learned quickly that there was a good time to leave the dance hall. A few, who were well tanked, became somewhat rowdy and a few tables and chairs were displaced with the skirmishes, making it easy to slip out amidst all the hubbub.

Bella Bella Indians were a matriarchal society. Traders to the area knew them by their original name of Bil-Billas or Bel-Bellahs and it is believed that the name Bella Bella is derived from this. In the early 1800s the Hudson's Bay Company, at Fort McLoughlin, traded furs with the natives, but eventually the trading post was closed. Here, as in many Indian villages in that period of time, the scourge of smallpox decimated their numbers cruelly. By the1880s a mission and hospital were built.

The native people later became successful fishermen in the commercial market. This was very much in evidence where, at the dock, there were rows of painted boats tied up. There was an air of activity as they tended to their fishing nets and catch. I was kept very generously supplied with fresh salmon, having been given seven or eight fish at one time. Like many others in the village, I wanted to do some canning and have a fish supply for the winter months. My attempts at filleting were terrible and two native ladies came to my rescue. With a quick movement of the wrist they had the job done in record time. They insisted on making me participate in order to learn the method for the future. When I pointed out some wiggly worms on the flesh of the salmon they just laughed and flicked them out with a knife. One lady offered to smoke the salmon for me at her personal smoke house. This would not only give the fish a flavour but would also preserve it. For a half smoke the time was one and a half days in the smoke house and for a full smoke that took three to four days. If the native people wanted to preserve the fish for later then it would take six days.

In the meantime I set about canning the fish. It was cut into strips, salted and placed in sterilized jars. After sealing they were then placed into a pressure cooker for the appointed cooking time. Many of the local people used an open canning bath on the stove in order to cook, but from the literature I read, the pressure cooker would be the safer method to avoid spoilage. Not being too used to these pressure cookers I found it a little intimidating. The temperature would rise to a higher level than required. In order to maintain the necessary level of heat I had to periodically release the safety valve, using a wooden spoon. I would duck each time the cooker hissed and spluttered, keeping an arm's length away. However I had the experience of using a pressure cooker at Baker Lake.

During the salmon season, many of the villagers left Bella Bella and went twenty-five miles southeast to a place called Namu. There was employment at the cannery there which had been in operation since 1893 and was considered one of the largest canneries on the coast of British Columbia. In 1911 the original cannery was rebuilt. There were rows of wooden houses on stilts in the water, all interconnecting with a board walk. Namu is an Indian word meaning "Place of High Winds." The whole coastal area was so beautiful and I was delighted to have yet another location to fly into in order to immunize the children. Once my work for the day at Namu was completed, I would just laze idly on the floating dock waiting for my plane to arrive. It seemed that the sky was so blue each time I travelled there and the water so calm but for the gentle lapping sounds against the dock. Lying there with my face to the hot sun, I could see the birds flying from tree to tree and my eyes would scan the horizon in search of a golden eagle. It was all very tranquil and this was my new-found paradise. Just as I drifted off to nap, I could hear in the distance that all too familiar sound of an engine, the droning becoming louder as the pilot drew nearer to land.

The only negative part of these jaunts was arriving home at six or seven in the evening, unpacking all the paraphernalia that accompanied me and having to cook my evening meal so late. On one of these occasions I discovered, as I set about preparing my meal, that I had run out of propane gas. After talking to the caretaker, who was responsible for the maintenance of the facility, I found out there were no more replacement tanks on our island and that I would have to wait until the following day for the gas to be brought from Shearwater. Meantime, I went to the hospital dining room and managed to find a few leftovers.

The next journey was back again to Klemtu. Most of the trips were for one day only, as I was able to accomplish my work in that time frame. Periodically I did stay a couple of days when I deemed the work to be more extensive. If possible, I invited an off-duty nurse from the hospital to join me. It gave me company in the evening and they, in turn, had a free trip, a change of scenery, and were free to walk about and explore the area while I worked. The local doctor had informed me that a number of children had head lice. I already was aware of the problem, this being part of my job to know. I arrived at the school for the examination of heads. I gave the special shampoo out to most of the pupils and staff as a precaution. When the bell rang for lunch the children ran outside to play. I was horrified to see several of them throw their treatment bottles into the nearby shrubs. How many times this action was repeated I will never know. Getting resolution of the problem then became very challenging. The students indicated to me that they were offended when receiving this medicated shampoo, feeling it was the white man's way of saying they were dirty. That suggestion was never implied and I tried to explain that this happened in white man's schools as well. I remembered the school nurse checking heads when I was growing up and some students having a note sent home. Unfortunately, the children not affected were the ones deriding their fellow students.

My trip into Rivers Inlet a week later was an interesting one. Situated southeast of Bella Bella, the inhabitants were the Owikeno Indians, a sub-group of the Bella Bellas. Their village was on the Owikeno Lake at the mouth of the Rivers Inlet, known always to me as Owikeno Village. I had planned to stay overnight on my own. At times, when I decided to stay, I would take along a film on a health topic, which I obtained through the National Film Board. There were also other interesting documentary films which were not on health matters made available to us. In the evening, when all was quiet after a day's work, I would arrange through the lay dispenser to have a health film shown and follow this with an interesting documentary. I always had a good turnout which was gratifying, especially when I was responsible for teaching health subjects. My superiors required accountability for the time spent in the various communities. I knew that the people were interested mainly in the social event, but it didn't matter. I had the opportunity to impart health knowledge as part of my professional role. I would serve coffee and cookies after and it was equally enjoyable for me to have their company.

I had only taken enough food for an overnight stay and got a shock when I was stranded there for four days. We had a storm with high winds and a heavy rainfall. During this episode a plane went down and the occupants were missing. On my original departure date no planes were flying due to the inclement weather. We had heard about the lost aircraft through the radio. The lay dispenser, who was also the chief's wife, on finding out I was stranded, immediately invited me to dine with her family and later handed me a baked apple pie to take home.

The Health Centre was the same type of construction as the one at Klemtu. Again, the furnishings were very sparse, but this clinic was on a site close to the villagers. I felt wary about leaving my home to visit in the evening due to the presence of cougars in the area. That fact was substantiated by my seeing many cougar skins draped outside the homes.

The next day was sunny and calm. Fortunately, in our location, we had been sheltered from the worst of the storm. The pilot knew of my departure date, but I waited all day in vain. No plane came and through radio communication I learned that all available aircraft were out searching for the lost one. I had no choice but to wait patiently, the way in and out being only by sea or air. Another family, in the meantime, invited me to join them at their table for my meals. I was hopeful about leaving the following day but once more the search continued. On the fifth day I was finally flown back to Bella Bella. I never heard whether the plane was ever recovered.

The winters were mild after the Arctic experience. Namu was closed for the winter season and the lighthouses were now out of my jurisdiction, making my workload less hectic.

When Spring arrived, I started travelling more to the small communities. I had deferred my visits during the miserable weather. I had plenty to occupy me with the various programmes, squeezing in a first-aid course for school-aged students in the evening, but the numbers quickly dwindled.

Monitoring of the village water supply was a regular duty of mine, and this meant walking to the local water site and collecting samples from all public sources such as schools, halls, the hospital and individual homes, which were tested on a rotation basis.

Back at Rivers Inlet I was invited to go trolling with the chief's son. We left at five o'clock in the morning in a small boat equipped with an outboard motor to troll the Owikeno Lake. How peaceful it was, with the calm water shimmering in the light rays of the morning sunrise. The trip was successful and by late afternoon I was enjoying the spoils of the day's catch, eating the barbecued salmon by the shore.

It was in this time frame that a nursing friend from the hospital suggested we take a trip to China. She had seen an advertisement in the paper inviting nurses from Ontario and Vancouver to join the trip. It was a thrilling idea and I eagerly prompted her to proceed with the arrangements. The proposed trip was in the early planning stages and being organized from Ontario. Although it was still quite a time away, we made out the necessary applications. One of the questions asked was regarding our political affiliations. With passports and the paperwork approved, we were given a visa to enter China. Immunizations against cholera, typhoid and paratyphoid were given and the resulting hot, swollen arm was a mere detail compared to the chance of a lifetime.

We were to be the first group of nurses to be allowed into China since the Cultural Revolution. At that time, China was not wide open to Westerners. Dr Norman Bethune, a Canadian, went to China in 1938, at a time when Japan invaded China. He worked as an army surgeon and was credited for saving many lives. He was revered by Mao Tse-tung and the Chinese people. Whilst performing surgery on a soldier in China, he cut his finger. Infection set in and in November of 1939, he succumbed to septicaemia.

Every so often I would have a visit from the Zone Director who resided in Port Hardy, on Vancouver island. The visits were different from most, as we did not spend the time indoors talking in the office. Instead, we walked the beaches, talking endlessly of many things past and present and any difficulties encountered in the work scenario were addressed promptly. He was encouraging and because he had been raised near to an Indian Reservation, many of his friends were natives. This, I believe, provided him with a greater understanding of the problems and frustrations often encountered by the nurses in dealing with a different culture. This type of support was greater than any I would later encounter in my career.

In the summertime I was able to go out boating with friends. We never ventured too far, but one visit was made to the Grave Island burial grounds. From the burial site we walked through the forest, amongst the tall trees which seemed to reach to the skies. The woods felt cool and moist due to the heavy overgrowth of vegetation. Moss clung and draped from the trees in a most artistic manner and the air felt so fresh and clean. To just sit awhile on the limb of a tree in such a setting was both relaxing and therapeutic.

Walking a little further we chanced upon some hieroglyphics on a rock. It was interesting to see these picture symbols that connected to the past.

On one trip across the water, we were joined by three porpoises. They just swam alongside of the boat as though inviting us to play. We stopped on a tiny island that was in isolation from all the others. It was so tiny that one imagined that if the water level of the ocean rose in the future it would be swallowed up and disappear for ever. With a little difficulty, the boat was docked and we clambered onto the island to inspect what looked like a square concrete structure. Being curious, we advanced to the entranceway. There was no door in place and we quickly realised that this was a burial site, as we saw several coffins stacked. One coffin, in an obvious state of decay, had a foot with a shoe on, protruding. Recognizing what we had intruded upon, we beat a hasty retreat. When we returned to the shore, we made enquiries and were told it was the Chiefs' burial ground.

There was no shortage of company for walking, boating and fishing. As well as the nurses, I had the teachers, and visiting personnel not to mention the four legged friends.

Summer came and went and we were now entering into the fall season. I decided to book a flight and have some holidays at the end of November and spend Christmas with my family. I had been looking after the doctor's very pregnant dog and during the evening, when I was trying to pack suitcases, the dog became very restless, wanting to go outside frequently. It was as well I had her on a leash as she attempted to crawl under buildings. I realized she was trying to find a place to give birth to her pups. I got some old blankets and placed them under my bed on the floor and left the room dark. At one o'clock in the morning, I could hear a licking sound coming from the bedroom. Curious, I went to investigate. Curled up close to the mother were two newborn puppies. I called my nursing colleague who wanted to be called day or night for the births. The two of us lay on the floor and watched intently as every five minutes she produced a new one. It was so perfectly orchestrated. As soon as one was born the cord was bitten through, the baby animal licked clean and when safely snuggled close to her she presented us with another, until a total of twelve was reached. The owner of the dog had arranged with some male in the community to dispose of all the females. I was so very glad that I would not be around to witness this event. One little female, I noticed, had beautiful markings resembling that of the mother's and I asked for her to be spared.

I arrived back from Britain and within a day I paid a visit to the young pups. There were three left and the doctor was about to bath them, hoping they might soon be adopted. He complained that no one would want a female and when I enquired as to why that would be, he replied, "Because they produce more litters." I asked him solemnly if the males were not in any way responsible for this state of affairs. Seeing that he thought the female to be such a handicap, I volunteered to take her home and give the necessary bath.

There were a lot of squeaks and squawks as I shampooed this eight-week-old bundle of fur. She was all towelled dry and lying on my chest wrapped in a blanket. This ordeal sent the pup into a deep, contented slumber. When the dog awoke I went to the phone and announced to my doctor friend that he need not worry anymore about the adoption of a female animal as I had just claimed ownership of her. This was the start of a long and wonderful companionship with Judy Freckles who would be my constant, furry friend for the next fourteen years.

On her daily walks her little legs would tire and when I picked her up I would carry her in my parka hood. I would pull the parka hood close to my face so that she would feel the closeness. She grew from that butterball stage and became a sleek dog. Speaking of a butterball reminds me of the time I left her at home for the evening whilst I attended a dinner with the hospital staff, at Shearwater. My nurse friend from the residence also had acquired a young dog. Being sentimental about our pets we left them together to be company for each other at my home. I had left one pound of butter wrapped in tin foil to thaw on the countertop. On returning home, no butter could be found, only a portion of the silvery wrap lay on the floor. It was obvious that the item had been devoured but which one was the culprit we didn't know. I knew my dog would do no such thing and strangely my friend felt the same about her pooch. When interrogated, neither of them would own up so we had to rest our case. We watched carefully the next day for some evidence which we were sure the digestive tract would yield up, but nothing unusual happened.

For the first six months of the dog's life she ran free within the village. I did not have a backyard to contain her and I did not feel happy about her being tied and left defenceless when other dogs roamed freely. As I did my home visits she would follow me in my travels, at times disappearing. She would often be seen around the village carrying my umbrella in her mouth or carrying home the mail which she had an uncanny knack of dropping in any available puddle. The local people were enamoured with her and offered to purchase her from me, but no money could buy the love I felt for my dog.

When she was about six months old I noticed, as she bounded into the house, something that looked like a piece of ribbon hanging from her anus. I realized immediately that she had a tape worm. I sent the specimen to a laboratory and talked with the veterinarian. He sent appropriate medicine which had to be repeated and I was advised to observe any stools passed. I had taken Judy for her customary walk and waited patiently for her to perform her daily duty. Unfortunately she did not comply by evacuating on the waste ground we visited, but decided to go nearer to my home, by the roadside, in full view of all the other residents. I inconspicuously searched with a twig for the offending worm segments, and just as I was getting underway with the examination a little old lady appeared. Leaning on her cane she asked, "What are you looking for? Have you lost something?" I felt very foolish and mumbled something about looking for the dog's play ball. I instantly abandoned my search. Fortunately the medicine did its job and the worms never reappeared.

We began having a problem in the village with rats. They apparently were coming from the garbage dump which, I was told, had been established too close to town. I was sitting quietly one evening when I heard a distinct gnawing sound emanating from underneath my sitting room floor. I asked the caretaker about this the next morning and he informed me that it was a rat. He set a trap, and although I never heard whether or not it was caught, after that I heard no further sounds. Someone in the community must have been very angry with me, believing, erroneously, that my responsibility was to rid the community of the perpetrators. An article inserted in the newly established local news bulletin made me the target of discontent. I had a good idea who this might have been. It was written that the public health nurse should do something about the rats that were running down the main street. I personally never witnessed these street runners, but then I might have been in the wrong place at the wrong time, missing out on this great event. I had notified the appropriate authorities in the south at headquarters and they in turn advised about the type of rat poison the local shop should obtain. I did have a vision, that, if too much pressure was brought to bear, I might end up like the pied piper, playing the flute with all the rats following me to the wharf and dropping into the murky waters below.

It was reported to me that my dog was seen eating a rat. On her return home one evening, she had a dazed expression and one eye which appeared droopy would not focus. Along with this she had bladder incontinence and I could only surmise that she possibly had gotten into some poison. I am glad to say she recovered by the next day.

I had just visited the small communities to do preliminary eye checks as the ophthalmologist was arriving the next week with his assistant. They would further test those that I referred and establish who was in need of spectacles. There were several potential candidates for glasses in Klemtu. The corrections were very important, particularly for the young children in school who needed to read the blackboard clearly. Many times children were thought to be slow learners when really they were either unable to see at a distance or hear properly.

I met the eye doctor, an elderly English gentleman and his young male assistant, at the dock and lent assistance by carrying some equipment. He wanted to stay at the Health Centre, he said, as that had always been his custom. I conceded that they could both stay. He spent two days at Bella Bella and on the third day wished to work at Klemtu. I chartered the aircraft and we flew in the following day. The pilot asked us to be at the dock at a given time for the return journey and was very emphatic about the time.

I did a clinic for the sick while the doctor attended to his field of speciality. The day went fast with the large number of clients to be seen. Those requiring spectacles had to make a decision in the type of frames that suited them and could not be rushed. I made the doctor aware of the hour, indicating we should pack and leave. He would acknowledge I had spoken, but carried on working. After a few urgings he finally packed his gear and we headed to the dock. The plane was waiting, but inside sat one very irate pilot who, on seeing us, exploded with rage at the delay in our departure. The wind had risen and he wasn't at all happy about the conditions for flying. I sat up front with the pilot while the other two sat at the back. I tried to soothe the aviator and rationalize that it was not good to be angry when at the controls. I too, was irritated at the unnecessary circumstances we found ourselves in. We were fast losing the daylight and with all the water between the two villages I did not relish the thought of again coming down in an aircraft.

The flight was quite bouncy and the doctor was mumbling something to me or to the pilot. As I turned my head I could see the doctor, who by now was sitting in a forward position with his arms resting on the back of my seat, peering through the window of the cockpit. He was perspiring and looking quite anxious.

The pilot relaxed for the remainder of the trip, although conversation was limited. I was not the guilty one but I suppose he judged the whole group as being tardy. At least we arrived home safely.

I had to start preparing supper for all of us. My freezer was located in the office and when I went to retrieve some food I found blood running down the freezer door. I was almost scared to open it not knowing what might lie within. When I did peek inside I found all my meat supply in a state of thaw. This precious meat supply, that had cost me plenty of money for the shipment, would probably have to be thrown out. What a calamity! What was the cause? It wasn't long before it became evident. When the doctor had set up his equipment on arrival in the office area, which was now three days ago, he had unplugged my freezer and had omitted to tell me. I was so upset, first with the delay in leaving Klemtu, then feeling somewhat tired on returning home and having to start cooking for three. Now I faced a mess that I alone had to clean up. I was equally annoyed at myself for allowing them to stay at the Health Centre.

There were two T-bone steaks which I had been keeping to share with my male friend, having planned a romantic dinner by candlelight. That idea certainly went out the window. Instead, I found myself cooking them for the doctor and his assistant who was a native from another reserve. He, at least, was sympathetic. I served them their dinner and left the building to visit with my doctor friend. Over a scotch I was able to let off steam. Not being used to much liquor, I soon became quite tranquil, but on my return home my mood was to change again.

The doctor was upstairs and the other young man had just come downstairs. The dirty dishes and cutlery were still on the table waiting, no doubt, for me, the maid, to return. This was the very scenario that I had experienced in the Arctic and was trying to avoid. I said nothing and cleared the dishes away. At that point I thought the dog would enjoy a nice bone to gnaw on but I didn't see them on the plates. I looked in the garbage pail and after rummaging under some paper I still could not find them. This was a mystery and I had to find out about their disappearance. On questioning the young native he just said, "You had better ask the doctor!" After all the dishes were done the doctor reappeared and I questioned him about the bones. "Oh that!" he said in his English voice, "I put them away in my brief case to take home to my dog!" I was flabbergasted! I asked him why he would not have left them for my dog and without flinching, he casually offered to part with one bone.

I attempted to save some of my meat supply and did manage to cook a couple of roasts that evening, which being thicker, had not fully thawed. A few friends as dinner guests would soon help to use the meat but I would now have to place another order.

The following day the ophthalmologist and optician were due to leave. Thank goodness! He came forward with his little change purse clutched in his hand and asked how much he owed me for the meals. Government employees were given generous travel and meal allowances and so it was not a hardship to repay me for the food I had supplied. He was quick to tell me that the previous nurse did not charge for breakfast. I was equally quick to point out that I was not in the hotel business. I still rankle a little when I think of a doctor's salary in comparison to mine and his expectations of my personal purse paying his way! I was not interested in contributing to his retirement fund!

A wedding was going to take place. The bride was a nurse and the groom a local boy. People busied themselves in different ways in preparation for the event. Her parents were to fly in from another province but the weather changed and it was evident they would not be able to attend. Undaunted, the couple decided to go ahead anyway. I, along with their friends, felt bad for them, the bride having to choose someone else to stand in for her father. On hearing about her situation I suggested that she and her bridesmaids might like to leave, bedecked in their wedding apparel, from my home rather than the nurses' residence. My house was, after all, next to the church. It would be a lesser distance to walk over the gravel road, which would have been awkward, given that she wore high heeled shoes and had to support her long gown and flowing train. Somehow it seemed more elegant and befitting to leave from a Victorian styled house. The bride was very happy with the arrangement.

The bride and her maids arrived at the house in the late morning. There was much activity as each in turn took over the bathroom, dressing in their finery and applying makeup. Solely for the bride to stand on while dressing, I rolled out a polar bear skin with a full head mount that I had acquired in the Arctic. There was much clamour and laughter, with visitors popping in with their well wishes and some bearing gifts. By early afternoon we all headed to the church for the ceremony, everything going like clockwork, with the bride actually arriving on time.

All around the Health Centre were Indian homes. My neighbour across the road owned a large dog. I say owned, or perhaps it just moved in. There were dogs running loose and the pregnant females had their pups wherever they found a suitable haven. The pups became strays and roamed about the community. Many of the children adopted an orphaned animal because in the puppy stage they looked cute. So often this happens in our society and as the dogs grow, they are not cared for, but seen as an inconvenience.

This large dog would follow me on my daily walks or on my home visits in the community. He had a very annoying habit of snapping at my legs as I walked, occasionally grabbing my pant leg in his mouth. It wasn't that he was vicious, he just wanted to play. I did feel that in time I might accidentally get bitten if he pursued this activity with greater fervour. I asked the owner to keep the dog more confined but it fell on deaf ears.

I was on one of my walks with him following close on my heels when I noticed him drooling freely from his mouth. He didn't appear ill and his energy level was the same, as evidenced by his barking and playfulness. He would come near to me, often licking my hand. It was then I noticed the saliva on my hands. I was concerned about rabies, particularly when his daily activities were not monitored and no one knew what other animals he could have been in contact with. I telephoned the veterinarian on the mainland. He indicated that there were other reasons for the drooling, but to be on the safe side the dog should be tied up, fed, watered and kept as normal as possible for the next ten days. If rabies were evident some signs would develop in that time frame and I would still have time to receive injections myself. I had seen film footage of humans with rabies and it was not a pleasant sight to see them in the throes of convulsions ending in death.

I approached the family to discuss the animal and its care. They heard me out alright and, laughing in my face, threatened to shoot the dog through the head. Of course if they had done that and if the dog had been rabid, the proof would then have been eradicated as the intact brain was necessary for examination and diagnosis. The family were very heavy drinkers and on my visit it was very obvious that they all were inebriated. I was informed that if I wanted the dog tied and taken care of I should do so myself.

I found a length of rope in my cellar and after some effort was able to tether the animal in their front yard which was positioned exactly opposite my sitting room window. At least I was able to observe the dog from a safe distance. I purchased a quantity of dog food and fed the mongrel daily and replenished his water supply regularly. I am quite sure the dog never had it so good. Those suffering from rabies are said to be hydrophobic and as I set down his water dish I almost expected him to go berserk at the sight of it. Nothing like that happened, and as the dog's behaviour and health remained intact he was allowed once more to run free. Of course now, he would not leave me alone, seeing me as his benefactor.

It was shortly after my arrival at Bella Bella that I actually learned of the Norman Hartwell plane crash. Because of that tragedy, courses on survival were offered to employees who were involved in northern flying. I signed up for the course which was held at a place called Blue Lake, located at Hinton, in central Alberta. The centre was run by the Department of Culture and Recreation for Youth.

The classes were held at different times of the year, but the group I was assigned to was having theirs on the first day of December. I had to fly to Campbell River and then to Vancouver. After an overnight stay in the downtown core of this large city, I travelled to my destination, in Alberta, by train.

It was a nice break to be with other nurses in my field of work and be able to compare notes. Happy as I was at Bella Bella, I realized after being in contact with a big group of professionals that I really was somewhat isolated from many aspects of life. At Blue Lake we were assigned a bed within a dormitory. We had been requested to take our sleeping bags which were government issue and consisted of goose down filler for warmth. That evening, after our meal, we assembled in the sitting room around a log fire, giving us an opportunity to get acquainted. A lecture was given along with a slide presentation on hypothermia and an outline of the programme for the next three days.

On day one we were paired off. Each person received a meagre food ration of one pork chop, one packet of soup mix between two, a spoonful or two of coffee and a small mixture of flour and baking powder which, when reconstituted, would be eaten as bannock. There may have been a few other scant items that I cannot recall. Each individual was given a rucksack to carry the food and other essentials such as a cooking pan, an axe, a compass, a large sheet of plastic with some twine, a flint and a small mirror. With our paraphernalia we were driven to an isolated area within a densely treed forest. In a clearing in the woods, a demonstration in the art of erecting a lean-to for shelter was given. We were instructed to locate our camps near to the convenience of a water source. We were then taught how to start a fire with a piece of flint. It all looked like good fun and very easy. We quickly dispersed and were given a few hours to find a suitable location, set up camp and get a fire going. This area had been used by other groups and dugout pits were already in place for bodily elimination purposes.

With all this new knowledge running around in my brain, my partner and I scouted for a suitable place, remembering the words of wisdom spoken by our leader that a nearby water supply would be convenient, as would a latrine. With the cold temperature it became a reality that frequent visits to the dugout would be necessary and in the darkness I had no intention of going too far afield to accommodate Mother Nature.

We found our little piece of land and set about finding two trees near to one another which would be used to build our shelter. Soon we were chopping small sapling trees to make a frame for the lean-to. They were placed in an order of assembly to have sides, a roof and an open doorway. With the twine we were able to bind them together making the frame a little more secure should the wind blow. Next came the task of covering the frame at the top with a good layer of branches to form a roof. Having completed this stage, we then used the heavy plastic given to us to cover in the side walls. Perspiring and feeling worn out with our efforts, we took a rest and admiringly looked over our handy work. We had at least a shelter now. Before placing our sleeping bags inside we cut some pine branches which we placed on the floor to give us a modicum of insulation and comfort. We made haste after our short break to collect wood for the fire, knowing we would have to keep it going as long as possible into the night. The effort of using a flint was very exasperating and I longed for a box of matches! We did manage in the end.

It was now growing dusk, but not dark enough to receive benefit from our flashlights. Once the elementary work had been achieved we gathered around for further counselling before doing a tour of each camp. With several fires now burning well, we had plenty of light. It was interesting to see the various shapes of the lean-tos. Some of the men made their abodes more cosy.

One of the members in the group was an Native Indian. I was very amused when on passing his camp I noticed he had his "billy can" dangling from a twig over the fire which was roaring, the flames emitting a much sought-after warmth. He was already well under way in the cooking of his dinner. There was a very appetizing aroma coming from the pot and we asked what kind of soup mix he was preparing. With a mischievous grin he admitted that there was more in the pot than soup mix. He had fashioned a catapult with a heavy gauge elastic which he had the foresight to assemble earlier. He must have been a crack shot because now he was about to enjoy some wood pigeon. How fortunate was the male person that shared his lean-to. They undoubtedly would not starve in a real life situation. He may, of course, have been telling a tall tale.

Rounds done and curiosity satisfied, we returned to our own camp and decided to make a few alterations to our shelter by making it smaller, cosier and less exposed to the elements. Important now was keeping a good fire going for cooking and warmth. We obtained water from the frozen river by poking a hole in the ice and then we were all set to have a little soup and a piece of fruit. This would have to last us until morning. Once more a bit warmer and fed, we gathered around the main camp fire as a group and entered into some discussions of survival techniques, followed by a sing-song and an early bedtime.

Because it was December and this was the north country, the temperature was below zero. The skies were clear, with the stars dancing overhead. In the distance we heard coyotes yipping and I thought I had heard wolves howling also. We had made the mistake before going to the group sing-a-long of putting some dead looking pieces of wood on the fire, which were readily available on the ground. We thought it would save us the chore of having to chop more wood later. When we arrived back at the shelter, to our horror we saw that our healthy glowing embers were no more. Instead, we had lots of smoke and between the coughs, splutters and gasps we were able to extricate the offending logs, disposing of them some distance away from our sleeping quarters. By salvaging a small ember we were once again able to stock the fire and produce a lively flame with new chopped wood.

And so to bed! My partner and I crawled into our separate, cold sleeping bags with a considerable amount of clothing still being worn. All was quiet in the camp but for the animals calling one another and the snores from some of the male campers nearby. We had very broken sleep due mainly to feeling cold. Every so often we would reach out for a log and add this to the fire. We lay with our feet pointing towards the outside and our heads facing inside the shelter. I was even more cold because of a previous impulsive action. The first time I had to use the outdoor latrine I had to strip right down in order to do what comes naturally. I thought at the time of purchase how warm my "long john" outfit would be covering my whole body. I gave no thought to the fact there was no back opening in this model. I hastily removed the offending garment and in disgust used it to boost the fire. It was all very amusing at first but not so as I lay and shivered.

I felt I had just entered into a deep plane of sleep when I was awakened by a commotion. It was breakfast time. Whoopee! Bacon, eggs and toast were welcome thoughts washed down with a jar of hot coffee. Re-entering the real world after my day dreaming, I jumped into action. Down to the frozen river again to get some water for the coffee and a quick face wash and mouth rinse. We were to have bannock for breakfast. Combining the mixture with the icy water in the plastic bag, a dough was formed. We made several little balls and I had the brilliant idea of mixing all the bannock at one time so to avoid the messiness later. The extras were put carefully aside and treated like gold. Using a long stick, we formed the dough around the distal end, placing this in the flames which were now leaping as the wood crackled and burned. I cannot really describe this meal which we washed down with lukewarm coffee. All one could say is that when you are hungry, anything can taste okay.

The fires had to be put out as we all gathered for our morning session. The instructors had made their rounds of the various sites and had found traces of apple cores and chocolate wrappers which had not quite burned and we were all promptly admonished. The idea was to live only on the rations in order to get a true feeling of hunger should we be downed in an aircraft. I was guilty of the same crime but that sweet dessert tasted so-o good.

On day two we were taught about edible plants and barks. Walking about the forest, they were identified to us. How to make a fishing net was followed by a demonstration of how to make and set a snare for rabbits. I thought at that point I would probably die of starvation, either because I wouldn't remember the "how to" or just because the thought of killing these soft cuddly bundles would be unbearable. Men are possibly better adapted to carrying out such actions, females being faint of heart.

In the afternoon, after having had a delightful lunch of coffee and raisins, we were then actively involved in making feather sticks. These were made from small branches of wood using a penknife to feather the ends. They were to be used as kindling in the initial stage of a making a bonfire. A large fire had to built on a high prominence with everyone pitching in to help. The whole scenario was to pretend we had crashed. The wing or tail of the imaginary plane had to be kept cleared of snow for identification and easy spotting from the air. We wrote the word "help" on an open area of the white frozen ground, should an aircraft be searching for us. In the event of hearing an engine overhead, we were to light the bonfire, which had to be sizeable in order to draw attention to us below. Each of us, in turn, had to fire off a flare from the flare gun. We watched the bright red colour gradually dissipate into the air. We were taught and practised with a small mirror, how to use the glare from the sun as a means to attract attention from above.

It had been a full day. Now back at our shelters, we set about preparing our evening meal once we had a good fire burning. This night we would really feast. Carefully stirring the remainder of the soup mix into the water in the "billy can" we added one pork chop still a little frozen. As an extra we would indulge in some bannock. Not so! My wonderful idea of preparing it ahead of time backfired miserably. We held in our hands, a solid block of bannock. The attempts to recover this morsel was in vain. Placing the product on a flat stick on the edge of the fire didn't work, as softened parts fell into the fire whilst other bits were burnt, making it inedible.

Gathering again around the main camp fire in the evening, many discussions arose, especially focusing on how we were all feeling at the camp. Two days of roughing the elements were annoying most of us. At first it was a novelty, but gradually the conveniences we were used to in our daily routines, such as indoor plumbing, bathing, clean clothing, central heating and adequate food to eat were but a few of the creature comforts we were missing. Here we sat looking somewhat dishevelled, smelling of smoke and in much need of underarm deodorant.

Back at our lean-to, my partner and I decided to get smart by making a few changes. Instead of sleeping in separate sleeping bags we opened one and placed it on the branches which acted as a mattress and the second one to cover us, both zipped together for warmth. We bundled for body heat and slept much better.

The psychology behind the exercise was to allow us to experience discomfort with the lack of food, sleep and coldness to endure and to understand what happens to the personality when faced with the elements, not knowing if rescue would in fact occur.

I could not begin to imagine what it must have felt like for Norman Hartwell and the young Inuk boy alone for so long in that frozen wilderness, injured, cold and hungry. I personally would never criticize his desperate need to survive by eating human flesh. Just as I believed I would not kill a rabbit, one does not really know until faced with the predicament.

In preparation for leaving on the last day the area had to be cleaned of all garbage and fires put out. We were to find our way out to the road only a mile away by using a compass. Fortunately we again travelled in pairs. Had that not been the case I am quite sure I would have been going around in circles until someone rescued me.

On arrival back at Blue Lake there was a mad panic to beat one another to the showers. A hearty meal was served, almost seeming like a reward for a job well done. With our gear all packed, we each made our way back to our respective health units.

Apart from vacations and the trip to Blue Lake there were not many opportunities to fly out to the city, unlike the situations with medical evacuations in the Arctic. However, I seized the chance offered to me by the hospital, to accompany one adult and a teenage boy to Vancouver. These patients had been sent for as hospital beds were now available for them to have ear surgery. The plan was for me to take them to the city, stay overnight as the escort and put them safely on the bus to their destination. Some of these patients had partial deafness due to repeated ear infections when they were children, resulting in perforated eardrums.

The checking-in at the hotel in Vancouver completed, the young man in my care stated that his relatives wanted to pick him up and spend a few hours with him. I refused to let him go until I met them and knew exactly what the plan was. In due course, the aunt and uncle appeared at the hotel and reluctantly, I handed over my charge, making a very definite time arrangement for him to return. Not surprisingly, he did not arrive back as scheduled. I waited patiently, phoning the contact number given to me, but there was no answer. In frustration I took a bus to the neighbourhood he was to be at. I combed the streets looking for him. As fortune would have it I spotted him with a group of other natives and although reluctant, he agreed to return with me to the hotel.

I had a morning wake-up call arranged for all of us. The young fellow made it downstairs but there was no signs of the older woman. I had to find her, as the bus would be leaving shortly after breakfast. I asked the receptionist to keep buzzing her room but there was no response. Another employee came to the desk and informed me that an Indian lady had just come in to the hotel after being out all night. With no more ado I headed to her room and quickly got her into motion. She was downstairs in a jiffy because she already had all her clothing on.

I sat opposite her at breakfast. She looked very dishevelled, her hair un-brushed and tousled, her mascara had run and her breath was none too sweet. Ah well, I ate breakfast in silence so as not to awaken her too much and I gave a sigh of relief as I waved them goodbye. My duty was over. Now I could shop before returning to Bella Bella.

I had been told that in the past, one or maybe two deaths in the village occurred due to botulism. The source of contamination came from what was known locally as "stink eggs." The salmon eggs were cleansed for two days with water running over them until there was no evidence of blood. A tablespoonful of salt was added to them and the eggs were allowed to ferment for four days. If bacteria was present or there was lack of refrigeration, the infected food produced an illness such as botulism and the individuals became critically ill. Health advice was disseminated to the public regarding the processing of fish eggs. There was need to use a pressure cooker and a high standard of hygiene, but old ways die hard and sometimes with a consequence to human life.

My dog continued to grow and in her presence I found unbelievable joy. I had always wanted a pet but felt as long as I travelled it would not be a viable proposition, but now I had allowed my heart to rule my head. In spite of the future travel difficulties I would encounter I was still very glad she came into my life unexpectedly. Apart from my going abroad, we were seldom parted.

My routine visits to the communities continued and on the next trip into Rivers Inlet I decided to take the dog along with me for company. After the event of my dog's tape worm I didn't allow her to roam freely anymore. I believed she either got the worm from eating dead raw salmon, often found lying on the shore line, or from the rat she was supposed to have nibbled at. Either way, when I stayed overnight I wanted to ensure her safety and well being. It was not always convenient for someone else to dog-sit her.

The pilot lifted her from the dock into the plane. She sat on the back seat beside me, eagerly looking about her and giving a few throaty sounds indicative of pleasure and excitement. I was buckled in, and as the plane took off I clasped my arms closely about the dog to prevent her from toppling over. It was again a small aircraft and as I had chartered it, only the pilot, myself and the dog were on board. The dog sat relatively quiet, panting at times from the heat of the day. As we began our descent into Rivers Inlet I noticed the dog licking her lips and becoming restless. I grabbed the plastic bag I carried with me, placing it over her snout. One, then two heaves and she vomited a small amount of bile. Thankfully she was travelling on an empty stomach. The retching stopped when the plane landed and with a bit of fresh air and her feet on terra firma, she was soon back to normal.

I actually stayed an extra day to stock the cupboards with supplies and managed to finish all the work sooner than anticipated. A few of the natives in the village were going berry-picking that afternoon and invited me along. We were mainly a group of women and off we went into the bushes with buckets in hand for the collection. As we were leaving, one husband joined us, sporting a rifle over his shoulder. I was taken aback when I saw this but he assured me it was just a safety measure with so many cougars in the area. I was glad I had decided to leave my dog at the Health Centre and out of harm's way.

The return flight back to Bella Bella was uneventful but it was comical to watch the dog sitting quietly, looking out the window as though she were travelling by car on a country road.

The holiday time to China was fast approaching. I had spent two years now at Bella Bella and I gave serious thought to moving on. I felt the timing was appropriate and it would be more economical to leave Bella Bella, take my vacation, then transfer to a different area rather than return. In the midst of my decision-making, the department was looking for a temporary candidate to cover a four-month period at Baker Lake Nursing Station. As I had previously worked in this location and was undecided as to where I should relocate, it was logical for them to offer me the posting. I quite liked the idea, but looking at the dog, I wondered how I would manage to travel so far with her, suitcases, trunks, and a large dog cage made of metal, but this arrangement was excellent, which meant that following my holiday to China I would go directly to my new position.

It had to be confirmed first that I could take my dog north and that the nurse there would have no objections. Back came the answer I had hoped for, that she loved dogs, and yes, I must bring the animal along.

While waiting at the dockside, I assembled the metal cage I had purchased and persuaded the dog, with a cookie, to enter inside before she was hoisted on board. Because this was not a charter flight, but rather a commercial passenger one, she had to be contained. Once on board she was placed at the back of the plane with the luggage. I was able to sit near to her and give her reassurance. She travelled very well and perhaps it was good that she had previously experienced a plane ride.

At the airport I collected my suitcases from the baggage carousel. While I was still wondering where to pick up the dog, the baggage door flaps opened again and there was my poor Judy in her cage, going around and around. She passed me once, then twice. I was unable to move the cage because of the weight, particularly when the conveyor belt was moving. One of the workers then appeared and assisted me in lifting her down. This done, I dragged the cage well away from people before unlatching the door and letting her out to stretch. She was so happy to be out of her confined space, judging by the tail wagging and the wet kisses that she bestowed lavishly on me. In two days' time I would be leaving her at the "Doggy Hotel" prior to meeting my travel companions on the China tour. We were to be briefed on our expected conduct while in a communist country.

CHAPTER ELEVEN
A SETTLEMENT REVISITED

The experience of the educational tour I had just completed had been most enlightening, spending four days in Hong Kong and almost three weeks in mainland China. On my return to Canada I was now ready to re-enter the workforce. Having picked up my furry friend, enjoying fully the reunion with her, I made my way north, taking in my stride the complications arising from travelling with a pet.

The welcome on arriving after the first leg of my journey, was not quite as friendly as I had hoped. Having collected my chattels following deplaning, I entered the passengers' lounge with Judy, my dog, by my side on a leash. She was always well behaved but now started growling and barking at people. I found this to be a little embarrassing and thought it strange, but I was quick to realize that she was troubled by the various passengers walking about wearing their parkas with the fur trimmed hoods up, covering in part the faces of the wearer. The dog was unused to this and perhaps felt somewhat threatened, although she had seen me wear one of these in Bella Bella.

I saw at a glance an older, stout woman standing alone and looking at the in-coming passengers. I noticed the Health and Welfare logo on her coat sleeve and, assuming this was my superior, I made my way across to her. Preliminary introductions were made cordially, but after spotting my dog she asked me in a pronounced English accent, "Is that thing yours!", at the same time staring at my dog as though it were a Martian just landed from outer space. "Yes it is", I replied. She then complained about taking the dog in her Government car and wasn't sure what she should do about her perceived dilemma. My dog seemed to be creating difficulties that I did not anticipate. After all, I was given permission to bring the animal, but once again I found there existed within the bureaucracy a poor communication between individual departments. The interesting part was, that we were frequently reminded to use our lines of communication, but it seemed that this did not apply to the higher echelons. There was much huffing and puffing and indecision on her part until I suggested that should there be a continued problem I could very well return from whence I came on the same aircraft. At that remark, she became amenable and we proceeded to her Government car.

I was first taken to the office for all the formalities, the dog accompanying me. It was then I was informed that the animal could not stay at the office and I agreed. I requested that they show me to my room in the residence where I could leave her and get on with the business in hand. The Office Manager, a woman, whose care I was now left in, stated categorically that I could not take Judy to the residence as this was not permissible. I was becoming somewhat irritated by now. What did they expect? The pet was with me as arranged, but now I could not have a room to place her in temporarily. I asked them for suggestions with regard to the dog and the immediate response was that she could perhaps go to the dog pound. "Dog Pound!", I exclaimed, "No way! Where I go the dog goes or I don't stay." I felt outraged at the thought of my well cared-for pet even being considered to join some mangy hounds that might have diseases or fleas. "I'll sleep on the office floor in a sleeping bag, but the dog stays!" I tersely announced. They deliberated for a while, eventually conceding to allow the dog to stay in the residence and pointed me in that direction.

Inside the two-storey building, I climbed the stairs to the first level where my room was located. When I opened the hall door I saw two cats playing there, so I called out that I was coming in with a dog. Instantly a female appeared and carried off the felines. She reappeared to greet me, fussing over the dog and remarked on her fine looks. Well, it was a matter of love me, love my dog. I knew I would get along very well with this other animal lover next door to me. I mentioned to her about the fuss there had been to bring my pet to the residence only to find another species roaming the corridors. She then told me that a girl further down the corridor had two budgies. I felt instantly at home in this menagerie. We worked out a warning system, whereby when I advanced with my hound, I would "holler" and the cats would be taken inside for their safety.

Late one night I could hear strange sounds and loud laughter in the corridor. Intrigued, I jumped out of bed, opening the door just a fraction just far enough to see a male riding a bike up and down the hallway. He was the boyfriend of one of the residents. So much for the third degree I had been subjected too, making me feel badly at breaking the protocols of residence living. Judy's behaviour was impeccable in comparison to the wild noises erupting from the human species. I did not mention the other pets to the department, not wanting to blow the whistle on the owners.

When I eventually arrived at my appointed destination the dog and I were well received by the senior nurse. Her nursing colleague had just left on a four-month training course and I would cover her position for that period of time. It had been fully five years since I last worked at Baker Lake Nursing Station and I had to admit it felt good to be in a familiar setting again. The clinic set up had remained unchanged as far as I could remember, as were the living quarters with the same furniture, still positioned as before. I felt I had returned home. On my way to the guest bedroom which I was assigned, I passed by my old bedroom. A wave of nostalgia crept over me, particularly when I spotted the quilt on the bed. On seeing it, the previous years were swept aside and I felt transported back into my original position. It made me laugh when I remembered the negotiations I had with the Hudson's Bay manager, in order to acquire the quilts.

I needed a fast refresher course on the basic routines of the establishment. New management invariably bring with them new ideas and make adaptations to suit their own functional needs. With this in mind I did not expect everything to be exactly the same.

As time passed I did not always like the changes I saw in the indigent people, but felt that we, the white man, had made this so. In trying to make them self-reliant according to our ways, some individuals, I think, became demanding, an attitude which I had never seen in them before. One such incident occurred while I was enjoying my lunch. A patient came to the clinic demanding immediate attention. She was well aware of the hours of operation but chose to ignore them. Loudly slapping the countertop she demanded some service. I had known this lady very well previously and she had never behaved in this manner. It is often said that a place is never the same when you return again and perhaps this was true.

By returning to this isolated community there is not too much that can again be written without being repetitious. However, I decided to focus on one event that occurred. There were just the two of us sharing the clinic duties and on call rotation. Also on staff was a part-time nurse specifically responsible for the public health duties. She was married and lived in the community in her own home, which meant she was not involved with being on call.

I had been there for a few short weeks when, during the night, the doorbell rang and rang. I could hear it faintly at first, but not being the one on call, I developed a knack of turning the unpleasant sound off. This ringing would not go away. I went to see what all the commotion was about.

A local lady, looking very anxious, nearly fell into the doorway. Bundled in her arms was a baby with lips quite blue and writhing in a convulsion. I took the child from her and quickly gave it some oxygen. By now the baby was lying inert, but showing gradual signs of the colour returning to the lips. The temperature, I found, registered very high. Following a brief history and further testing it was obvious that the baby had meningitis. I had the mother start a tepid-sponge bath to reduce the fever while I quickly went to dress and at the same time waken the nurse who was officially on call. I banged loudly on the door several times before finally getting a groggy response.

The baby was quite ill, going from one convulsion into another. While I administered the oxygen, the head nurse contacted the hospital doctor. In the past we used the radio to communicate with the Zone Director. Now, with a new system in place, communication had improved greatly, with direct telephone links to the hospital in Churchill and medical personnel. When finished with the call, he prepared to give the child an injection of Phenobarbitol intravenously. I did not feel comfortable with this route of administration, as in my training we were not taught nor allowed to administer this way. However, I must say that many of our duties which we had to tackle went beyond the scope of our training. He indicated that he was well experienced in this matter. We differed in our diagnosis, he believing the baby was teething and I was convinced that the condition was more serious. He administered the medication to control the seizures. The anticipated response was not what we expected. The child went into respiratory arrest and for a moment we thought we had lost the child. The heartbeat was still evident and we immediately commenced artificial respiration. Fortunately, we had a quick and positive outcome. We later found out that the child did have meningitis.

A plane was requested for a medical evacuation. Normally we took turns acting as an escort and I was due for this trip, but my colleague informed me that morning that he would be accompanying the child. Apparently, in the process of making arrangements by phone, the Supervisor had asked him to accompany the baby so that he could attend a management meeting in Churchill. Tired from always being on the move, I was quite happy to relinquish this journey.

Prior to my colleague leaving with the ill child, the phone rang and I answered. It was the Supervisor requesting, that whoever was travelling with the babe to the hospital should bring with them certain supply requisitions. I acknowledged her statement and replied, "That will be the head nurse as you requested." There was a moment of hesitation before she answered, "I made no such request. It is entirely between the two of you who travels."

Shortly after returning from the airstrip, having seen the patient and escort off, a local male attended the clinic, requesting a refill of phenobarbitol tablets which had been prescribed and used by him to control his seizures. I had known this man from working there previously and was aware of his illness. Fetching his medical record I noticed that his medication had been recorded as being filled that same week. He would not have been due for a repeat order, so I questioned him as to why he had none left, discussing with him the label directions. He was, I knew, a very upstanding man and he adamantly denied any knowledge of getting a refill except one month before which was his routine. I believed him and issued him with a fresh supply.

There was something "rotten in Denmark!" I couldn't quite put my finger on it, but there were a number of things happening that needed explanation. I did notice that my co-worker seemed quite excitable at times, eyes a little bit too bright, while at other times he would be shivering, bent over and his demeanour subdued. Then there was the incident the night before where he was very difficult to awaken and seemed dazed with a far-away look. Now he was telling me a story of having to attend a meeting and the supervisor denying this. As I searched my mind further, I could recall that on more than one occasion, always happening on a Saturday, when I walked my dog across the sea ice, an activity which only took half to three quarters of an hour to complete, he had seen a patient with a medical problem. The condition was always serious enough to warrant an injection of morphine, yet there was no sign of any admission to our clinic nor did a follow-up visit ensue. At first I thought he must do things differently, for I would not have given a morphine injection to a patient unless absolutely necessary and certainly would not have sent the individual home at once. Rather, I would have kept him or her for observation over a period of time.

The part-time Health Nurse arrived for work and over a coffee we sat down and talked. I confided in her about my concerns. She had the bright idea of doing a total drug count. All narcotics and other drugs of addiction were required to be under lock and key. A register was kept and each time one of these drugs was given, the patient's name, dosage, time and type of drug were recorded along with the signature of the administrator. At the same time an entry would be placed in the patient's file along with the history of the medical complaint denoting the need for this medication.

In my previous capacity as Nurse-in-Charge of this same facility, the RCMP checked and signed these drugs to be correct once a year, but apparently this protocol was no longer in effect.

As we methodically checked each category of drugs, we were horrified at what we found. One bottle contained a variety of different-sized pills, some with a slightly different colour. What they were was anyone's guess, but we could not be sure they represented the labelled contents. Then there were a rash of entries claiming that ampoules of a narcotic, at staggered times, were smashed en route and replacements were ordered. I had never experienced breakages in transit and seldom did I ever have to use narcotics on patients. We tried to be unbiased in our thinking, tempting ourselves to believe that perhaps the circumstances were authentic, albeit bizarre.

Following the discovery of many irregularities during the count, we then diverted our focus. We compared the most recent entry of names in the narcotic register against those in the patients' records who were purportedly the recipients of a strong pain killer. There were practically no matches, that is to say, no entry was made in the patients' records of those medications having been administered, nor information depicting an illness or injury to warrant a narcotic. In fact, many clients were not in attendance at the clinic at all. We then assumed that these names had been randomly picked and written into the narcotic book. In fact, our observations were that each entry looked as though it had been written at the same time, but with different dates and times given. Further discussions ensued. We were quite clear about the obvious facts before us and that an investigation was necessary. Being the full-time employee involved with the clinical aspect of work, it fell on my shoulders to make the necessary decision and report.

It would appear to be an easy task, given the evidence and suspicions, but living and working with a colleague makes the situation more personalized and awkward, mixed with disbelief. I had to act quickly as the senior nurse would be returning the next day.

I had a heavy patient load to attend to on my own, keeping me busy throughout the day, but the problem niggled at me. By the end of the day I arranged to meet the RCMP officer and asked to talk with him privately in his off-duty hours. We were friends, so having this discussion was made easier for me.

I gave him the scenario, going on to say I felt I had a duty to the clients, to myself and indeed to my colleague whom I considered medically sick if indeed he was taking these drugs. By the end of the conversation I knew what had to be done. My view was that the identification and reporting of the findings would be a positive move for the presumed addict, so that he might receive appropriate care.

I called the Supervisor and invited her to visit the settlement the next day, indicating it was a matter of some urgency. I requested also that she keep my colleague in Churchill on some pretext. Because it was possible that our telecommunication could be picked up by others, I was reticent to discuss the matter further or make any accusations. She insisted on having more details and of course I could see her perspective. I insisted that I could not afford her the privilege of more facts at that precise moment but reiterated the urgency of the matter which required a drug count. I believe then she understood the gist of my conversation.

Around noon the following day the Supervisor arrived and to my horror, she had the Senior Nurse in tow. My nursing colleague entered the house ahead of our boss in an excitable state, almost in a panic as he announced to me, "Ms Smith is here and she wants to check the drugs!" I tried to act very nonchalant, feeling rather guilty that I had orchestrated this move and I was not surprised to see him in this state. I said, "Oh that is okay, it's usual every so often to have a drug count." My colleague thrust into my hand a plastic box containing twelve ampoules of a narcotic drug and at the same time said, "We were right out of these and I thought I'd better pick these up when I went to Churchill." At that moment it all came to me. We were out of this drug. As there was a medical evacuation, my colleague seized the opportunity of flying out to get further supplies from the hospital pharmacy, thereby having instant access to the drugs rather than wait for the request to be processed through the normal channels, which took a few days. This explained the lie he fed me about being requested to accompany the sick child.

I served tea in the sitting room and while sipping, the three of us made idle conversation. My heart pounded so hard that it sounded, to me, like the beating of a drum in the quietness of the room. The senior nurse left us and proceeded to the clinic where he said he had to make a long distance call. It was the ideal opportunity to dialogue with my Supervisor on the subject. After a detailed account of the events she nodded that she understood. When my colleague returned to the room he was instructed to follow the Supervisor to the clinic and commence the drug count. It was very obvious that the nurse was upset.

We ate supper after the drug counting was completed. None of us had much of an appetite that evening and I found myself just moving the food around on my plate. Nothing was being said. There was an air of suspense. One member at the table was in a panic, with his career perhaps at stake, one felt guilt at the necessary exposure of a colleague and the third had to make a hard decision. With all these diversions of thought, conversation was almost non-existent.

Finally the meal was over and the Supervisor announced she wished to talk with me privately, both of us disappearing into the clinic office. I requested that I be allowed to talk to my colleague about the day's events and express to him the need to expose his misuse of drugs. I wished to show my support. The Supervisor raised her hand to hush my diatribe and instructed me that on no account was I to mention this matter to him. She was going to talk with him immediately afterwards and remove him from the Nursing Station in the morning. She would make arrangements later for me to have some assistance at the clinic, but in the meantime I was instructed to write down the sequence of events leading up to her being called in to investigate and submit a report to her as soon as possible.

The nurse in question carried on as though everything was normal and the next day he announced he was going south to have some medical tests done, followed by a vacation. There was no animosity displayed and I did not know if he was aware of my involvement.

Three weeks went past and I heard very little, other than the nurse had confessed to taking a small amount of leftover narcotics after treating patients. He had now been officially removed from his position and was to receive medical care and counselling. His personal belongings remained in his room.

During these weeks I received a letter from the nurse whom I was replacing. On the outside of the envelope addressed to me she had written Acting Nurse-in-Charge with the word acting underlined no fewer than six times. Before I ever read the contents of the letter this struck me as odd. I did not recognize the writing but felt someone was making a dig at my newly-acquired position, which held no prestige for me. I had been Nurse- in-Charge in numerous establishments before and I had taken on this job as a temporary one. I had been happy not to be in a position of seniority and it was perchance and not by design I found myself wearing this cap again. Opening the envelope, I read through three pages. The unfriendly letter basically mounted a series of accusations against me. Some negative reference was made about my dog, which must have come from my colleague, since removed. I was then instructed by the writer to put the furniture in the living room back the way I had found it. Now I was really confused on this issue. The same pieces of furniture stood in exactly the same position as the day I arrived. The arrangement that had existed for years was satisfactory to me. As I read on there was a list made of seven types of alcohol, which I was accused of drinking, demanding that I, in no uncertain terms, replace them. Her friend and colleague must have passed on these lies during the long distance call made previously and now this total stranger was falsely accusing me. Interestingly she chose the wrong person to accuse, as I was practically a non-consumer of alcohol. Due to migraines I seldom touched liquor, particularly wine, which brought about blinding pain for me.

I was very angry at this letter but decided not to respond to her. Instead, I contacted the Nursing Supervisor and requested her to call a meeting with my accuser, on her return north in a month or so. I would then be departing. She, in her infinite wisdom, did not think this was necessary, but I insisted. My name was being tarnished falsely and news had a habit of travelling quickly in the barren lands.

Prior to the narcotics event, my colleague had been visiting the RCMP and came home with a bottle of wine which he claimed had been a gift from the officer. I later found out that this was very inaccurate and in fact the nurse had gone over to borrow the wine. It was all becoming crystal clear.

Meantime the promised help was due to arrive on the Easter weekend. Unfortunately the weather was bad and no planes were flying. She was an Irish nurse and a friend that I had known from Bella Bella. She arrived in the Northwest Territories after me and had secured a job in an adjacent community. That weekend was a very hectic one as I had to deliver a baby and the newborn was not breathing normally. I had to be up during the night to monitor the little one, being unable to airlift it to a hospital at that time. In the midst of this, a little girl was brought in who had been scalded with hot water. There was a bit of furore, with the child screaming in pain and fright. The parents, too, were very upset.

We had sterile packs made up for various medical emergencies, this being one. It helped to simplify the problem when all materials were readily at hand. Covered in dressings and bandages, she fell asleep from the sedation I gave her, and I was able to get an intravenous started in her now that she was quietened. It was lucky that the burns were not of a severity that she would require skin grafting. There was a medley of minor accidents requiring dressings or sutures on that long weekend, banishing all hopes for a relaxing Easter.

My good friend arrived to aid me and take a turn on call so that I might have an undisturbed night's rest. I still had not received any update on the previous Nurse-in -Charge. It was annoying to be kept in the dark. Now that I had a witness I wanted to search out his room for some proof. I had not wanted to enter his room alone, but waited until now. Together we looked in the bedside drawer and there the evidence was plainly in view; there were syringes, empty vials of two types of narcotics, along with analgesics and other sedative drugs in pill form. In a tea chest in the corner of the room, I spotted a bottle sticking out. Curious, I looked more closely and there were seven bottles of booze that I had been accused of taking, neatly placed, but not really concealed. We looked no further, I had gotten the answers I needed. I felt somewhat hurt that I had enjoyed friendship and laughter with this senior nurse and then his contributions of erroneous, malicious information was given to my detriment. I had to conclude that the pathological lying was all part of his addiction.

Leaving my friend behind to man the Nursing Station, I took my leave. I was en route to yet another northern settlement in British Columbia, called Kincolith. However, I still had to have an encounter with my accuser at headquarters.

We were formally introduced and without wasting time I produced the letter she had written, reading its contents back to her as though to serve as a reminder of her own nastiness. In a clear voice and facing her I said, "Please make your accusations to my face and in the presence of a witness!" She moved uneasily in her seat, apologizing profusely, admitting her colleague had given her this information. I gave her a frosty stare and revealed that she would find the bottles of alcohol exactly where her cohort had stored them, emphasising again that I did not drink. I intimated to her the fact that her friend was a drug addict and went on to say that she could not possibly have shared her work space and living space without knowing that. She made no comment.

Both of us were staying in the Churchill residence for the night. Burying the hatchet, I invited her for a walk along the shore line. We avoided the topic and just enjoyed seeing the polar bears quite some distance away. Churchill is well known for its polar bear population and although magnificent looking beasts, they are also very savage. The area was well posted, warning of the dangers. Some bears came into town. Often under these circumstances they were trapped live, tagged and marked before taking them to a distant place. This would identify to the game and wildlife officers whether the same one had returned.

CHAPTER TWELVE
KINCOLITH

As usual, before leaving my current place of employment I had another position lined up, so as not to break continuity of service. This time I was headed to a small Indian village called Kincolith, located north of Prince Rupert in British Columbia, deep in the mountains and heavily forested. Again the isolated location did not lend itself to roadways and accessibility was by sea or air.

History has it that Kincolith was also known as "The Place of Skulls." The Haida Indians, native to the Queen Charlotte Islands, in British Columbia, had a raiding party up the Nass River looking for slaves. The natives aboard the vessels of their captors, created havoc in their attempt to escape while crossing over the sea. The Haidas, afraid of their boats capsizing with the struggle, pulled into shore and killed the captives. The decapitated heads of the victims were displayed on poles thus giving the name "Place of Skulls."

The day I arrived was sunny, with not a cloud in the sky, presenting me with a picturesque view of the new community. The plane which carried three passengers and the pilot landed smoothly on the water. As I stood on the dock with my suitcases, one trunk, one dog and a collapsed metal dog cage, I looked about me and had hoped to be welcomed by a friendly face from the Health Centre. Alas no one appeared, nor was there a vehicle made available to me for the transportation of my luggage. In exasperation I asked a local native if someone usually came to meet the new arrival. He just shrugged and pointed to a sort of transport system which resembled a flat bed on four wheels. It had a long metal shaft with a handle that was used for pulling this contraption. He was kind enough to load all my gear onto the trolley with some assistance from another native standing nearby. I felt very grateful to them, but the help ended there. Pointing with a gnarled finger, he directed me to the Health Centre which really wasn't too far away. Gritting my teeth, my thoughts were, "Well, with your pioneering spirit you chose to live in the great Canadian north, so get on with it." With Judy in tow, I grabbed hold of the trolley and headed in the direction of my new home. The pulling was not made easy by the fact that the roads were made of gravel and full of little ruts, causing me to stop several times to check that all the baggage was still on board. As I neared the health unit I saw a tall female coming from the building along the road. She was in pursuit of a Dalmation dog heading towards mine. I concluded the animals name was Tucker and her expletive rhymed with it. I swallowed hard on hearing her profanities being directed at the hound and I muttered to myself, "What have I come to?" Within minutes she came forward and introduced herself to me and visa versa. I had surmised she was the nurse. She took command of my luggage, pulling the contraption and my personal effects to the final destination.

In British Columbia the clinics were referred to as Health Centres, but unlike Bella Bella, where I only did prevention work, this facility had the same duties and responsibilities of a Nursing Station, which meant treating and diagnosing patients in the absence of a doctor. I had allowed myself to believe that in a preventive programme there would be no on-call duties and life would be somewhat less hectic, but I was deluded to some degree.

The building was a modern structure on one level. The living quarters were an extension of the clinic area, and were quite different from anything I had experienced in other types of residential living. Each nurse had her own separate quarters which allowed privacy. There was a communal sitting/dining room for visiting personnel.

It was while my new colleague was giving me the grand tour of my quarters that her Dalmation dog showed himself to be somewhat chauvinistic in the presence of a lady dog, proceeding to lift his leg in the hallway. He barely had a chance to mark his territory when a yell was uttered by his master and he was sent quickly, shamefully on his way. "Oh dear", I thought. Was this going to be an ongoing problem where marking boundaries would become a ritual? As it turned out I had little to fear, each dog accepted the other and became wonderful doggy friends, respecting each other's right to an area.

I found out very quickly that some community members did not come to the clinic during working hours, which meant that medical problems, not of an urgent nature, were often treated late in the evening, clients electing to turn night into day. I thought I could adjust my sleep routine to accommodate this, as flexibility sometimes could be an advantage. Not liking to rise early in the morning this could have been a good arrangement for me, except that the radio in the office, which was our only means of communication, had to be manned at eight o'clock each day.

The nurse that was showing me the ropes planned on leaving at the end of the month. I needed to get a handle on the functions of the facility and of the administrative duties. There were some aspects that were basic to each clinic, but each community and tribes had a different approach and outlook within their own societies. It was up to newcomers to learn about these ways.

Within a week of arriving I wanted to go on a much-needed long walk with my dog. Before setting out to explore any new place I would generally check with the local Indians as to the type of wildlife there might be roaming about. On this occasion I relied on my co-worker's information. She had been there for two years and claimed that there were not too many places to walk. When the tide came in, it reached well inland to where the soccer field was situated. I didn't like the idea of walking there in case I would be caught by the incoming tide. There was, however, a nice trail in the bushes that she would take me through, mentioning on the way that she had heard rumours of a bear in the area but had never seen any indications of one.

We were ambling along on this fine Saturday morning. The dogs were up ahead, ranging and sniffing everything in their path, at times chasing one another. My colleague, Beth, and I chatted on the way. She was a little ahead of me as the path, being narrow, meant we walked single file. Suddenly, I stopped dead in my tracks. Along the side of the path and slightly hidden by bushes was this large, black, hairy object, a little too near for comfort. I managed to blurt out, "What is that?" followed by, "Oh my God it's a be-be-bear!" I instinctively called the dog to heel and Judy dutifully came, whereupon I attached her to her leash. My friend's dog took off in chase of the bear once it had got the scent, and according to his owner, it was usual behaviour for him to ignore her admonitions. He was still a very young dog, not yet too interested in discipline. Had my dog not been on the leash, she too would have given chase, judging by her straining and leaping about in excitement. All this happened in minutes, and meantime I stood frozen to the spot, my knees knocking. When I say knocking, they literally were. I didn't know whether or not to follow the other girl who by now was in hot pursuit of her pet. The bear had, of course, taken off and probably was even more frightened than we were, but their behaviour can be unpredictable. Needless to say, I seldom went along that trail again.

The only other place to walk was through the small village which consisted of houses, one shop and local offices pertaining to the community affairs. The houses were connected by various board walks which made walking very easy. The lack of good walking space made me feel very confined, especially when I had a large dog requiring vigorous exercise She was a mixed breed of Husky, Alsatian and Collie.

Life was quieter than I had anticipated because the population was in the vicinity of three hundred. I had only been there a month and just prior to Beth leaving, we had a doctor arrive to see patients. As in other centres we kept a book, listing those clients who required to be seen by a physician. We busied ourselves setting up appointments for each patient the day prior to his arrival.

Being trained thirty-odd years back and with the old school attitude on protocol instilled in me, I still retained some feelings of awe in the presence of doctors, placing them unintentionally on a pedestal. Gradually though, that respectful feeling was leaving me. Perhaps, having done the duties of a doctor myself for so many years I realized that nurses did wonderful work in these isolated posts, particularly having to wear the cap and carry out the duties of many professionals, such as radiographers, social workers, mental health counsellors, to mention a few, as these services were not available. This, I believe, made the northern nurses something special. If this comes across as being a little boastful then I have succeeded in creating an awareness of the nurses' roles in our society; those who are not given the same status as doctors, but nevertheless are the backbone of any health service. Their financial rewards should be matched to services rendered, many of us having studied just as long as doctors.

This diminishing respect for the medical profession was accentuated for a variety of reasons, when the doctor arrived at Kincolith. When he introduced himself to me I am sure my mouth must have gaped open in surprise. Before me stood this man, looking in every way like "Hippie." He had long crinkly hair tied back in a pony tail with an elastic band. He wore a heavy plaid shirt similar to those worn by lumberjacks, a baggy pair of trousers made of denim, held up by a pair of braces. On his bare feet he wore a pair of thong sandals, exposing his very large toes.

He wasted no time in starting his clinic work. A number of women in the waiting room shyly asked me if that man was the doctor. After affirming that he was, several left. I can't say I blamed them one bit as I would not have allowed him to attend me, particularly when some of their complaints were of a female nature. Needless to say, word got around and the clinic was not at all busy.

The first evening, Beth and I prepared supper and the doctor was our guest, along with a community friend. In this small village, as in Bella Bella, we paid for our food supplies and also for the shipping costs. It was quite usual for guests coming to stay with us to make a gesture of supplementing us with some fresh fruit or vegetables as they would be partaking of our supplies. This fellow brought with him his personal effects in a rucksack and a partially eaten ring of garlic sausage, which he carefully stored in one of the fridges.

Dinner was served, and being polite hostesses we passed all the various cooked dishes of food first to the guests. Our doctor friend acted as though he had not eaten in a while and proceeded to literally load his plate from the variety of foods before him. By the time I was seated and the dishes were passed to me, I was fortunate to get a teaspoonful of potatoes and vegetables. I must admit I was more than a little ticked off at the sheer face of greed that looked across the table from me, chomping away on his food in a way that could not possibly be described as civilized. I was tempted to give him a book on "Miss Manners." This further display of uncouthness made me realize that having a doctor's degree does not necessarily equip the individual in the art of social graces, as in the days of old whereby many doctors came from well-to-do backgrounds. If this was the new modern way, I was not impressed nor do I believe it would have impressed many of the very dignified men/women still in the medical profession.

Everyone was finished dining and as the conversation was becoming a little sluggish, we decided to take our leave of the doctor. The room we dined in was to be his sleeping quarters on a sofa bed. As we started to make it up with linen, he announced that he would not require us to do so. He would sleep on the bare mattress with a blanket over him. To give him the benefit of the doubt he may not have wished to inconvenience us, but somehow he did not strike me as that time of chap. We continued in spite of his protests to make up the bed with sheets, for hygienic purposes for those who would follow.

He left within two days, thankfully. As a parting gesture, he offered the shrivelled up remains of what once was a healthy piece of garlic sausage. You would have thought we had been proffered a ring of gold. Perhaps he was unaware that he had eaten well at our expense, which irked us, particularly his salary being handsome compared to ours, a salary which he did not earn on this trip.

My colleague left soon after this incident and I was reassured by the department that help would soon be forthcoming. When I accepted this position it was with the understanding that within three months after arrival in Kincolith I would be permitted to take my summer vacation. My travel arrangements had been confirmed earlier.

It really was a most beautiful, peaceful place to be. There were bald-headed eagles in abundance flying overhead, giving us below a view of their magnificent wing span, before perching themselves atop the tall evergreens which engulfed the village.

I decided to give my kitchen a good cleaning one evening, starting with the fridge and stove. With my preoccupation of the job in hand I had not realized how late it was. I sang a few Scottish songs and the dog, contented to be with her master, sprawled lazily on the floor beside me. She suddenly sat upright and gave a low throaty woof. She repeated it a few times. I heard nothing and carried on as usual. But again she woofed, this time a little louder. When she started a third time I thought maybe there was good reason. I looked through the kitchen window but saw nothing. I headed down towards the clinic area. The building was in the shape of the letter "L" and from the far clinic window I saw a ladder placed against the wall beside the kitchen window and I heard heavy footsteps run off. I became frightened and ran next door to where a retired teacher was living. I frantically banged on the door and the teacher who had been asleep finally answered. I told him what had happened. He quickly dressed and searched the area. Two different sets of footprints were found in the wet ground beneath my kitchen window. I asked him if he would stay the rest of the night, by now feeling a little unnerved should the intruders return. He agreed and once again I made up the guest bed.

I informed the council in the morning and I was told it probably was a specific man and his son who were "peeping toms." One of the men I knew had a mental disorder. After that incident I never felt comfortable living there alone.

I was already packed for my vacation. The week before, I went down to the dock to talk to the pilot about my expected flight out with the dog. The pilot informed me that he would take my dog this time but on the return journey he would not do so. He explained that some residents were complaining about dirty dogs being allowed on the aircraft. His business depended a great deal on those people and he felt compelled to abide by the new ruling. My option on return would be to take the dog in by ship. Whether it was true or not, I was told that the dog would be tied up on the deck. I had heard enough and basically, all things considered, I decided not to return to that area.

Helping me to finalize that decision was the fact that no second nursing assistance seemed to be on the horizon in spite of all the promises. I radioed the Prince Rupert office to remind them that I would be leaving on vacation soon and that I would be requesting another posting on my return to Canada. I went on to express my concerns about leaving the Health Centre unmanned because there were narcotics in the locked cupboard. When I say locked, the mode used was a long length of bicycle chain threaded through the door handles. Given that someone had been lurking outside the premises recently, I was reticent to leave without the department being fully aware of the situation. The radio station band which I spoke on was supposed to be private, but my conversation was heard. I received a call from one Councillor who was very angry with me, stating I had no right to give the information about the "peeping tom" to my boss. In their eyes they felt that this was bad publicity and they were afraid of being without any nurse.

With Judy in tow I took my leave in July. Due to my brief stay in the community I did not experience any pangs of sadness as the plane took off. "Where to next?" I wondered.

CHAPTER THIRTEEN
GLEICHEN, ALBERTA

After much deliberation I accepted a position in Southern Alberta, again with the same department. I enjoyed my work in the north immensely; it had given me many rich experiences, but the constant heavy workload was becoming too restrictive. I was single and the social aspects of my life were being neglected. At the end of a normal workday there were always more duties to be done, sometimes spanning another two shifts, making it a twenty-four hour working day. At that time there was no financial reward for the overtime.

The new position required me to have a valid driver's licence and without hesitation, I took the necessary instruction in British Columbia. The ability to drive gave me a new freedom. Gone were the skidoo and bombardier as a form of transport. Now I had four wheels, places to explore and shopping near at hand, instead of ordering through a catalogue. No more restless nights with being on call and no more intense decision-making that involved human life.

I remarked to my colleague, who chauffeured me along the highway, that this was going to be quite a different lifestyle We were bound for the Siksika Reservation, a mere sixty miles from the city of Calgary, in the province of Alberta. As we sped along I observed the similarity of the wide open prairie, likening it to that of the vast Arctic tundra landscape, but instead of caribou roaming about I saw huge herds of cattle.

We had now arrived at the Indian Reservation. I was able to identify the various agency buildings we passed, by the large, painted logos standing high, visible from a distance. We pulled up in front of a two-storey building. I recognized it to be the local Indian hospital which was funded by the Federal Government. At the main entrance we were greeted by the Director of Nursing who in turn introduced me to the hospital staff. I was given a tour of the wards before being shown my living quarters, in the upstairs of the hospital. When I went to retrieve my dog from the car a discussion arose as to where my dog would be lodged. I was instantly informed that she could sleep in the caretaker's workshop building. I was shown the workshop which also served as a garage. Observing the car grease on the floor, debris, general clutter and detecting strong chemical odours, I was not happy at the arrangement and insisted the dog stay with me. Reluctantly, I was allowed the privilege. In fairness I must say that in order to access my room I had to go through the main doors of the hospital and it was not the best arrangement. I was finally left to my own devices, to unpack and settle in.

Because the dog was not welcome in the residence for obvious reasons, I tried to make our stay as unobtrusive as possible, confining her at all times to my room except for toilet needs. On seeing the fire escape stairway directly alongside my room, I decided to take the dog outside by this route, but on the second day the poor animal lodged her little paw in a gap in the wrought iron stairs, uttering the most painful yelps and howls. Annoyed at this situation I found myself in, I decided to take her out by the front door and chance being the recipient of any hostilities. Had the dog slipped on the fire stair in panic it would also have compromised my safety, resulting in both of us falling from a height.

The next day, I met my colleagues at the Health Centre. The building was nothing glamorous but rather a double wide mobile trailer unit on the hospital grounds. The staff consisted of the Nurse-in-Charge, two women from the Blackfoot Reservation, both in training as Community Health Workers, and one native Secretary. I was given my own office where I spent some time learning about policies and procedures.

Having been given the keys to the government car assigned to me, that evening, after work, I decided to take a drive through some parts of the reservation and find my bearings. The roads were not quite what I had expected. Instead of tarred surfaces there was gravel, which I had never driven on before. Undaunted, I took off and when coming down a hill, I applied the brakes. The next I knew, I was in the ditch at the opposite side of the road, facing in a different direction from the one in which I was originally travelling. The first lesson had just been learned about the application of brakes on gravel surfaces, but fortunately without any mishap to me or to the car. I had to apply the brakes very gently and travel slowly until I was accustomed to this type of road surface.

My evenings were spent searching for a place to rent, and at that time it was almost an impossibility to find accommodation. I walked around the adjacent town of Gleichen, making enquiries. Perchance, an English woman who had befriended me, introduced me to a female teacher who was looking for someone to share her rented space. She welcomed me and in less than two weeks I was moving into town, very relieved to be leaving my restricted quarters.

I was now settled into my abode, which was a very old building and whilst reading and enjoying the quietness in the sitting room, I was startled to hear odd sounds coming from within the walls, but exactly from where I was not sure. My housemate told me not to worry as it was only a woodchuck running around between the walls. This little creature, I learned, was a North American marmot. She went on to say, "Oh by the way you may hear sounds in the basement, but don't worry, it's only an iguana that was left by the previous owners." "An iguana!" I said, swallowing hard and asked, "How big is this thing and will it come upstairs?" "No! No! It stays there." she replied. My eyes narrowed as I looked straight at her and asked, "How do you know it's there? Have you actually seen it?" She admitted she had only heard this as speculative talk.

On one occasion I had reason to descend the steps into the basement. Not knowing what an iguana looked like, I was nervous, imagining the creature would be the size of a crocodile. My dog was game for most adventures but when she refused to accompany me downstairs I was highly suspicious that this creature was lurking in what was described to me as an old well in the floor. Nothing ever did appear, but then I decided to leave the basement area well alone. Only one time when home from work with illness did I hear some funny sounds resembling a dragging movement from the bowels of the earth. I didn't bother to explore lest my housemate would return home and find the remnants of my bathrobe and one missing tenant.

I was gradually finding my feet in the new job, although it was not made easy. In fact it was hard, as I was left to flounder, given no encouragement or direction. How I longed daily for the life in the north again.

A comfortable routine established, I worked fairly independently over the next few months. One morning I received a call from my headquarters. In the introductory conversation with my Supervisor she mentioned, "You will of course now be acting in charge of the facility." I was puzzled until she explained that the Nurse-in-Charge had resigned. She was equally surprised that I did not know. Fortunately my native Secretary was a godsend and helped me through many hard times in the office, always steering me in the right direction until I became familiar with the various aspects of my new role, while others remained less friendly. There was resistance to a new person being in charge.

During the following months and in my new capacity, I attended meetings with the Chief and Council, along with an administration representative from my department. The meetings were regarding the proposed new health facility. This building would amalgamate the clinics for outpatients, run by clinic nurses and the community health programmes, making this a replacement for the closing of the old hospital. It was a hot political issue, causing a diversity of feelings from the residents of the reservation. By the time we moved into the new building many were not convinced of the wisdom of such a plan. It was a matter of economics, but by creating this new facility, which was to cost a tidy sum, the native people felt somewhat threatened by the loss of their hospital which had been in existence since the 1920s and had been the birthplace for many. Apart from that sentiment the new Health Centre would be open from eight in the morning until twelve midnight, with a nurse being on call during the night for emergencies.

I attended the initial turning of the sod ceremony and ultimately the building was erected. On the seventeenth of June, 1977 the clinic was officially opened. There were the usual official speeches at the event which was attended by the staff, the Blackfoot Chief and Council, as well as other Chiefs from the Treaty Seven Bands and the Parliamentary Secretary to the Minister of Health and Welfare. Other dignitaries, as well as some of the public, were there to observe.

The health unit, named Siksika Medicine Lodge, represented the modern concepts in promoting the trends toward preventive health care. The Blackfoot people had health services dating back well over one hundred years, delivered to them by their own medicine man. In those early days many people died from smallpox and diphtheria. In 1869, Chief Crowfoot requested the help of Father Lacombe and the Anglican missionaries after a smallpox epidemic decimated much of their population. Also in the early 1880s, the Blackfoot were faced with the scourge of tuberculosis and in 1895 the first hospital was built at the northern end of the reservation. Eventually it became inadequate to accommodate the sick and therefore a new hospital of fifteen beds was opened in 1924. In the late 1920s further expansion of this facility took place and this was the hospital that now the natives had to see replaced. One could well understand the insecurities that many elderly residents must have felt, particularly with a bureaucracy that they did not trust because of past encounters; signing treaties in good faith with the government of that time, and their subsequent disillusionment when these treaties were broken.

When my Supervisor visited, she suggested that I should consider taking a diploma course in public health. She stated that I had shown capability in my field of work and in administration but there was a heavy focus on obtaining a degree or diploma. I declined to enter into more training, particularly when the government did not pay me for all the nursing certificates I held, yet they benefited from my existing extra trainings in certain aspects of my work.

The Blackfoot Nation consists of three tribes, namely the Blood, Peigan and Blackfoot. All speak the Algonquin language. In the early days they were a nomadic people who hunted the bison which provided them with clothing, food and shelter in the form of tepees.

The Blackfoot, who fought tribes such as the Cree, Kootenay and Assiniboine, were considered great warriors. The best known of their Chiefs was Crowfoot. History tells us that he was not originally from the Blackfoot tribe, but was born in the year 1830 of Indian parents who belonged to the Blood Tribe. He was given the name of Shot Close which he kept until he reached maturity, for names were considered a possession. When a person died, the name was given to someone else within the family. The father of Shot Close, who was named Packs A Knife, was eventually killed in battle when he was still very young. His mother, in due course married a Blackfoot warrior. Following that marriage she was to return with her new husband to live amongst the Blackfoot tribe. Shot Close was to remain with his grandfather and be raised by him. When the young boy learned of this arrangement he followed on foot after his mother and new father, eventually catching up to them. Although they wanted him to return to the grandfather, he refused, wanting to stay with his mother. Eventually, the grandfather came to live with the Blackfoot. A little later, the young boy was given the name Bear Ghost. This second name was a Blackfoot one given by his stepfather. Another name bestowed on him was Packs a Knife, that of his deceased father, following his first exploit in a raid. Soon afterwards he was given yet another name which was shortened to Crowfoot the name by which he is best known.

On September twenty-second, 1877, The Blackfoot Nation signed a treaty with Queen Victoria's commissioners at the Blackfoot Crossing. In signing, they gave up their title to thousands of square miles of traditional Blackfoot land. In exchange, the Indians were given Treaty Rights which meant they were allotted land known as reservations. Health, education, hunting and fishing rights were to be honoured by the Canadian Government and they would also have their economical future sustained. The Indians were to respect the law but could also abide by their own traditional ways, co-existing with their European neighbours.

On July sixth, 1977, one hundred years after the official signing of the treaty by Chief Crowfoot and other chiefs, a re-enactment of the treaty signing took place at the Blackfoot Crossing, which is part of the reserve land. My parents, who were visiting from Scotland, and I were presented with official invitations to attend the event. This allowed us to sit amongst the native guests and very near to the site of the actual ceremony. I felt very privileged to witness a re-enactment of this historical moment and my father recorded the event on his cine-camera.

We waited for the ceremonies to begin, but they could not until the special guest, His Royal Highness, Prince Charles arrived. Suddenly, there was a stirring in the crowd and shouts of "He's here!" The Prince, riding in an open horse-drawn carriage and waving to the crowd, passed close to where we were seated. Queen Victoria, the reigning monarch at the time of the original treaty signing, was the great, great grandmother of the prince.

The most regal of the sights for me, that day, was on seeing an elderly Blackfoot, astride his horse, slowly descend the nearby hill, proudly making his way down. He wore a beautiful headdress with the feathers cascading down his back. In his hand he held a staff with many feathers attached. My excitement mounted as I watched this magnificent entrance into the present day arena. Many natives today still retain that sense of aboriginal pride while others have given way to alcoholism, losing their self pride and allowing so much bitterness to develop between the races.

Many of the native people were prosperous in their farming work, while others were employed with various local Governmental Departments. Funding for the different programmes came from the Federal Government mainly but the Provincial Government also contributed. They were a progressive band and were seeking self-government for their future.

Although I was used to the cold Arctic conditions I also found the prairies very cold in the winter. I hated the tedious task of having to scrape the car windows and warming up the car before I set off on my rounds. There were many situations that created frustrations and stress for me working in that environment. Each day, in my attempts to promote health, I met with non-compliance for a variety of reasons. One was due to the lack of public transportation which meant the health services had to be brought to the people in their homes. Because many were on welfare they could not afford a private vehicle or the maintenance of one. In the white society the majority of the people attended the clinics for immunizations, pre-natal instruction, tuberculin testing and x-rays. Of course that was not a foolproof system, either. Going out to the homes was basically like travelling through a farming community, having to contend with isolated roads and houses spread far apart throughout the district. The authorities were gradually building more houses closer together to create a greater community atmosphere.

Telephones were not a luxury in many households, therefore I could not pre-arrange my visits under these circumstances. Rather, I had just to take a chance that my patients would be at home. Sometimes, after a twenty mile drive, I would arrive to find a locked door with no one there. In other situations I would be informed that the baby was sleeping and instructed to come back later. In trying to explain in some instances that the child was very behind in the immunization programme and in spite of several attempts on my part to upgrade these, I would be chastised for not letting them know in advance.

Meantime, the bosses at the headquarters in Ottawa exerted great pressure on the nurses. It was imperative that the statistics show how many had been inoculated. If the statistics were low there was a call to do more in spite of the fact, to use an old cliché, "You can bring a horse to water but you cannot make him drink." Some mothers were opposed to having their children inoculated at an early age and consciously refused to have this done.

Sometimes my work involved dealing with animals. It made me wonder if I should have been a veterinary. Three such incidences come to mind. I had been travelling daily to a particular home located nearly twenty-five miles from the clinic. My middle-aged male client was supposed to have close follow-up care due to his past history of tuberculosis. He was very elusive and it was important that I locate him. Unabashed after one or two failed visits, I continued, fitting this visit in with my other duties for the rest of the week. Each day there was no one at home, but I did notice that the old grey mare was always standing in one corner of a pen surrounded by an eight foot fence. It looked as though the animal had never moved her position from day one when I first saw her. There was no sign of food and the gate to the water trough, an old bath tub, was closed. Finding no one at home I turned my attentions to the animal in question. I climbed over a fence at least eight feet high. Thankfully I was still agile enough to do so. After assessing the situation I climbed down and gathered all the pieces of scattered hay I could find on this farm complex, only to clamber back over again. When I threw the food in, she responded and walked towards the inviting dinner I had just provided for her. I then tied open the gate and with a few persuasive clicking sounds with my tongue, coaxed her to enjoy some water. Happy that I had helped one of God's little creatures again, I left feeling that not all had been lost that week. Further inquiries from a nearby neighbour indicated that the owner would be home the next day.

On another very hot day with the temperature hitting ninety degrees Fahrenheit, I was again doing home visits on another part of the reserve. I decided that I would have to head home after this next visit, unable to tolerate the heat any longer. Perhaps coming from a country with a more temperate climate affected my ability to take the extreme heat. As I approached the next home I saw the lady of the house standing at the door with three of her children. She seemed to be a little put out and I found out why. She wanted someone to come and shoot the young horse that was lying in front of her home because she thought it was ill and dying. The very thought of an animal so young being shot upset me greatly. I summed up the situation and decided that the horse was suffering from heat exhaustion. I asked the boys to bring me a bucket of cold water, which they did willingly. I poured water over the animal's body and then taking large scoops of water in my hands got him to drink. At this point I realized that we had to get her out of this unrelenting heat and until we did, recovery was not about to take place. I was somewhat perplexed as to how we could move this animal all the way down to the field into the shade of some grain storage bins. The animal appeared to be weak. Well, there was nothing else for it but to walk it down manually. The three boys, the mother and myself pushed and shoved and managed to get the filly onto her feet but she wouldn't budge from that spot. I instructed the boys to take a leg each and I would take one. Moving a leg, one step at a time in rotation we walked the animal to shelter. "Right leg, now left, now back left and back right" I called out. It must have been comical to see but those kids were as delighted as I was to have helped. The filly had some tear marks on her neck as though torn by barbed wire but obviously they had been treated previously. The animal must have strayed from the mother. Before leaving the family I checked again on the horse and she seemed to have recovered and was eating. I spent my evening attempting to track down the owner and discovered he was in his tepee at the Calgary Stampede. I eventually managed to make contact with him.

The third encounter was with a horse, standing by the roadside. The poor animal appeared to have hoof problems. I stopped the car to have a closer look at the animal. I made the mistake of going behind him. The horse kicked with his hind legs, missing me by a fraction. I reported the animal's condition to the appropriate authorities as I am sure he was suffering.

I enjoyed visiting the various areas on reserve as each one was so different. In certain parts there were small groupings of houses like a parish. Gradually the old homes were being replaced by new ones but on many occasions there was overcrowding, which played havoc with the septic tanks, designed only to contain a certain capacity and for a specific amount of resident usage.

Often the young members of the family would move in with their children to the grandparents' home. There just were not enough houses for them all. It reminded me of the post war days in Britain where housing shortages were in existence, and my parents, too, had to move in with my grandparents when I was very young.

Trees on the prairies were very few and far between and with the extremely hot summers the grass was very dry and scorched. It was not unusual to witness grass fires, often caused by carelessness. With the wind blowing and fanning the flames it did not take long for the fire to spread.

There were also a number of house fires that occurred, the causes arising from numerous factors. This only added to the shortage of homes as many were totally gutted. I can recall one house fire where, from my house in town, I could see the flames leaping into the air. I jumped into my car and raced over to lend assistance. All but one person managed to escape from the home and sadly, the father died inside. It was terrible to witness the house blazing and in the midst of all the commotion with police, ambulance, fire trucks and hoses everywhere, to hear the shrieks of anguish from the relatives who were not only screaming that someone was still in there but attempting to re-enter the house to save their loved one. All I could do was to take them, struggling, to the clinic to be sedated. What utter misery and trauma it was for those left behind, wondering if their relative suffered before dying and feeling no peace because of that thought. It was reported to me that the deceased was found positioned beside the window, as though attempting to get out.

In the 1960s the First Nations were given their liquor rights and therefore could go to the local bar in town and drink or take their purchases home. As part of a civilized world everyone has rights and so too had the Blackfoot, but it was a right that would often play havoc in their lives. Violence often erupted and as a result deaths occurred with frequency either from homicides or by suicide. It appeared up until the liquor rights were given, deaths were more due to aging or health related causes, but the alcohol changed that status. Suicides carried out were often, shootings, hangings or overdoses. On occasion, when returning from the bar in town and intoxicated, an individual was sometimes killed or maimed by the oncoming train, the railway separating the town from the reservation.

Because of the use of alcohol by some natives, we nurses were often subjected to racial abuse by the inebriates, deriding us as a white race and showering us with verbal abuse on numerous occasions. The antipathy was directed at the white man for stealing their land and was a usual issue. Many times in the process of delivering health care to the individuals I was reminded that I was on Indian land and was trespassing. I would be told repeatedly that the white man also caused the addiction to alcohol. One cannot deny the hurt of a people who felt duped by government, nor blame them for the mistrust that evolved. It was unfortunate that we, being the messengers and who were not responsible for the political situations, had the bullets fired at us. We also understood that as humans, when we are injured, we lash out at others and blame. It was part of a process and it was easier to forgive the treatment than retain hostilities.

In my nursing career there were many situations which gave rise to humorous stories. I was not present when the one I am about to relate happened, but which was later told to me. Dentures were given free every two years or so if needed. One toothless Indian lady arrived at the health facility requesting she have a new set made. She was informed by the secretary that she was not yet due for a replacement. Not accepting this she spoke louder with annoyance, so that the Nurse-in-Charge was called upon to settle the matter. Checking the patient's file once more she assured the woman that her dentures were relatively new and her request could not be considered. The woman insisted she needed them to eat. It was then established that she had loaned her false teeth to her friend. The Nurse-in-Charge seized her opportunity to bring this matter to a close by saying to the woman, "You better go and ask for them back." The woman quickly countered that remark by stating, "I can't. They buried her yesterday!" I never heard whether the lady in question got another set but for that story alone, it was worth breaking the rules.

During a home visit I became very concerned about the well being of an elderly lady who lived in a small shack and had a severe physical impairment, restricting her getting about. I had noticed how deaf she was and decided to get her examined for a hearing aid. This lady referred many times to her religious beliefs on my other visits. The conversation that followed was, "Would you like me to have you fitted with a hearing aid?" No reply. I repeated my words. "What did you say?" she asked. I repeated my words. "I didn't know what you said!" she answered. I repeated it a fourth time, somewhat louder. She heard me this time. "Oh no", she exclaimed, "My hearing is okay now, the Lo-ord healed me." It was not for me to say otherwise, so I dropped the subject.

I was out on my usual home rounds when I stopped to visit an older gentleman. He and his wife were heavy, habitual drinkers, but nevertheless they were grand people. At times they were a little coarse in their language with me, but because I knew them in sober times I could make allowances for their behaviour. On this day Bert was home alone, or so I thought. I knocked on the door and a raucous voice from within shouted, "Come in". Knowing the family history, I was not sure as to what I would find when I entered. He was standing in the kitchen leaning on a pair of crutches, his leg in plaster due to a fracture. He greeted me in a friendly manner and once conversation was under way I was aware of a cat mewing. It became so intense that I was completely distracted from my conversation. I had had enough. "Bert", I said, "I can hear a cat mewing!" He replied, "Yep, I've got a cat." I could not see it but I knew it was in the kitchen area. As I walked across the floor towards the fridge the sound became louder. "Bert you don't think it got into the fridge by mistake do you?" He laughed so hard. "No! No!", he replied. Not satisfied, I asked if I could take a peek inside the fridge. He gave me permission. No cat was to be seen. Then I had the brainwave that it had to be in the deep freezer compartment. Once again I ventured to look. In the meantime Bert is bursting his britches laughing at the intensity of my search. Still no cat. I next went down on all fours and with a flashlight he provided me with I finally traced the rather loud meows to underneath the fridge where the poor cat could not disengage itself from all the wiring below. It must have climbed up on the countertop, then onto the top of the fridge and fallen down the back. How long it had been there was anyone's guess. I said I would try and move the fridge to release the animal, but it was quite heavy and he could not assist. From the background I heard a low pitched utterance. Someone else was in the house. Perhaps that person could help me. Bert agreed and limped off to arouse his friend who was pleasantly inebriated and sleeping it off. The friend staggered through, stifling a few good yawns. He was good natured about it and fortunately I knew him well. He came to my help and in-between he could not resist a few words to me of a personal nature. I good-naturedly scolded him and with a laugh, he pushed the fridge aside and out popped a frightened feline. I wanted to pick the kitten up to soothe it but it darted for safety into the next room.

Occasionally visits were of a serious nature but still had a humorous side to them. Sometimes we were called upon to inform a relative that a loved one had died. Such was the case when I visited an elderly man who also was the Medicine Man. I had travelled by car down the gravel road and over grassy bumpy terrain to reach his house to let him know that his wife's sister had died. His wife was not at home and at first I thought this gentleman was not either. After several loud raps on the door there still was no response. The sign outside the door read, "No doctoring today." I opened the door and proceeded inside, calling out his name. I could hear a slight sound coming from the sitting room and on entering it I saw the person I needed. He was sitting on the couch and before him were different denominations of paper money all arranged in neat little bundles. As I announced the reason for my visit, he was not at all fazed. Apart from a brief glimpse in my direction, he continued with his count---ten, fifteen, twenty dollars. The scene was quite amusing. I repeated the message a second time only to get the same reaction as before. Ah well! I just left him alone absorbed with his financial matters!

The prairie land was often dry and it did not take long for the grass to change from green to yellow, then a brown colour, with the heat. I travelled over dusty gravel roads mostly every day to different areas and I found a special beauty in the vast landscape. It altered with the various times of the day. On a clear day one could see the Rocky Mountains in the distance.

After heavy rainfalls, travel was made difficult in places, forcing me to leave the car at some point and walk the rest of the distance to do home visitations. I recall an episode when my colleague could not leave the clinic because of a pressing meeting. She asked me to attend a patient of hers requiring an injection, essential to his care. I left the car on a side road and proceeded by foot along the side of a barbed wire fence and over a quagmire. Each time I took a step I would leave behind my Wellington boot. Hanging on to the barbed wire fence I would then extract it slowly. There was a loud suction sound and a plop when it finally released, almost knocking me off balance. In this manner I eventually made it to the house. It was a painstaking half hour just to go a short distance, and in the end the patient refused his treatment. To make matters worse it was raining heavily. I did not have the right to compel him to take the injection even though it was to his own detriment to refuse. Dumbfounded, I left to begin my muddy trip back to the clinic. Looking in the car mirror I saw a sorry sight. My face was mud splattered and my curls were now strands of straight wet hair, but I still managed to smile at life's follies.

At a later date I was called upon to attend this young man at the request of his mother. He was threatening suicide. I was able this time to drive close to the house due to the drier weather conditions. I found the man sitting outside on his rocking chair looking blankly into space, holding a large calibre rifle over his arm. Seeing this, I wondered what I had gotten myself into, and felt uncomfortable knowing there was no one nearby to give me assistance should I require any.

I talked to him gently in an attempt to persuade him to put the gun down, inviting him to come with me in the car to the clinic for his medication. He really didn't want to enter into negotiations and told me simply, "Maybe I'll kill myself and maybe I won't", and with a flick of his head and a movement of his arm where the gun rested he asked me to leave. I didn't stop to argue, but on turning my back I did not know what he might do. I gave a sigh of relief on reaching the car and a greater one when I drove off. I had to contact the psychiatrist first and await his instructions. Being a danger to himself and others I had to notify the RCMP and they took over the case, which meant incarceration for the patient for a period of time in a hospital. When the police were informed about this type of situation, requiring their services to act as an escort, they did so in plain clothing and transported the patient in an unmarked car. The patients were not criminals, only sick, and that status was accorded them.

There were a number of patients with cancer who came home to die and this meant more involvement for the health team. Unlike the larger communities, we did not have a Home Care Programme on the reserve even although it was badly needed, nor of course a hospital. The Home Care programme was quite separate to my role but one in which I was very heavily involved, although not of my own choosing. I became very attached to those who were dying, feeling as though I, too, was an extension of the family and their deaths emotionally impacting on me. I believe one develops a deep closeness to families in the community when visiting their homes and getting to know the various family members. A nurse sees first-hand their interactions with one another and with their the dying relative, and through those observances we assist them to cope.

The home care duties began encroaching on my time and still the administration couldn't see that or didn't want to. I had spent much time with one terminally ill lady who worried greatly about the future of her children in her absence. It was undoubtedly heart-wrenching to watch the weeks pass by with the time of her death coming ever closer. She was very aware of this and not wanting to forsake her children by dying. The moments that nurses share at these times are sad, but rich in the sense we are in the intimate position of knowing our clients well: their lost hopes, their fears, witnessing their tears and at the same time giving human comfort. We were able to physically see to the most private of their needs, giving emotional strength, encouragement and at times spiritual aid. There were instances of verbal attacks from agitated relatives who were trying desperately to come to terms with the imminent demise of a loved one.

I recall after a full day at work I volunteered I to do one night shift per week in the home of an ailing cancer victim, there being no one else to relieve his elderly and frail wife. During the night he slept for short periods of time and when awake, I made him comfortable, reassuring him, making him tea and giving him the necessary narcotic injections to control his pain. In between his sleep he enjoyed our conversations. Then the house would be still again as he drifted back to sleep, except for a strange sound I was hearing. It was coming from the lower level. I crept downstairs only to find the cat sitting at the bottom, enjoying a meal of a bird she had caught earlier. There were feathers all around and unable to watch or bear the crunching sounds, I left her to finish her meal. From time to time I would venture downstairs just to check on the new family of kittens lying, snuggled against their mother, who was purring contentedly. It was a pleasant distraction and helped to break the monotony of the long night.

Each week saw more deterioration in my patient with an increase in his pain. I contacted the doctor during the day and invited him to visit the patient before he started his afternoon clinic so that he might assess the gentleman's need for an increase in his narcotic. It was not a standard procedure in Canada to do medical home visits as it is in Britain. The doctor never went to see his patient nor did he order any increase in pain relief, even although the patient's home was located a hundred yards away from his office. When I approached him the day after, he said he was too tired. This same doctor belonged to an evangelical order and frequently he used the phrase "I am a Christian!" When I arrived at the home to do the nightshift I was severely berated by the patient's wife because I could not give him extra morphine. I felt for her but I had to adhere to the written order and to the law.

I was taught in nursing that one must make allowances for the sick and distraught relatives and to learn not to take the anger personally. It was considered that people, underneath the outer shell were good human beings but coping with severe illness and a dying person was difficult and traumatic. Nowadays, relatives who express concerns and show reactions would be deemed *abusive!* The changes and viewpoints which abound in our society today are not necessarily for the best. Key words and catch phrases gain momentum and quite soon the word *abuse* becomes a dictum with no real substance.

I decided to attend a two-day assertiveness training programme, sponsored by the Federal Government. It happened to be scheduled at the time I was doing my night shift. This meant that after working all day and being on duty all night, I would drive to Calgary, leaving early in the morning with no time to eat breakfast. On the first day I felt very tired and I yawned a great deal. During the session we were asked to take part in a relaxation exercise. Everyone had to lie on the floor and the instructor's voice droned quietly in the background as he spoke. It was a good feeling and when the exercise was over I did not quite hear the call to sit up, but continued to lie there, sound asleep. It couldn't have been very long before I opened my eyes, feeling a little horrified at what I had done. The instructor was bemused and said he had not realized how good he was at getting students to relax. Apologetically I told him of my lack of sleep from the shift the night before.

Time passed at Siksika and months became years. By now I had met and married my husband who was the Headmaster of the local town school. My yearning for the north had returned but it was not possible to go back. I found it hard to adjust to living in the south.

There was always plenty of work to keep my thoughts at bay. I visited a home at the far end of the reserve in order to immunize a little boy who was very behind in his programme. Before reaching his house I had stopped to visit with the grandparents who lived less then half a mile away. They were not home but the father of the child I was about to visit was there. He was acting very peculiar. A moment later, rolling up his sleeve, he indicated to me that he needed a fix. I twigged to his possible use of drugs. Having quickly extricated myself from the scene, parting amicably, I drove over to his home.

At the house I was greeted cordially by his wife who invited me in. I went through the preliminary questions, checking the child over to ascertain that he was healthy. Next came the unpleasant task of sticking a needle into the little guy. He had a good set of lungs and used them to show his displeasure of the treatment. At that precise moment the father, whom I had just left, burst in through the door and into the living room. On hearing his child cry he went, as they say, "ballistic." Pointing his finger at me and sticking it in close proximity to my face, he screamed loudly, "Get the hell out of here before I kick your backside down the stairs!" Knowing well of this man's previous violent history, I packed up quickly and headed to the foot of the stairs to put my shoes on. He repeated his warning and followed me to the doorway. I waited for the clunk of a boot on the back of my head but fortunately it never came. Fortunate for him, too, as I would not have hesitated to lay criminal charges against him. I left very shaken, my heart doing cartwheels and my head pounding. I was not easily intimidated by people and I was feisty in the face of adversity, capable of looking after myself in most scenarios, but I had always been cautioned not to respond when drugs most likely were a factor in the behaviour.

The original ambulance, located in the town of Gleichen, offered a very simple service and the owner, who worked alone, did not have the basic life support skills required. In an emergency situation a clinic nurse often accompanied the ambulance driver and it was during a nursing shortage that another colleague and I were coerced into being on call for emergencies during the night. As a Health Nurse I was not in any way involved in the aspects of illness, the promoting of wellness being my role.

At two o'clock in the morning my deep slumber was disturbed unceremoniously when the telephone rang. I had set the tone loud deliberately so as not to miss calls. I was soon wide awake with the noise. It was the ambulance driver announcing he had a call from a native patient with abdominal pain. He wondered if he should bring her to the clinic or would I accompany him to the home and do the assessment there. Because there was not a nurse on duty at the clinic as planned when the facility was built I agreed to go with him. I quickly pulled on my clothes and was ready when the ambulance pulled up at my door.

We drove fifteen miles on the highway before turning onto a gravel road which had a winding, steep descent to the homes which were spread out below. In part, we travelled over rough, deeply rutted, grassy terrain to reach the patient's home. The journey was in complete darkness except for our headlights. There soon appeared a light from one house which we thought was the one we wanted. We were correct in our assumptions. When we knocked on the door, an older lady, with a pleasant demeanour, answered and led us to a young woman lying on the sofa. Although the lights were dimmed I noticed right away the beer bottles strewn about on the floor. As she was not one of my regular clients, I introduced myself as the nurse. I proceeded to ask about her pain, but received very little input from her. When I suggested that I palpate her abdomen to establish the focal point of her discomfort, she rudely pushed my hands away and exclaimed in a loud, slurred tone, "You are nothing but a horse doctor!" I responded by saying, "Neigh, that is not true." I knew that I would not get her co-operation due to the fact that alcohol had been consumed, so I returned home. I still had my work the next day and by the time I returned to bed it was nearer to five o'clock in the morning. I was very annoyed to say the least. The older ambulance driver and his family were disturbed, but that was his privately owned business and his specific line of work. Call-outs were to be expected. My household was disrupted too with my husband staying awake to see my safe return. Because of all the activity the dog was up and begging to go out, possibly thinking that a new day had dawned. It is difficult to return to sleep once the adrenaline is flowing.

Many months later a similar incident occurred just as I was about to start my summer vacation. I had worked overtime specifically in order to leave the workplace at one o'clock in the afternoon. I had planned to go on a camping trip with my husband which actually was to be the honeymoon we never had. I had my hair set and wanted to complete the packing and food preparation for the journey. I had just begun to assemble the ingredients needed to do the baked goods and make a meat loaf when the telephone rang. It was the nurse on evening duty, by herself, at the clinic. She asked if I would go to the summer camp where the Indian Days were being held. She explained that an elderly woman, some twenty miles away, was having a heart attack and might need to be escorted to the hospital. I explained that I was officially on vacation and suggested she call someone else, particularly a clinic nurse. She had already done that. One nurse had refused to go and the second one was going out to some function. There was no one else in the nursing field living in the community. Reluctantly I conceded to go, showing again my altruistic nature and hoping that the same might be done for a member of my own family in such a situation.

When we arrived in the ambulance at our isolated destination it was raining very heavily. When the vehicle came to a stop and as I was alighting from it, some natives started to open the rear doors of the ambulance, eager to deposit the ill patient therein. It was obvious that many had been celebrating and were inebriated. I was taken to the tepee where the old woman lay. She did not understand much English, being of the older generation. I asked her relative to interpret for me and in the process one sometimes had to reiterate the line of questioning in order to gain clarity from some of the answers. The assisting relative told me in no uncertain terms that she would not interpret any further and that I should do my job and take the woman to the hospital. There was much contempt showing in her face and oral expressions. I went on to examine the lady in spite of her non-compliance and decided she was not in danger. The heart attack, in my opinion, was in fact a bilateral pneumonia but I could not be certain. I made the decision that she would be best served in a hospital setting as opposed to the cold, damp tepee where she was unlikely to get care from those around her. She would have the added benefit of having her heart checked. She was placed in the ambulance with me accompanying her and whisked off to hospital some thirty miles away, for admission. I made a request of the local tribal policeman, who had appeared on the scene, to follow me in his car so that I might use him at the hospital as the interpreter. He was most agreeable and I appreciated his willingness, the family seemingly unconcerned.

On reaching the hospital, I delivered my patient into the care of the nursing staff and gave my report to the senior nurse. The old lady, I assumed, was being settled into a warm comfortable bed. By the time I was ready to return home in the ambulance, my eyes just about popped out of their sockets, because there, large as life, was my patient sitting in the back of the tribal police car. I went back into the hospital to find out what exactly was going on only to be told that the lady refused to stay and be treated. Under these circumstances a patient cannot be kept against their will. I shook my head in total disbelief and in disgust. Because I did a favour for an un-appreciative human being, my hair-set was totally ruined with the rain, I had lost about two and a half hours of preparation time, and had not eaten my evening meal. I was harassed and insulted and all for nothing. I requested overtime, under the circumstances. The amount received barely paid for my ruined hair set and certainly did not compensate me for my personal lost time. Needless to say, I did no further ambulance duties.

After work I usually took my Government vehicle for refilling, to the petrol station just two miles outside of town, ready for the next day. Printed on each side door of the car was the Health & Welfare logo. On this particular day there was a queue and while I sat patiently in my car I noticed two scruffy Caucasian men standing beside their parked truck off to the side but near to me. They were pointing and laughing at the logo on the car and as my car window was open I heard their derogatory remarks. It seemed to be the Welfare component that they were focused on. They were becoming offensive in their language and one went as far as opening his front trouser zip in order to expose himself. I rolled my window up and turned the other way but the young pump attendant chivalrously jumped to my defence by telling them not to treat a lady this way. The next action happened without warning when one of the men grabbed his rifle from the back of his truck. At that point I leapt out of my car and ran inside and called the police. The men vanished very quickly with the police in hot pursuit. They were caught and one was incarcerated overnight in jail. I had to give a statement to the police.

I reluctantly attended a programme on alcohol and drug abuse called Nechi which was presented in modules. It was designed to help the native counsellors to deal with clients and their addictions. As health professionals we were obligated to attend due to the nature of our jobs whereby, it was thought, we would have a better understanding of substance abuse and its ramifications on the individuals and their families.

One of the courses was held at Camp Yumnuska, near to Banff National Park. Sometimes the sessions would continue all day until bedtime. Often high emotions were displayed amongst the participating native counsellors when they bared their souls in anguish. Some of the counsellors themselves had been alcoholics. These individuals by choice were seated upon the sacred buffalo rug and they in turn invited a person whom they trusted to sit with them. On one occasion I was called upon, by a young woman, to sit and hold her hand. It was difficult to sleep following such emotional encounters. By attending these sessions I found them to be more unsettling than helpful.

One positive interaction I did have was with an Indian Elder in his eighties. He was a lively individual and quite spry for his age, well versed in the English language, this eloquence not often heard amongst the older generation. His role at the Nechi training was to talk a little about the Indian culture and offer prayers. One evening he asked us to gather around. He then untied one of the sacred bundles which contained the pipe of peace, the pipe stem and sweet grass. I cannot recall the other contents within his bundle, but apparently these bundles could contain many things such as eagle feathers, the skin of different animals and other objects of a sacred nature, their significance known only to the owner. Because these bundles were sacred only certain people owned them. There were rituals to be observed at the opening of these bundles and the same applied when a bundle was passed on to another tribe member. At the bundle opening I witnessed, the peace pipe was brought out and the pipe bowl was filled with tobacco and lit. The pipe was pointed to the north, south, east and west, then turned in a circular motion before being smoked. The pipe was passed to each of us in turn and before handing the pipe to the next person it was rotated in a circle. I did not actually smoke the pipe but rather went through the motions which was acceptable.

Our sessions were held within a circular building, similar to a tepee. We all sat in the circle and at the start and end of each day, a blessing took place, using the sweet grass for purification. The grass was obtained from the prairie land. When dried, it was woven into a braid and when burned, it emitted a sweet smell. We would stand in the circle and, as was customary, all rings and other pieces of jewellery which we wore were removed before taking part. While our heads were bowed in prayer, one native lit the sweet grass and as it smouldered he approached each member of the group and proffered it. With cupped hands we wafted the smoke over our body and at the same time symbolically brushing ourselves with the smoke: arms, legs, head and body. This was repeated silently until all had participated. Then we joined hands and a prayer was said in the Blackfoot language. The day's events were then under way.

The Blackfoot natives I worked with often talked about the ill treatment they received in earlier days. They discussed how they were forced to attend the residential schools run by the nuns and priests and suffered as a result of the strict disciplines imposed on them. They were forbidden to talk their own language and were even punished for doing so. This sometimes meant that the children who did talk their native language would not be allowed to go home at the weekend to see their parents. They also mentioned that children sometimes had their faces painted in a ceremony that had significance to their culture. The children were made to remove this. It is little wonder that the natives throughout Canada feel as they do about us and continue to lobby for justice.

At one time the Blackfoot and other tribes, as part of their culture, participated in the Sundance. The native braves underwent a form of self torture by having the skin in the chest wall pierced and small pieces of wood made from willow were inserted under the skin. These willow inserts were attached to ropes and ultimately to a main central pole. In the old days this ceremony was held in the medicine lodge but the practice was eventually outlawed by the church. As the native people are now beginning to assert themselves and move more towards self determination they are reviving some of their own cultural ways, the Sundance being an example.

Last summer I was lucky enough to have had the honour of receiving an invitation to a Sundance being held on the Blood Indian reservation. These are deeply meaningful and symbolic ceremonies which were explained to me as the four-day gathering went on. I would not adequately be able to write about all the intricacies and significance of these practices, but they can be better studied from book sources in libraries.

The use of Sweat Lodges are still in evidence today. At certain times, these Sweats, as they are referred to, are put on for purification purposes and are attended by both sexes. A small structure in the shape of a dome was made from willows. The dome was then covered with blankets on the outside to insulate. In the middle of the floor, a pit was dug which eventually would accommodate the stones. These stones were heated by fire outside for three to four hours. The hot stones were brought inside and placed in the pit and sprinkled with sweet grass. The people then assembled inside and before the ceremony began, water was poured over these hot stones, producing steam, thus creating a hot, humid atmosphere. A song was sung and a prayer was said, then the door was opened to let the prayer go out to the people. This was repeated four times. Sometimes the prayers were for the sick or a request may have been made for some other specific reason. At the time of praying one was not allowed to leave the Sweat Lodge, even although it was too hot. I was to attend a Sweat at the Sundance, but before I could enter I had to wear a long dress according to custom. A nightdress is acceptable, but as I had neither with me I was not allowed to enter.

I often wish that I had learned more of the Blackfoot ways, but sometimes at the end of a busy, frustrating day it was good to escape and relax. The social life in a small town was mediocre. My main social events came mainly through my husband's work, providing me with a little respite from the ever growing strain in the workplace.

I spoke in the introduction about the loss of my dog and of the many deaths within the Indian communities I served, but one little boy's young life stands out. By age ten he probably went through more pain than many of us do in a lifetime. His parents were both alcoholics and the children often were sent to a care shelter. They would run home, preferring their familiar surroundings to any substitute placement. His older sister was pregnant and the mother died from a drug overdose. I can readily recall the event, as I was asked to assist in the attempts to resuscitate the woman, which were in vain. The little boy spoke to me about his mother lying so still in her coffin, as he tried to absorb the fact that she would not be coming back. Shortly before that incident his twin brother had been removed to a foster home. He had leukaemia and it was important that the sick boy was not in contact with illnesses and was well cared for. His family environment did not provide that level of care. This boy was too young to understand why his brother and playmate should be taken away. Sometime after his sibling left, an older brother hanged himself on the porch of the home. My young friend, who saw his brother hanging, gave a detailed, descriptive account of what he witnessed. The mother could not deal with the pain when she ended her life, but who would ease the deep hurt this boy was feeling? His father continued to drink and was not there for his son.

So often children are victims of their environment. It must be very hard for them to create a good life for themselves when encouragement, love and caring are lacking and there exists an abundance of negativity. In very recent times, whilst visiting this area in Canada, I met this boy, who was by now a young adult. He remembered me. He had overcome his family turmoil, did not drink and was attending advanced education.

I enjoyed attending conferences, especially at some of the chosen locations. It usually was a week's respite from the daily routine, with good company and excellent food. On one occasion we travelled by car to Jasper National Park where we were provided with very pleasant accommodation in an idyllic setting amongst the trees, mountains and lakes. The time of year selected was not the best. We had to travel high, mountainous roads and we were confronted with areas of extreme icing across our path. If anything had gone wrong, there was a huge plunge to the valleys below.

On this trip I was the driver of the company car and had three other nurses in tow. Suddenly the car started to slow down, finally coming to a complete standstill, but I did manage to get it to the roadside. We all tumbled out only to discover the coolant pouring out from underneath the car, leaving behind a big pool of green liquid. While we debated our predicament, we realized we were miles from a phone or human habitation. Luck was with us, when another car from our clinic drew up alongside. The crew decided to drive on and find the first available telephone and send back a tow truck. Meantime, we settled down by the roadside and pooled our junk food to snack on. I don't recall how long it took a tow truck to appear, but after hoisting the car for removal the driver crammed us into his vehicle and took us to the nearest town. From there we rented a car and proceeded on to Jasper.

By the time we reached our destination it was ten o'clock at night and we were cold and hungry. There was no welcoming party to greet us. All the food from the banquet, which was planned as a reception for all of us, was gone. We felt rather bad at missing out on a scrumptious meal and ended up making do with a hamburger and greasy chips.

Over the years I saw many bosses come and go. Each one believed that their own values and opinions were the ones that would work at our clinic, where the political climate was fast changing. As a result, my health was being affected due to the many external stressors over which I had no control. In my opinion I felt subjected to inequality in the workplace. It had become a place of constant racial tensions and as an employee, I had always to watch my step and show political correctness. When a group of Blackfoot natives made a decision to have two non-native Government employees, at different times, removed from their position for no good reason, it was an indication that discrimination was very much alive and being allowed to happen. These were two of my colleagues.

I personally was called to headquarters for something minor that had transpired between myself and an aboriginal. A question was put to me by my employer, "What will you do if a Band Council Resolution dictates your removal?" I asked my employer if they wished me removed from my position, before I answered. My employer was emphatic that I was a very good employee and he did not desire this. My response then was that I would sue the Band Council for inappropriate dismissal. He mused that this had never been done before. The threat did not come to fruition but it did nothing to enhance my desire to stay in this unhealthy atmosphere. I held my position for fourteen years and was one of the longest-staying employees.

There prevailed double standards. One for native people and one for non-natives. The natives were encouraged to attain self-determination, and rightly so, but one became paralysed by the political correctness and attempts to do my job became, for me, a futile endeavour. The situations I faced are too detailed and too political to discuss in this book, which I want to be light-hearted. It is best perhaps to say that more nurses at that time needed to come forward to discuss the existence of reverse discrimination meted out by a bureaucratic system.

Today we are seeing more and more political correctness being thrust at us. In doing so, I believe there is a danger of losing our freedom and own cultural identity. I think we can share our land with other cultures but we must not abandon our own ideologies in the process. I find it quite appalling that some of our own countrymen would even suggest that we should not use words pertaining to our own Christianity. I speak as someone who has been an immigrant and my own expectations in my adopted land of Canada were that I accept their ways.

In January, 1990, a thirty-four year career had abruptly and without ceremony come to a finale. It had ended on such a sour note. It was not the way I had envisioned it would be after giving dedicated service to the Government, but the politics were becoming unbearable. I had given my heart and soul to the job and I wanted only to provide a service to the public in the best way I could, given the restrictions I faced. Exit "Nurse Nora", as I was affectionately called by the children in the Arctic. Those were the days when I wore rose tinted glasses and there existed for me only good and no evil, but the latter experiences in my career somewhat changed many of my views.

CHAPTER FOURTEEN
CAMBRIDGE BAY

A lengthy stay in Scotland was planned after my husband's retirement, but I became increasingly restless. Still yearning for the north, I applied for a position in the Northwest Territories. In due course an interview was arranged, to be conducted by transatlantic telephone. I felt a little intimidated at having to answer questions to a committee of four with whom I had no visual contact. I was unable to see any facial expressions which could have indicated how they were receiving my answers, as they verbally tested my competence as a nurse. I did not believe I had a chance against the other five applicants, especially as they were already living in Canada. Imagine my surprise when I was offered the position as Community Health Nurse at Cambridge Bay. Retirement was short lived!

On descending from the aircraft at Yellowknife the cold, crisp air made me gasp. When driving to the hotel, I could not believe the transformation of the community, nor could I have envisioned in 1968 that it would become such a bustling city. Several years before, an inquest was held in the hotel where we stayed, into the Norman Hartwell plane crash. The event, discussed in a previous chapter, generated much news coverage at the time.

"Those travelling to Cambridge Bay can now board!", came the announcement. There began a steady stream of travellers, dressed in parkas, making their cold walk to the aircraft. As I fastened my seat belt, my usual exuberance had left me, being replaced with a feeling of trepidation.

After an uneventful flight, my husband and I were met at the Cambridge Bay airport by the Nurse-in-Charge and were promptly transported by truck over a winding road, covered in hard- packed snow, to the community and our residence.

The building was a large, two-storey high metal structure, comprising several flats. In bold lettering the sign attached to the wall of the building read: 13B Omingmak Street, our new address.

I was allowed one day to settle in and collect from the incoming flight, my meat supply, purchased in Yellowknife. Gone were the days when generous food rations supplied by the government arrived by sea-lift or were obtained through a purchase order at the Hudson's Bay store. Locally, food items were extremely high in price. As we were not provided with a cost of living supplement, it was more cost effective to have our own goods delivered.

When I arrived at the airport the next day I was rather discontented, as my meat and other staple food supplies did not arrive as promised. I was assured that by the next day I would have them. On the second day the supplies still had not arrived and a tracing of the goods had to be implemented. It turned out that they had been delivered elsewhere and when I finally received my supplies, I found the meat to be a strange colour. I refused to accept that shipment of meat, not knowing whether or not it had been thawed and refrozen. I was unable to obtain a proper history as to what exactly had happened to the meat. A new order was placed promptly and I received everything in good condition the following day, the shipping costs being absorbed by the airlines.

The hamlet of Cambridge Bay, situated on the south eastern tip of Victoria Island, was not an inhabited settlement until the fifties. A few Inuit gathered and lived around the area to hunt and trap. The area, rich in seal, caribou and fox, had become a centre point for trading furs. In the mid-fifties, a radar station had been installed as part of the Early Warning System, named the Dew line. The fishing was considered excellent, the lakes and rivers being abundant with trout and arctic char. There exists physical evidence to support the fact that the Inuit had been around there for centuries, judging from finds of tent rings, stone house villages and food caches.

The flying distance from Yellowknife to Cambridge Bay was about five hundred and forty nautical miles over a bleak, snow-covered landscape. We were presented with a certificate stating that we had crossed the Arctic Circle. I had previously been given a small card commemorating this experience, when travelling to Resolute Bay in 1970.

Although it was May, everything was covered in snow and the bay was still frozen. The brightness from the long daylight hours filtered in through the curtained windows, making it hard to fall asleep. Tin foil, once again, became an effective method to darken the room and the rustling sound with each breeze reminded me of those earlier Arctic days where I had spent my youth. During my second week, I was on call and I worried about this, dreading the thought also of an emergency flight.

When being briefed in Yellowknife, I registered my concern over having to fly on mercy missions. I was reassured that there was an air ambulance service in operation, but there had been talk of the nurses taking over this duty again in the future. By the time I arrived at Cambridge Bay it had become a reality. It meant travelling to smaller, surrounding communities, such as Spence Bay, to escort patients to Yellowknife whenever the occasion arose. The name Spence Bay conjured up the memory of nurse Judith Hill, who had been working there, before stopping in Cambridge Bay en route to Yellowknife on the fateful night she tragically lost her young life. Perhaps with aging I was becoming more insecure and I was beginning to feel that working in the north was more for the younger age group. I was becoming more cautious. Had I worked there all the way through my career, it may have been different. Having been absent from the northern environment for some time, I realized that the comforts and amenities of southern living held a certain allure.

I was interested in gaining more knowledge of my new geographical location, its inhabitants and in general, the history of the area. The information obtained often was from the Inuit or others who had resided in the community for a length of time.

The mode of land travel was similar to other regions in the Arctic, but I was to experience, for the first time, a ride on an all-terrain vehicle. These were heavy machines with three large wheels suitable for driving over the rough, rocky tundra. The newer models came with four wheels and were considered somewhat safer and more stable. It wasn't long before my husband and I found out, first-hand, as to what they meant by stability. A staff outing had been organized and we had been given the loan of a vehicle to drive. Bundled up very warmly, as it was still quite cold in spite of the sun shining, we mounted the contraption, my husband being the driver. There was nothing to it. After all we could ride a bicycle and drive a car, so this would be simple. A few words from the owner about its operation and off we went. The initial part of the trip was on what could be described as the main road. It was fairly bare of snow. We started out, moving cautiously as one often does when driving an unfamiliar vehicle. We came to the camber of the road which was quite pronounced. The vehicle started to have a mind of its own. My husband couldn't control it as it headed across the road and downwards into the ditch, landing us in deep water. It was cold, being the run-off from the melting snow on higher ground. The ditch served as a catchment area, deep and wide, resembling a pond. There we were, in full view of the entire party, sitting in the water astride the vehicle. I was not altogether calm. I had visions of us sinking and drowning. With everyone pitching in and laughing with us, the offending piece of metal was retrieved. To play it safe from further mishaps, we both became pillion passengers with some experienced drivers up front. The pillions were not padded at all and I could feel each and every bump as we chugged along. Although there still was snow and ice around, the layer was thin and bare in places, revealing the shale stone underneath, making travel rough and uneven.

In the midst of this snowy landscape, eyes searching the horizon, one could see only more barrenness. This vast, bleak plain before us somehow made me realize how powerful the elements of nature really were. I can only imagine the hardships there must have been for the past generations of Inuit who lived under the harsh conditions, yet they seemed to be a happy people.

We were not headed for any particular landmark, rather it was an outing in the crisp, fresh air and for the camaraderie. On the homeward journey we deviated from our route, driving over slightly higher ground. There, not far from us, stood the magnificent beast of the Arctic, the musk-ox, still wearing his heavy coat. They were quite awesome to see in their natural habitat, chewing quietly on the lichen. We stood still lest we disturb them or cause them to charge at us in defence. As they half turned around we were able to see their large curled horns. The shed wool is called qiviuk. When spun and knitted it provides great warmth.

On returning home, my husband and I walked as though we had just dismounted from a horse, feeling rather numb in parts. I learned, too late, to do posting as though riding. Had there been a next time, I would have brought ample padding to sit upon.

There were two main stores in the village, one being the original Hudson's Bay store, now renamed the Northern. Looking at all the different wares for sale, I was reminded so much of my first journey north to Norway House and it revived in me a nostalgic fascination. These stores were not as elaborate and sophisticated as those in large towns and cities, but rather they had a simplicity to them. They carried grocery items and meat supplies with selections of frozen foods. Magazines were stacked in one area and in another you could purchase some warm clothing, such as wind pants, parkas, socks, boots and the like. In yet a different area, tools and necessities, such as candles, kerosene lamps, bicycles and rifles, as well as furs, were displayed. Many of the pelts, either wolf or fox, were hanging on a pole at the back of the store. It was most enjoyable to browse amongst all this, giving me a sense of the pioneer days, visualizing the old trading post. I imagined the Inuit exchanging their furs for items of flour, lard, food staples, materials, clothing, equipment and bullets. Perhaps, in spite of the language barriers back then, communication existed and friendships developed.

I saw many familiar sights as I walked about the community. The husky dogs were a mixture of breeds and none looked like the traditional sled pullers. Caribou meat, cut into strips, was laid out on wooden frames to dry, whilst the caribou furs, previously scraped and cured, lay about, some of them blown out onto the frozen bay. The furs were necessary for warmth when the Inuit camped or travelled by Qamutik.

There were two churches and a Royal Canadian Mounted Police detachment with three officers, as well as a local school. Further along the road from us was the hotel which could accommodate forty people. With three different airlines operating between Cambridge Bay and the south, it brought tourism to the area.

A visit to the local cemetery, some distance away, proved to be interesting. Some of the graves were covered over with rocks, as I had seen in Baker Lake. A simple wooden cross gave the pertinent information of the deceased lying beneath. A more recent grave, that of a child, was adorned with wreaths made of plastic flowers. On some graves lay personal items, such as a pencil, pen, a hat or a toy, which had been in the deceased's possession at the time of death, giving a brief reminder of their earthly existence. In the distance one could see the lines of crosses standing silently, like sentinels guarding their own, amidst this bleak, rocky landscape broken only with the presence of an occasional spring flower. With our backs to the village and focusing only on these graves and the land beyond, it was hard to comprehend a human existence within these elements before the arrival of the white man, who brought the modern amenities of heat and electricity, not to mention food stores. Yet, at times I envy their simple and tranquil life as they knew it.

We ventured a little further from the cemetery and after we crossed a bridge, we lost sight of the village. We came across a number of Inukshuks. These were stones piled one on top of another, resembling a human figure. They were used by the Inuit as land markers when they followed the caribou. We eventually came across two families who were at their land camp. Upon finding out they were fluent in English, we talked for a while before they invited us to join them in their tent for some tea and bannock. The atmosphere was very friendly, with the men teasing and joking back and forth. Filled and warmed with a good brew of tea, we headed home. The temperature had now cooled considerably.

I found out there existed the skeleton remains of a boat on the far side of Cambridge Bay harbour, the area which was called Old Town. After delving further, I learned that the ship had belonged to the Norwegian explorer Roald Amundsen. History tells us that he led the first expedition to reach the South Pole. He, along with his compatriots, discovered the pole in 1911, beating Robert Scott in the race by a few weeks.

Roald Amundsen began studying medicine, but abandoned his studies and took to a life at sea. In the 1900s, he sailed for three years in his ship, called "Gjoa", passing through Cambridge Bay en route to the Northwest Passage, and was the first individual to navigate it. His later ship, named the "Maud", after the Queen of Norway, was used for further Arctic explorations. This ship was a schooner, that is, with three masts. She carried on board two airplanes, as well as up-to-date wireless equipment in order to transmit the Arctic weather conditions to those in the south.

The "Maud" was sold to the Hudson's Bay Company in 1925. The name was changed to "Baymaud." It was used first to carry supplies to the company's outposts in Western Canada, later being used as a warehouse and eventually as a wireless station to send out weather reports while anchored at Cambridge Bay. In the 1930s it sunk in the harbour due to some leaks. My walk took me to the edge of the water where I could see the remains of the wooden framework protruding through the snow. I edged nearer in an effort to touch some part of this historical vessel, but the ice was too precarious to further my attempts. I remember being taught in my history class about Amundsen. I never thought I would be a stone's throw from his sailing vessel. The steering wheel from the ship was presented to the Norwegian people. Amundsen died as a result of an airplane crash in 1928, during an air-rescue attempt of an aviator.

In recent years I visited Norway and while there I searched out the museum that housed the steering wheel of the "Maud", and saw it displayed.

The "Gjoa" is located at the Norwegian Maritime Museum, in Oslo, and I was also fortunate to see this vessel. It was returned to the Norwegian people in 1972. Looking at this small vessel it was hard to believe that it journeyed from the Atlantic to the Pacific oceans.

While attempting to sail the Northwest Passage, Amundsen wintered on King William Island, in a natural harbour which was named Gjoa Haven, after his ship. There is a small Inuit community there.

I had been at Cambridge Bay just four weeks when I decided to leave. I was finding the pace of the diagnostic clinical role too demanding at this point. The key factor, too, was that I had not yet overcome the traumas I had faced in southern Alberta and the negativity of that experience still lingered within me. Although my stay was very short, it was a worthwhile journey, if even for the historical knowledge that I gleaned.

CHAPTER FIFTEEN
FORT HOPE, ONTARIO

I was back from the Northwest Territories, living in Calgary, Alberta, basking in the warmth of the sun, when I received a most unexpected call. It came from Health and Welfare, in Sioux Lookout, Ontario, offering me a casual position at Fort Hope. I declined, feeling Nursing Station life was too vigorous for me. I was invited to ponder the offer. I agonized over the decision, wishing they had not approached me. It meant leaving my husband behind for a period of time. In the end I accepted.

After reaching Winnipeg, Manitoba, I made the appropriate connection to Sioux Lookout. Being a late evening flight, it was totally dark outside, making the journey seem endless. I dozed off soon after we were airborne but my sleep was suddenly disturbed. We had hit turbulence and the aeroplane started to lurch quite badly. Because the aircraft was small, accommodating only a few passengers, one could feel the effects much more. I had flown in bad weather before but this was perhaps the most unpleasant weather condition, I had encountered and the most apprehensive I had ever felt. We had to miss out landing at one community due to the storm. I was very thankful when the aircraft finally touched down at the appointed destination.

I spent two nights in Sioux Lookout while the supervisor deliberated as to which community I would be selected to work in. There was a shortage of staff in various places within the region. I had accepted the relief position on the condition that the placement would be with other nurses. Finally she informed me I would be going to Fort Hope which had a compliment of four nurses.

Deplaning at Fort Hope, I saw the usual turnout of curious bystanders. I was met by the local caretaker and transported, on a short, but rough ride to the clinic and my attached living quarters. I was greeted warmly by the staff who, over a cup of tea, chatted and insisted I would be the new nurse for the adjacent community. By their description it was apparently even more isolated and more inaccessible than the destination I had just reached.

I was rather taken aback as I had very definitely been appointed to Fort Hope. I wondered if once again there was a lack of communication.

The community of Fort Hope had a population in the vicinity of one thousand and was located in a very picturesque setting, surrounded by trees and lakes. Many of the houses were old and painted in a variety of colours. I found out later that many still had only outdoor toilets, which was an incredible disgrace for the 1990s. The people were Oji-Cree and their language was quite musical to listen to. There were two tiny stores supplying a number of goods, including groceries. My accommodation, although a modest bedsit, was comfortable and adequate. A hall doorway connected the residence to the adjoining clinic.

In less than a week after my initial arrival I was flown into the "other village", which was called Landing Place. I was accompanied by the Nurse-in-Charge from Fort Hope, who would stay one night with me to make the customary introductions. Because there was pressure exerted on me to take over this facility, I elected to stay a week, keeping an open mind, although this position was not in my contract.

The Fort Hope clinic supplied medicines and manpower to this very small reserve. Normally a nurse visited there every Monday and returned to Fort Hope on the Wednesday. I learned that the department wanted a nurse stationed there permanently, which was unbeknown to me and explained why every effort at local level was being made to convince me I would enjoy the challenge.

LANDING PLACE

We landed after a thirty-minute air journey and made our way to the facility, again by truck. There were no nice cars ever involved in transportation. We were heavily laden with medical supplies, personal effects, bedding, sleeping bag and some rations, just in case the plane came down. There had been a plane crash in recent times, I was told, in which a nurse and a priest were killed.

As the driver pulled up in front of the Nursing Station, I could see it was a double-wide mobile trailer unit, but not one of the modern ones.

Once inside, I met the native staff members, a Secretary and a Community Health Worker, both very young. At first glimpse, I was not at all enamoured with my accommodation nor the clinic set-up. By evening, I had misgivings of having entertained the thought of working in this location. It became all too evident why the other staff wanted to unload this position onto a new unsuspecting employee.

I was not afforded safe or sanitary conditions and it was inappropriate for the administration in my employing department to expect me or anyone else to live in what I considered substandard conditions. I mentally catalogued all that was wrong and still today have a clear vision on what I encountered.

The sitting room, dining kitchen, two bedrooms and bathroom were all located next to one another. The furnace room, situated across from my bedroom was loaded with inflammable substances placed next to the actual furnace. If there had been a fire in my living quarters the only accessible exit was through the front door. The door did not have a proper locking device, but merely had a hasp with a large rusty nail inserted through the hole, which did prove difficult to open.

The windows were small and narrow and difficult to open. The curtains, which were falling off the rails, did not adequately cover the windows to afford privacy.

The fridge had rotting food inside as well as a build-up of mould. Dirty dishes were in the sink while others were strewn all over the counter top. The carpet in the kitchen was badly stained by the drips from the coffee pot. The sitting room was cluttered with items such as children's toys, disposable intravenous bags, past their expiry date, a spade propped against the fireplace, and furniture such as chairs and sofa were arranged in rows, similar to that of a waiting room.

In the bedroom I was to occupy and lying on top of the bed, was heavy furniture belonging to the sitting room. In order to make up my bed, I had to lift the furniture back to its rightful place. There were no drapes on the bedroom window at all.

The bathroom was a disaster area, so much so I recoiled from showering on the first night. Dirty, wet towels were draped everywhere, with toothbrushes and toothpaste cluttering the very dirty sink. The toilet itself looked as though it had not been cleaned in a long time. The shower cubicle was covered in long black hairs. I very soon found out that the staff, although not resident there, nor paying rent, used the bathroom during the day and showered before going home. The employed housekeeper was unable to work at times, although still drawing a salary, because she was busy baby-sitting at home. I learned that the bedroom right next to mine was used not only for visiting staff, but also for the admission of patients. If they were ambulant, they too would use the same bathroom.

While trying to rationalize the absurdity of all this, my supervisor felt it was perhaps best to get everything out in the open at once. Sitting me down with a cup of cocoa in the evening, she mentioned nonchalantly that each afternoon, after their long lunch break, the girls on staff came and watched a television soap opera for an hour in my living quarters. I looked at her and said, "Could you run that past me one more time?" Yes, I had heard correctly. While the team members were enjoying their entertainment I would be working alone at a patient clinic. I looked at her coolly as I announced, "That is going to change. In fact, my quarters are to be off-limits, totally!" She begged me not to make waves. As I digested her response, I thought to myself, "It will be a tidal wave tomorrow!" Because of the years spent in the north, I was able to make a fair comparison of the living and working environment, and the conditions encountered at Landing Place were unacceptable. She agreed to have a talk with the two staff members but I discovered later that nothing had changed.

I had been told from the beginning that this reservation was very politically charged. In an instant, the words I heard at Norway House many years before resounded in my ears, "Don't rock the boat!"

I wanted my living quarters cleaned and the cleaning lady was called in. Her work schedule started late in the afternoon, that is to say when she deigned to make her appearance. She was also responsible for cleaning the work area after all the clinics were finished for the day.

When she arrived on duty she started work on cleaning the fridge/freezer and the rest of the living area at my request. We were by now preparing our evening meal and as we sat down to eat it, we were aware of our eyes burning and watering. A strong chemical was being used to sanitize the toilet, but more is not always better, as the cleaner quickly found out from the senior nurse. The waste from the toilet went into a septic tank and too much disinfectant was not advocated.

I did not get to bed until the early hours of the morning as I was busily cleaning dishes, cutlery, pots and pans, and generally tidying my surroundings. I managed to find suitable curtains from the clinic area to cover my windows. My accommodation was somewhat more comfortable but much yet had to be done.

I had only been in bed an hour when at three o'clock in the morning the clinic doorbell rang. When I answered I was greeted by a young woman and her elderly father. He wheezed and coughed and a full examination revealed he had pneumonia. With the appropriate medicines prescribed, I sent him home, confident that his daughter would take good care of him.

These interruptions in sleep were part of the job but the time spent with the patient was probably less than the time it took me to get back to sleep. There was often an element of worry when alone and making a diagnosis especially when so far removed from a hospital. Sophisticated equipment was lacking.

By noon, my nursing colleague was on her way back to Fort Hope. I would have to call on my own knowledge to deal with whatever came through those doors. I was ready to start the afternoon clinic and the first patients had arrived. I needed some assistance, such as pulling medical files and making new appointments, amongst some other duties expected of the staff, but none was forthcoming. The girls were otherwise occupied, watching their soap opera. I went into my quarters, turned off the television and asked them politely to return to their work posts.

I needed to address the problems and nip them in the bud, as it were. With the clinic over, I held a staff meeting. I delivered some rules and regulations about the television viewing and the free use of my living space. There was tension in the air and it was obvious, from their facial expressions, that my new rules were not acceptable.

I have always enjoyed working and puttering around and with little social amenities in the community, I kept busy. In the evening I decided to make myself more familiar with the clinic area, checking emergency equipment and the medical supplies. The oxygen supply was always an essential item. I found the tank, set up for emergency use, empty. I searched in the store room for the spare ones and to my chagrin, the only spare was registering almost empty. This was no laughing matter when faced with an emergency situation in isolation without such a basic entity.

I checked the outside of the trailer unit and found the steps to my door and the clinic ones well were worn and not very safe. Part of the siding on the basement of the trailer was missing, showing all the insulation. It was a perfect place for mice and stray animals to bed down.

Two days down and now I was into the third. The staff of two, who were not nurses, were making all the rules, yet I was held responsible for the facility and patient care. If mistakes were made by them, I would be held accountable. I was not in favour of the secretary prescribing antibiotics. Hourly it got worse. In the midst of the clinic proceedings, a woman, having recently delivered a baby and newly home from hospital, arrived on the doorstep having a secondary postpartum haemorrhage. It was not, thankfully, a dramatic bleed, but the cause probably would require medical intervention. When I went to give her the necessary medication by injection to stop the bleeding, none was available. The native worker, on finding it was outdated some time before, had thrown it out and never had it replaced. Considering the distance from medical help, I decided to send my patient out to hospital, ordering a chartered plane to the Sioux Lookout Hospital. Arrangements were made and a nurse was being sent in to act as a medical escort.

I had decided enough was enough, and asked the secretary to book me a seat on the scheduled flight coming in that afternoon. Protesting, she reminded me that I was not due to go for a few days. I assured her that I was not staying on at any costs.

With my patient's problem under control, I quickly packed up my belongings and was feeling somewhat relieved to be going. To say the events of those last three days were over would have been premature. More yet had to follow.

Being in a small community, there were no ambulance services. I requested local transport and due to the nature of the client's problem, I wanted a smooth, slow ride for her. I suggested that the driver arrive with a generous margin of extra time. I was most impressed when I saw the vehicle parked outside the building quite early. The man in charge had to remove two sets of seats from inside to accommodate the stretcher. In between getting the patient ready for the trip I ventured outside to ascertain if the seats had been removed, only to find that the two men were struggling, but to no avail. It appeared they did not have the right tools. Still there was time yet. Half an hour later, I had confirmation that the plane was on its way. This called for another check on the transport situation. Lo and behold there must have been five men on the job and still the seats were in the same place.

I left them to their own devices and started to prepare the stretcher. It was closed so very tightly that I called for reinforcements. For all the grunts and groans and trials of strength, using our feet as levers, we could not get it to budge. Just at the right moment two non-native men walked in, who were, ironically, checking the place for safety. I hastened to mention the state of the furnace room. With the extra manpower we got the stretcher opened, only to find that one of the small support legs was broken. Placing a make-shift object underneath the broken leg for balance, the patient was then loaded on to it and taken to the waiting "ambulance." The men had finally and successfully removed all the seats.

During all this commotion the radio announcement indicated that my own flight, travelling a different route from that of my patient, had already landed. With everything loaded onto the waiting vehicle, I was about to say goodbye to the workers, but they had other plans. They had locked up the clinic, business being put on hold, presumably, and they quickly climbed aboard the vehicle which already lacked adequate space. I said, "You can't close the clinic!" but it fell on deaf ears.

When we arrived at the airstrip, the air ambulance was sitting off to the side and the pilot and nurse were standing outside, chatting. To the right, much further down the runway was the other plane, its engines running, making a lot of noise. Once my patient was safely on board I commenced my report to the nurse escort. She had brought the vial of necessary medicine which I lacked at the clinic. Just as I was drawing the liquid into the syringe to give the injection, someone shouted, "Your plane is leaving!" "What!", I gasped. "It can't be. It's not leaving without me!" With that, I instructed the nurse to give the injection as she was a fully qualified nurse.

My aircraft had the steps up, the door was closed and it had started to taxi slowly along the runway facing us. I raced down towards it, waving my arms madly in the air. That at least did the trick. The pilot stopped, and when eventually the door opened, a head peered out. "Yes, what is it?", he asked me in a drawl voice. I told him I had to finish my report, and I was booked to go out on his aircraft. I asked him to wait but he wasn't too happy as he had a schedule to keep.

I ran back to the first airplane and gave the final part of my report. Completing this, I then did a marathon all the way back to plane number two. I had quite a physical workout that day. As I started to board, I asked if my luggage had be placed on board. No one knew, so I hastened back to the terminal shed, only to find it empty. I left, assuming that it was on board. By the time I sat down, my head was throbbing so much it felt as though it was going to explode. With the nausea I was experiencing, I thought I might need to use the little white bag in front of me. I was so relieved to be out of my unpleasant situation.

So much for the initial staff welcoming party at Fort Hope. No wonder they had been so anxious to encumber me with this Health Centre. Nothing ever came down the paper trail that indicated any intent to place me there and I assumed it was contrived at local level to use me, the "new girl" on the block. The "new girl", however, had been around the block much more often than any of the others, due to long service, and was not so gullible in the end!

Settled back in Fort Hope, I was inundated with questions from my work cohorts as to why I would not stay the whole week at the other reservation, but the nurse who recently covered that clinic, I suspect, was well aware of my reasons. I felt that the other staff who had frequented there over a period of time should have addressed many of the problems and taken a firmer hand. As a temporary staff member I was not about to stress myself with the situation. Had I been a single career woman I think I would have found Landing Place very challenging and with my type of personality would have had the place running smoothly. Having been a nurse for over thirty years I choose not to live with the aggravation.

Just as the Nurse-in-Charge was leaving for two weeks of vacation, she coaxed me into feeding and caring for her large dog which was part Husky and part Labrador. There was another dog which she included in her request. He belonged to one of the Indians and spent more time at our residence than with his owner. He was skinny and she indicated that the owner neglected him. With that, she took off not giving me an opportunity too agree or disagree to this arrangement.

When I walked her dog, Beth, the other dog, who answered to the name Jack, joined in, the two frolicking like a pair of pups. I was bemused watching their antics. To feed one more was not a chore. At bedtime they both selected a place in my bedroom to sleep. Beth, sprawled on her side, lay close to the side of my bed, while Jack selected his niche underneath. It wasn't long before they were both sound asleep, tired no doubt from their day's activities. The snoring became unbearable, but in a short space of time I experienced something much more unpleasant than that. I am not quite sure what Jack may have eaten when running free but, whatever the diet was, it moved along his digestive tract with speed. Frequently, as I tried to drift off to sleep, I would hear the musical sounds of Prrt-Prrt-Prrt-Prrt! interrupting the snores. What followed made me cover my head with the sheets. I prayed I would fall asleep and be spared any further noxious odours. I would soon find out this would be a nightly occurrence, but I did not have the heart to put him outside. Sad to say, several months after I had left Fort Hope, I heard that Jack had been killed by a skidoo while on one of his freedom runs. Even although I was not there, I felt sad, but also glad I had given him some tender loving care in his lifetime.

When I arrived in September, the scenery was very beautiful, with the lakes still open and the trees, such as the birch, just beginning to take on a look of burnished gold. The population was small and from my room I could see the houses scattered throughout the village. The ones next to the main road were all laid out in a neat row.

My main source of social activity came from the staff and the school teachers I had met through my work. Getting together in groups for entertainment thereafter became very much the norm. We graduated from coffee visits to pot luck suppers and weekend walks, allowing the bonds of friendship to grow. Walking was a little restricted, but we often chose to go through the village, past Slipperjack's Poolroom and onto the only good road which was built for the logging trucks.

I felt quite at home in this setting, The only thing missing was my husband, but at least we talked often on the telephone and communicated by letter. By the time the mail had arrived, I already had an update on his news via the phone.

The days were always so busy and time passed quickly. My first time on call at Fort Hope proved to be hectic. I had just concluded my day shift and barely reached the door of my quarters when someone barged in to tell me they were bringing in an unconscious person. Within a few minutes, a woman in her thirties was carried in. She was actually quite conscious, but acting a little wild. The story was that she had been drinking and had ingested a large quantity of an analgesic. It was hard to get any sense from this lady, doubly so when I had to wrestle with her to prevent her from leaving. From time to time she was giggly and then she would become quite obstreperous. My colleagues had just left for a walk. I certainly needed some assistance. The woman was given a charcoal preparation by mouth, almost forcibly, as she resisted so fiercely. In the end, it was debatable how much she had received internally. The room and bed she was lying in, looked like a war zone with articles upturned. The sheets were blackened from the charcoal she spit out, and my face, hands and white coat were similarly splattered. She did however, recover.

Before going off-duty again, a child had now appeared at the clinic accompanied by his concerned parents. The problem was an accidental overdose of iron pills. Syrup of ipecac was given but did not yield the desired effect. This child was reluctant to give up his stomach contents. The doctor on call in Sioux Lookout decided we should send the child to the hospital to be on the safe side. While I was arranging for air transport, a third emergency arrived, a newborn having respiratory problems. The babe was given appropriate treatment to aid his breathing and combat the infection but, being so tiny, I elected to send this baby to hospital, taking advantage of the available transport.

Attending patients when on call could be very exhausting. There were medicines to administer, charts to be made up and an accurate record of events had to be entered. Continual recording was made as long as the patient was in care. One also had to deal with the many concerned relatives who showed up at the clinic, and be able to handle them with tact, in spite of having little time to spare.

Although we had our own local transport, the driver, when off-duty, had to have a message sent when his services were required. Although only a few people had a telephone, there was always rapid communication within any of the places I worked, especially when the nature of the illness was serious or if there had been an accident. It seemed at times as though the whole village would turn up on the doorstep. With all the interruptions it sometimes was quite an impediment.

By the time my two little charges were medically evacuated and the older woman sent home, it was ten o'clock at night. When all the paper work was adequately completed for the clinic file, the work area had to be cleaned. It could be just tidying or there could be several items to wash and re-sterilize, as well as mopping up blood and secretions from the floor. Empty oxygen cylinders had to be replaced as well as any medications used for emergencies. The clinic had to be in good functional order and ready at all times for the next casualty. This was not something that could be postponed until the following day. Only after all chores were attended to could one retire. I had only eaten a light lunch and missed my evening dinner. At this point I did not feel like cooking an entire meal, but instead I settled for some light refreshment. It already had been a sixteen-hour day, with very few opportunities to rest. I was still on call for the entire night but as it turned out, all was quiet.

Other staff had their share of emergencies, but I only depict my own, although many of the events that happened on my shifts were, I am told, rare happenings for that area, occurring perhaps every two years. It was just the luck of the draw.

When on call one evening a serious episode occurred. I received a call from a diabetic lady in a predicament, finding her insulin supply depleted and feeling very ill. A driver with a stretcher was dispatched to her home. Arriving at the clinic she indeed appeared very ill, due also to many other medical complications. She previously had a kidney transplant and also had a severe heart problem. We did carry spare insulin of the type she required. She was vomiting copious amounts, and an intravenous was started. Once all the preliminaries were completed and I had a clearer picture of the crisis, I made contact with the medical staff at Sioux Lookout and made arrangements to airlift her to hospital. Air transport was not readily available and an anxious waiting game ensued. The hours ticked by, with her condition showing signs of deterioration. Unfortunately, the woman had refused to attend the clinic the previous day, although urged to do so by family members. Rather, she waited until a crisis situation became evident. She had been hospitalised often and perhaps had become resistant to further admissions.

The clock ticked by slowly and then I could hear that oh-so-familiar sound overhead. The driver, on hearing it also, hastened to the clinic, bringing with him some extra men. The patient was a very obese woman and the extra attendants were necessary to get her onto the stretcher and subsequently into the waiting vehicle. It was quite cold and frosty outside and at least he had the foresight to warm the truck. I bundled myself up warmly, too, and, with the low temperature, I felt that the snow was not too far off. It was one o'clock in the morning as we sped off to the airport through the sleeping village. A nurse would be waiting on board the plane to escort my client from thereon in.

There is quite an air of excitement from the time the patient is first brought to the clinic, all the way through to the handing over of their care to some other professional. This feeling of excitement is heightened as you see the plane parked in front of you, engines making a loud, powerful sound. The aircraft doorway opens and the steps are flipped down. Just when you believe you are the only one awake at this ungodly hour, people seem to appear out of nowhere and gather round to get a glimpse of the individual on the stretcher.

A voice in the small gathering said, "That's my auntie. Can I talk to her?" "In a minute, after she is on board in the warmth", I found myself replying as I made my way up the steps to the nurse waiting at the top. We went inside where it was quieter and I briefed her on the knowledge I had of my patient and the care she received at the clinic. That completed, I wasted no time, but signalled the men to bring the stretcher on board, where a transfer to their stretcher took place efficiently. I squeezed my client's hand and whispered a word in her ear, reassuring her she would be okay, before taking my leave.

The steps disappeared, the door closed as I ran back to the truck for warmth. The plane began to taxi down the runway, turned, hesitated and the engine sounds changed. It then speeded past and was airborne with the ease and grace of a giant bird. "Godspeed", I thought privately. I made my way back home, shivering a little with the cold air, lack of sleep and with a residual feeling of excitement. I felt tired and yet, after the event, there was still too much adrenaline flowing to retire immediately to bed.

Dropped off at the doorway, I hastened to straighten the clinic again, making sure everything was at the ready. I didn't have too long to wait. The clinic door burst open and my driver requested the stretcher once more. Someone had just informed him that a female was "passed out" and suspected of sniffing gasoline or taking drugs. He darted off into the darkness of night, only to return swiftly with the unconscious patient. We placed her in one of the beds so that I might examine her fully. Her lips were a bluish tinge, prompting me to give her oxygen at once. I had never quite seen anything like this before. The girl lay completely rigid. When I lifted the back of her head, her whole body uniformly lifted straight up. There were garbled messages as to what she had taken and her boyfriend, who had had been involved, was sent for. There was a total lack of co-operation from him, he probably being scared of the police finding out. Finally, after rationalizing with him, he admitted they were sniffing gasoline. As I continued to give the oxygen it was fascinating to watch how her rigid body reverted to its normal state, except for occasional spasms. An intravenous drip was set up and monitoring of her condition lasted for four hours.

She was awake now, but acted as though she were intoxicated. I made breakfast for her and myself. By now I was quite ravenous, not to mention being quite tired. The intravenous and oxygen therapy were now discontinued. By ten o'clock in the morning I discharged her home and I literally crawled into bed. I had worked non-stop from eight o'clock the previous morning, a total of twenty-seven hours. I was on call for the following twenty-four hours, but someone took over my daytime duties while I rested. Thankfully, the next evening was quiet except for an occasional "runny nose", needing little care.

The weeks were flying past and I was enjoying the work tremendously. It was strange, but I felt more at ease at Fort Hope than I had at Cambridge Bay. Gradually my confidence was returning, but I still did not feel fully comfortable with the responsibilities when on call.

While I was at the school attending to health matters, an elderly lady was admitted to the clinic for observation. There was nothing specific she complained of but she just did not feel well. That night I was on call and therefore it fell on me to send her home later that evening if her vital signs were normal.

I sent a family member to get some clean clothing and in the meantime I instructed the health workers to give her a bed bath. This was offered as a kindness and readily accepted. Many did not have bathtubs or running water, having to boil their water to wash. I made her some macaroni and cheese which she enjoyed. The girls were dressing her when they shouted for me to come. I dropped what I was doing, hearing the urgency in their voices. The old lady was having a seizure and quite a bad one at that. We managed to get a wedge between her teeth and turn her on her side before giving her oxygen. She came around, but it was now necessary to keep her as an in-patient. Following that first episode, she continued to have seizures. Medication was given to help control these after consulting with the hospital doctor. I wasn't very happy about her colour and felt there was a change in her medical condition. I advised the doctor again, mentioning that I would evacuate the patient. We were allowed flexibility in the decision-making process because we were on site and better able to evaluate the patient's condition.

I had dealt with many seizures before but I was concerned, not knowing what was causing these. When requesting a plane, we had to determine if an escort was needed and what level of medical care en route was desirable. In this instance I asked for the paramedics. Staff with basic life support were also available but I declined this offer. Transport was not readily available but they would keep me posted.

An hour later the phone rang. A plane was leaving from Thunder Bay, Ontario, and would arrive soon. There is such a feeling of relief in knowing that your patient is going to receive more advanced hospital care than we could offer. The phone rang again some time later and I expected this to be an announcement of their estimated time of arrival which I had calculated would be imminent. It was the airport all right, calling from Thunder Bay. They explained that they had been more than half way to me when the ground crew discovered that after refuelling, the petrol tank cap had not been replaced. The plane had to return to base immediately. By the time the aircraft went all the way back, probably refuelled again, and made the return journey to us, it was approaching midnight.

I was a happy person when I saw the air ambulance crew finally walk through the clinic doors. One paramedic checked the woman's vitals signs and attached some electrodes to her chest to get a heart reading. Meantime, in the adjoining room I gave the report to the other paramedic. As we were discussing her case a shout came from the other room. When we entered, we discovered that the woman was in respiratory arrest. The two paramedics rapidly worked on the lady. Thankfully she came around and after stabilizing her, she was taken to the waiting aircraft. I am happy to say that the woman did recover. Because my own departure was imminent I did not find out the final diagnosis on this lady.

The snow was lying quite heavy on the ground now, changing the landscape. The skidoos could be heard and seen crossing the frozen lakes. In the summer, the natives who had boats were able to travel long distances and were able to explore what lay on the other side of the lake. For the rest of us, the frozen water now gave us the opportunity to walk further afield.

I was now at the final day of the first eight weeks of my contract. In fact, I had completed nine, extending my time to accommodate someone on staff taking a few day's leave. The day before had been very dramatic. An older man had been found face-down in a snow bank and on arrival at the clinic, there was no heartbeat. No one knew how long he had been there or whether it had just happened. The little nurse who was temporarily in charge called the doctor at the Sioux Lookout Hospital, while two of us carried out cardiopulmonary resuscitation. We were not getting a response. An intravenous was set up and drugs were injected into him by this route. The drug stimulated the heartbeat, but as the drug's effects wore off, we were unable to sustain his life. After a great effort by our team, my part being minimal compared to the young nurse's, he had to be officially pronounced dead.

Because of the unexpected death and the fact he had not been under medical care, nor had a known medical condition, the tribal police were now involved. This meant an autopsy would be requested by the coroner. Nothing was to be removed from the patient or the room, or touched in any way. The door was sealed with tape by the police. However the family were allowed in and the body was attended to in spite of the ruling that nothing was to be touched. The next time I saw the man's body he was wrapped like a "mummy". Cultural ways had prevailed.

Outside, in the clinic hallway and in our living quarters, family and friends had gathered. Anguished sounds and much sobbing resounded everywhere in the building. It must be very traumatic, especially immediately after death, to consent to an autopsy on a loved one to rule out foul play. The family were having a hard time dealing with this necessity.

While the nurses were busy in other ways, I gathered the many people into the large teaching room. I explained to them everything I knew, from when the deceased was first brought in, and the reason for the autopsy. This death impacted on the staff, too. I asked if an elder would say a prayer for the deceased and for the grieving relatives. I did this in respect of their culture and spirituality before returning to assist with the work.

It was arranged that his body would be flown south that night, with a police escort. When everyone left, there was such an eerie silence. Each of us was somewhat subdued as we left the clinic for the privacy of our own room.

The next afternoon I was packed and ready, waiting at the airport. I had hoped to see the staff again but there were no guarantees I would be returning to this particular Nursing Station. It had been a fully loaded experience. I had in my possession the securely packaged medical file of the deceased man and upon arrival at Sioux Lookout, I was to personally hand over the file to the Senior Nursing Officer.

It was good to be back home with my husband, in spite of having contracted a severe respiratory infection. I did not return north, but it was not of my choosing. To write of the many injustices I met with and my nine years of battling the bureaucracies, so far to no avail, would leave this account of my experiences with an negative undertone. This is not my intention.

I am retired from my nursing career now, but my experiences in the Canadian North are my greatest ones and I relive the memories often. The paths that I chose gave me the opportunities to live and work amongst the Aboriginal people. My life has surely been enriched by the exposure to the varied ways of life.

GLOSSARY

Inuksuk	Rock pile used as marker
Qamutik	Sled
Inuk	Of Inuit descent
Inuit	The people
Inuktituk	Inuit language
Kamiit	Boots made of sealskin
Maktaaq	Whale blubber
Kilalurak	White whale
Qulliq	Oil lamp made of soapstone
Amauti	Parka type of garment with large hood to carry baby
Qiviuk	Musk-ox wool
Aanniasiuqti	Nurse used in Resolute Bay
Naja: Pronounced. Na-yuh	Means little sister Name for Nurse in Baker Lake
Qallunaat	Caucasians
Ticanogan	Cradle Board to carry papoose
Skelp	To spank

BIBLIOGRAPHY

Norway House Jail: Hudson's Bay Archives, Winnipeg.

Manitoba Cultural Heritage and Recreational Historical Branch 1985

James Evans- Cree Syllabaries: Wikipedia, free encyclopaedia

York Boats: Hudson's Bay Archives. Author John Foster.

Yukon Stern Wheelers. End of an Era. Canadian West Magazine 1987: Author Ronald Barnett.

A History of the Yukon: Origin of Yukon name. Native American Super Site.

Yukon: the First People. Page 21 Bering Strait

George Carmack, Tagish Charlie and Skookum Jim. Author T.W. Paterson.

Ghost towns of the Yukon 1977.

George Carmack an American. Junior Encyclopaedia. Hurtig Publishers 1990.

Chilkoot Pass route to goldfields. Junior Encyclopaedia. Hurtig Publishers 1990.

White Collared Workers in Klondike. Video-City of Gold. Published by National Film Board of Canada.

Gertrude Lovejoy known as Diamond Tooth Gertie: Author, Douglas Fetherling. The Gold Crusades.

Klondike Kate alias Kathleen Eloise Rockwell. Article from Canadian West Magazine, "Queen of the Klondike". Summer Edition 1986. Author John Stevenson.

Yellowknife, also known as Tatsanottine named after a small Athabascan speaking tribe. Excerpts from Britannica: Micropaedia Ready Reference 15th Edition.

Dr John Rae. Reference from Internet Orkneyjar. The Heritage of the Orkneys.

Massacre by Dog Rib Tribe. Britannica: Micropaedia Ready Reference 15th Edition.

Gold Rush, Yellowknife 1934-1936. Canadian Encyclopaedia. Publisher Hurtig.

Baker Lake, NWT. Shaman meaning" He who knows". Britannicia Encyclopaedia Volumn 26

Chesterfield Inlet NWT. Named after Earl of Chesterfield. World Book of Encyclopaedia 1993 Edition. Article by Gary Stringer.

Chesterfield Inlet NWT. First discovered by Thomas Button. Britannica 15th Edition

Marble Island NWT. James Knight Explorer. Reference from "Dead Silence". Authors Dr Owen Beattie and John Geiger, Viking Published by Penguin Group Toronto, Canada

Sioux Lookout. Legend concept from Sioux Lookout 50th Anniversary Book. Article written by Nan Shipley. Free Press.

Bowes-Lyon family in Sioux Lookout. Excerpt from Sioux Lookout 50th Anniversary Book as told to Lisa Carlbom by John W. Lyon, eldest son.

Resolute Bay:

Parcoll Huts. Musk-ox study at Polar Bear Pass: Article by Don Cockerton.

Relocation of Inuit. Film: Broken Promises. National Film Board, Canada

Sir John Franklin Expedition in search of Northwest Passage. Ships Erebus and Terror.

Captain Crozier.

Franklin at Battle of Trafalgar. Joining Navy aged 14years.

Last sighting at Lancaster Sound by Whalers.

Lady Franklin search party.

References from many sources including Britannica Micropaedia Ready reference 15th Edition Page 940

Franklin's travel to King William Island and perishing.

Exhumation of bodies at Beechey Island and causes of death from "Frozen Time", by Dr Owen Beattie and John Geigor. ISBN 0-88833-253-X. Publishers Western Producer Prairie Books.

Somerset Island. Origin of name. Information from Historica- the Canadian Encyclopaedia. Author S.C. Zoltai.

Bella Bella BC

Word Potlatch by early Europeans from book Potlatch by George Clutesi. Gray's Publishing Ltd 1969 British Columbia.

Namu Fishery. Reference from "Drums and Scalpels". by Dr Geddes Large. Mitchell Press Ltd, Vancouver, Canada.

Namu. Indian meaning of name from Wave Length Magazine, British Columbia.

Kincolith. Place of Skulls, from British Columbian Place Names. Reference by GPV and Helen Akriggs, Victoria BC.

Blackfoot Reservation. Crowfoot Names. Taken from book, "Crowfoot" by Hugh Dempsey. Publishers Hurtig. Third Printing.

Blackfoot Tribes and Language. Junior Encyclopaedia Vol.1 1990. Publishers Hurtig.

Fought Cree, Kootenai and Assinboine Indians. Junior Encyclopaedia. Vol.1 Publisher Hurtig 1990

Amundsen Roald. Norwegian explorer. Abandoned medical studies.

Expedition to South Pole 1911.

Died 1928 in aviation crash. Taken from Junior encyclopaedia of Canada page 63. Publisher Hurtig 1990

Purchase of "Maud", name change and eventual usage as warehouse and Arctic wireless weather reports. NWT Data Sheets. Department of Culture and Communications. Published by Outcrop Ltd, Yellowknife NWT

ABOUT THE AUTHOR

Nora Philip Fry was born and raised in Scotland and did her nurse training in Aberdeen and Edinburgh.

She later emigrated to Canada, travelled extensively through Europe, visited China in 1974 and spent twenty-four years working with North American Indians and Inuit in isolated communities in her chosen profession.

She returned to live in Scotland three years ago.

Naja is her first book.

Her hobbies include, quilting, cross stitching, tapestries, genealogy, travelling at home and abroad and walking.

Printed in the United Kingdom
by Lightning Source UK Ltd.
114564UKS00001B/58-99